Meager Beginnings

A Memoir

Annie Baldwin

Meager Beginnings is dedicated to every one of my family members including Mama, Dorothy Sikes Coomer, Daddy, Buford Franklin Coomer, and my siblings: Franklin Eugene Coomer, Thurman Harris (Bud) Coomer, Raymond Lewis Coomer, Ruby Lee (Coomer) Paul, Robert Lee Coomer, Ruth Evelyn (Coomer) Huey, William Henry (Nuse) Coomer, Dollie (Coomer) Weems, and Harvey Joe Coomer. Without them I would not have had a story to tell.

I also want to dedicate it to my wonderful husband, Arthur Earl Baldwin, who put up with me while I was writing my family's story. A special dedication goes to my son, Kevin DeWayne Baldwin, his wife, Cindy Diane, and to my precious grandchildren, Clayton Earl Baldwin, and Kathryn Sue (Kat) Baldwin. These are the five people who I love most of all.

To my cousins and to the people who live in and around Lindale, Texas, who encouraged me to write this book, I want to thank you for doing so.

One

The July sun was hot, unrelenting. As she picked blackberries, the thorns pricked her fingers. She did not have any shoes to wear, and the sun was extremely hot. Her feet had painful blisters on them. She put them in the shade of the berry vines as much as possible. The baby began to stir within her. She had not seen a doctor, but having seven babies before this one, experience told her the time for birth was soon, perhaps today or maybe tonight.

The year was 1942 and a war was raging in Europe. The only thing this meant to her was that necessary commodities, like sugar and gasoline, were being rationed. When the war was over this would disappear. The war would not touch her family who was considered white trash tramps working in the fields of East Texas. She hardly thought about it. A later turn of events would, however, imprint this war in her brain for the rest of her life. Today it meant nothing.

The baby stirred again sending pains through her back, but she couldn't quit working. Picking blackberries was the only way she had at this time of making money to buy needed staples. Thoughts of her husband came to mind. She hoped he wasn't at a bootlegger's house buying whiskey. Tonight she would need him sober if this baby decided to show its bottom to the world. Another pain and she doubled over. *No*, she thought, *wait until the day is over and a little more money is made.*

Her husband drove up in their old car, a 1929 Ford. She watched as he got out. *Please God, let him be sober.* He had assisted her in all the babies' births. She had never seen a doctor with any of them. One baby had been born on a wagon bed, one on the kitchen table, another when they were living in a house made of cardboard. Her own brother had help deliver her last child. This baby would be born in their tent. A tent with a dirt floor!

As he came to her, she felt relieved. She could tell he had not been drinking. They had been married since 1923. He was short, only about 5'6". His nose was large and his ears stood out some, but he had sky blue eyes, dark complexion and a handsome face. His teeth were crowded in his mouth, yellow from smoking too much tobacco. She was dark also, but her eyes were as black as night. Both of them had skin that was leathered from being in the sun too much.

When he was sober he wasn't a bad fellow. Being drunk brought out the other person inside him, and then he would be mean to her and the kids. She loved him to a fault, even forgave him each time another woman came between them. Before she had met him, he had tried marriage for six weeks staying drunk the entire time until the girl's mother had run him off. *Had he ever divorced his first wife?* He said he had, and this was all she had to go on, his word, having never seen any divorce papers. *Well,* she thought, *I'm about to have his eighth child, so we're as married as anyone I know.*

As he came to her in the field he smiled showing all the yellow teeth. "I think the baby will come before tomorrow," she told him. No reaction from her husband except to say, "I'll take the kids to the tent and start some beans to boil." *Good,* she thought, *at least I won't have to cook supper.*

Back at the tent with the kids playing in his sight, he gathered wood to make a fire out in the open. After the fire was blazing he produced an old pot from inside the tent and filled it with water to boil the beans in.

Another baby, he thought, *I hope it's a girl.* He had five boys already. Another girl would bring that number to three. He knew that after supper he would have to prepare things inside the tent.

The beans were boiling now. How he wished he had some ham or dry salt meat to go in them. One family who lived in a nearby tent smelled the beans and started walking toward him. It was a large pot and he had a lot of beans boiling, but he also had a lot of mouths to feed, and he didn't like sharing his food with his neighbors. About this time a frog came hopping by. He grabbed it and threw it into the boiling beans, guts and all. The frog spread itself out and peed as it met death. It would serve as a substitute for ham. The neighbors couldn't stomach eating beans with a frog in them. They turned and went back to their tent.

After the other family members came back to the camp that evening, they ate silently. The husband had fried bread in a skillet to go with the beans with the meat in them. The children dared not to complain about the frog. They knew their Daddy was the boss of the family, and if he told them to eat, they ate. The oldest boy, Franklin Eugene, now eighteen, felt his stomach tighten some as he began to eat, but he never spoke a word.

The man-boy sat as he always did, hunkered on his feet and legs. He never sat on a box to eat or when he was whittling or having idle conversation with anyone. Franklin Eugene kept an eye on his Mama knowing the baby would be here soon. He had been close by when all the others had been born. Tears came to his eyes as he thought of the pain she would endure this night. He knew too that it would be his job to walk into town, which was three miles away, to get the young doctor who had a practice there. The family had never lived this close to a doctor before. He hoped the doctor would have something in his bag to relieve his mother's suffering.

The mother's bed was made on a makeshift pallet on the dirt floor. After eating supper the kids played in the yard for a while, but all were put to bed early. A blanket on a wire across the inside of the tent separated the children's pallets from the parents "bedroom." The younger kids would sleep unaware of the miracle of life going on so close to them. The older ones would stir uneasily in their sleep knowing tomorrow there might be another child to keep while their Mama worked in the field.

Around two a.m., with pains wracking her body, the husband sent Franklin Eugene into town on foot to bring back the doctor and his black bag. He never thought about taking the car, as that would be a waste of gas. Three miles were not many to walk when one was used to walking almost everywhere. He walked swiftly. He had to. His precious mother was hurting.

In a tent nearby, a fourteen-year-old boy got out of his bed and went outside to relieve himself. Hearing the screams next door, he automatically went into the tent to investigate. Once inside, he realized the baby was coming and he had to help it get born. This lad was a good worker and naturally curious. He worked along side the man, neither one hardly uttering a word. The lad felt sorry for the woman who had now stopped screaming, but, as he knew, was still feeling a lot of pain. Just as the baby popped out, the doctor arrived, in time to cut the cord and take credit for the birth.

The fourteen-year-old promptly left the tent, went to the edge of the woods, threw up and returned to a pallet that was in his own tent and fell asleep. He did not realize two hours had passed; it was now four o'clock, almost time to get up and to get back to the blackberry patch. He also did not know if the baby were a boy or girl. He just had not stayed around long enough to find out.

The night of the morning of the birth her husband shared a pint of whiskey with another woman in the woods close to the campground. Inside the tent the woman looked into the face of the baby. Brown eyes to brown eyes, a bond forming that would never be broken. The mother didn't mind that her husband was with another woman. After all, it had been quite some time since she had been able to give him pleasure. *A new baby girl was a very good reason for a man to celebrate his manhood.* Besides, she had to save her strength, for tomorrow she had to return to the fields to begin picking berries again. They had to eat!

There were not any baby blankets to wrap the baby in or anything that could be used for diapers. As she gave her baby a kiss, snuff ran from her mouth, across the infant's cheek. The naked baby went to sleep, cuddled in her mother's arms, unaware of her meager beginnings.

Two

It was July 10, 1942, near Lindale, Texas, a small town in East Texas when I breathed my first breath of air. Lindale is located exactly halfway between Dallas, Texas and Shreveport, Louisiana, a hundred miles from each city. The kind young doctor marveled at the fact that although small, I was very strong. As he washed me and put me, still naked, in my mother's arms, he thought, *she'd make it; she'll survive.* Several years later this same doctor would deliver a Heisman Trophy winner who would bare his namesake. The Heisman winner would be Earl Christian Campbell. The young doctor was Earl Christian Kinzie. That is my one claim to fame, being delivered by the same doctor who delivered Earl Campbell, the famous Houston Oiler running back.

My daddy, Buford Franklin Coomer, asked the doctor how much he owed him. Dr. Kinzie replied, "How much can you spare Mr. Coomer?" Daddy thought it was a nice thing for this doctor to address him as Mister. After all he was just a laborer. My daddy looked in his billfold and gave him $13.00. The doc told him he could give him some more when he got some. Daddy would later laugh and say that he guessed he never got any more money because he never gave Dr. Kinzie anymore for me. Some might suggest that Dr. Kinzie actually charged too much for me. Remember this was 1942.

The doctor would remain friends with our family from then on, and although he was poor at the time of my birth, he would later become a rich man, not only in money, but also in that kindred spirit of giving that would make him the most beloved man of our community.

Within two days things were back to normal. Mama was back in the field with the older kids, and the younger ones were tending to me. I was allergic to cow's milk, and of course, Mama didn't have time to breast feed me. Therefore, they bought a goat to be milked so I could be fed. To this day my siblings know where I got my stubbornness from, an old goat.

Right from the beginning I would prove to be a little different from the rest of the clan. I would have a more natural curiosity, and although afraid of my daddy, I would at times challenge him, making him mad. The story goes, although never confirmed, that Mama's grandparents came from Holland. I was dark skinned, and sometimes when Daddy was really upset with my actions he would call me his "damned old black Dutch daughter." I didn't care. I didn't like him much anyway, but I wondered at times why it bothered me when he was extra irritated about my trying his patience. Sometimes I would just stare at him and him at me. Brown eyes to blue ones with no words being spoken between us until he would walk away wanting to strike me and my being afraid that was exactly what was going to happen. And sometimes it did.

My oldest sister, Ruby Lee, who was nine when I was born, hated him too. She wanted him to die. One day someone told her that if a person drank spider webs with his alcohol he would die. All day she rounded up spider webs that were plentiful. She ground them up and poured out some of the whiskey replacing it with the webs. He drank it. She watched happily. This was the day we would be rid of him forever. Around midnight he woke up from his drunken stupor with a very bad stomachache. He screamed, "Kids get up, your Mama has poisoned me." Ruby Lee said, "Thank the Lord!" Of course, after throwing up, he lived. For several years my sister lived in fear that he was going to remember what she had said and punish her.

It took the rest of the kids a few days to get used to me. Besides Franklin Eugene and Ruby Lee there were Thurman Harris, who turned sixteen the day after I was born; Raymond Lewis was fourteen; Robert Lee was six, Ruth Evelyn was four, and William Henry turned two thirteen days later. If William Henry was jealous of all the attention I got, he didn't show it. He was glad that he no longer was the *baby* and that name could be passed on to someone else.

Franklin Eugene and Raymond Lewis had blue eyes like Daddy's. All the rest of us had brown eyes like Mama's, but we all favored. There was never a question as to who our mama and daddy were. We all had double names, as was the custom in those days. Lots of kids had common first names such as Ruth, Ruby, and Robert so the second names were necessary so that the right kid would come when called in the afternoon by the parent. At least this was what my mama explained to me. The name they gave me was *Annie Bell.* I've hated it all my life.

My mama's brother, Uncle Jean, lived in Dekalb, Texas, about 100 miles north of Lindale. He was very close to her. They had been very poor growing up. Their daddy had died a few months before Mama was born. There were two older boys and another girl. The girl, named Kate, had been put in a state mental hospital where she would remain until she died. I'm not absolutely sure of her problem. Mama told us she had gone crazy reading the Bible. The story went that she would disappear when they were working in the field, and she would be found in the house reading the Bible. I always thought it was sort of sad for the Lord to punish a person for reading His Word. But stranger things have happened. The two older boys had left home as teenagers and were never heard from again. They left, Mama said, to try to escape the poverty.

Grandma Sikes, Mama's mother, cleaned houses for people in town. Mama got to go to school through the fourth grade. After that Grandma moved to the country to work. At the time there were no school buses in the area in which they lived to take kids to school. So, Mama never got to go to school again. She had been a good student, having loved school. She was very sad about not getting to go, but as was to become a good character trait of hers, she accepted what had to be. She went to work with her mother.

Uncle Jean and his wife, Aunt Pearl, had six girls and one boy. Uncle Jean always said that he had six girls and every one of them had a brother. These Sikes cousins would become close with us as we grew up. One of the girls would later remark after she was grown that as children our families were all that we had had.

We had cousins on Daddy's side of the family too. We always called them the Coomer cousins. We didn't see them as often as we saw the Sikes cousins, but we loved them just as much.

Daddy's life before he met Mama is a little suspect. As we were growing up, he told us a lot of things that have never been confirmed. He was born in Cobb Station, Kentucky. His daddy, Henry Coomer, had had three wives and three sets of kids. All three wives had died. One son was born before the first wife died. His name was Henry also. With the second wife, my daddy, Buford Franklin, was the oldest. Then there was Bessie, Harley, Leona and twins, Peggy and Ellen. The children of grandpa and the third wife were Earnest, Thelma Lorene and Lillie Mae. Thelma, for some reason, would change her name to June. Lillie Mae died, according to Daddy, from a drug overdose.

How the first and third wives of Grandpa died, to my knowledge and belief, was never disclosed to me. Quoting from my daddy, his mother died while trying to give birth to another set of twins. After she was dead, the twins had been cut out of her with a butcher knife. There was not a doctor available, and the midwife thought she could save the twins. The babies were dead.

Daddy stated that he and another man stole wood from a shed on the property that belonged to the man for whom they were working. They used the wood to build his mother a coffin and they put her and the babies, identical looking boys, inside. It was raining very hard on the day of their funeral. When the wooden coffin was lowered into the ground, water rushed onto their bodies, and Daddy thought at the time that if they had not already been dead, they would surely drown. Daddy was married by the time his daddy took his third bride and Grandpa had his third set of kids.

Sometimes the stories about Grandpa became really crazy. Daddy told us how mean Grandpa had been. He had boarded a train once and cut a man's guts out and pushed him off the train. Another time he had killed a man who had gone crazy and was shooting people. A reward had been offered for anyone who would kill him. After my brave Grandpa had done just that, the sheriff of the county told him that he had better leave the area before the dead man's kinfolks got there to get revenge. Of course, the sheriff just wanted to collect the reward money himself.

According to Daddy, Grandpa Coomer had gone to prison in the state of Kentucky. He had helped build the first electric chair that was built in that state. Grandpa also had escaped prison and was never caught. He and his wives and kids were always on the run.

My granddaddy had been mechanical. Well, my daddy told us that he could have built a car if he had had the parts. As a child, listening to these stories about him, I always wished that he were alive, since we always needed a good car.

All my grandparents had died by the time I was born. Daddy had killed Grandpa Coomer. Grandpa had cancer. He was hurting so bad that a doctor let Daddy give him a shot, probably morphine, which ended his life. Daddy never regretted doing it. After all, the man was suffering.

When I was small and we were still living in the tent, Aunt Pearl had a baby, and it was either born dead or died soon thereafter. Daddy and Mama made the trip in the old car to attend the funeral, leaving us kids by ourselves. Ruby Lee was in charge to cook and to care for us.

No one knew what happened, how the tent caught fire and burned to the ground. One of my older brothers, Raymond Lewis, got his hair burned when he went into the tent to try to find me, not knowing that Ruby Lee had already removed me safely.

Cans of rationed gas were sitting outside the tent, and it was a miracle they didn't catch fire and destroy the whole campsite. There was no way my parents could be notified. When they returned to the camp, they hit a tree with the old car when they realized their tent had burned down. None of their children were in sight. They found us at another family's tent. This family had taken us in and fed us while Mama and Daddy had been gone. This was the same family that Daddy hadn't invited to eat beans with us. This same man helped Daddy repair the old car.

In a few days my family sold the goat and left Lindale. By now Mama had shoes on her feet, and although she didn't realize it, she was in the family way again.

I'm not really sure about this, but by now my daddy either had had his teeth pulled or had them knocked out in a fight. All I know is that as far back as I can remember Daddy did not have teeth. He never got them replaced. However, he could eat an apple or meat as well as the next man. I was also told that Daddy had gotten his ribs broken in a fight. So, when kids asked me why my daddy didn't work, like have a job, I would say, "He can't work, he has broken ribs."

Another thing I was told was how Daddy and Mama met. Well, actually, she had met one of Daddy's sisters first. She had told Mama about her good-looking brother and his ex-wife. At Mama's initial meeting with Daddy she had said, "I know who you are, you have been married before."

That very night, Mama and her boyfriend, a guy named Robert, went to church. Daddy went too and watched from the back row. Mama and Robert got filled with the Holy Ghost. Daddy thought this would be a good time to make his move. When the church service was over, that's exactly what he did.

Daddy told Robert, "I am going to walk Dorothy home." "You are not, she came with me and she will leave with me," was Robert's threatening reply. According to Daddy, "he knocked the Holy Ghost out of Robert and walked Mama home."

Mama always told us she forgot about Robert right away, but I always thought it kind of funny that she had named one of her sons Robert. I reckon it must to have been at a time when she was reminiscing about the being filled with the Holy Ghost.

Three

It was Easter Sunday in 1943. Daddy got the family up early as usual, before daylight. The rooster had not even crowed. However, this would not be the same old usual day for us. The oldest son, Franklin Eugene, was leaving on a bus, going to fight a war into which he had been drafted. Having gone to school only a limited amount of time and being basically illiterate, feeling he had nothing to contribute to this war, he had not considered volunteering.

Mama fixed breakfast, biscuits and gravy. She gave me a bottle and felt her stomach for any movement of the baby she was carrying. The goat was gone so I was drinking Carnation milk and Kayro syrup. The family ate, dressed and reluctantly went to the bus station as a single unit.

Franklin Eugene told us all good-bye and promised to write home from time to time. My mother knew this would be a chore for him. He went through the door of the bus. On the steps he turned and smiled as he waved good-bye. We watched as the bus left town. We would never see him again.

Mama, who had thought this war would never mean anything to her family, had been wrong. She now had two sons in the service: Thurman Harris had enlisted in the Navy after Franklin Eugene had been drafted into the Marines. She needed her boys home with them. How could she survive without them? She felt distaste for whoever had started this war, but what could she do?

During the next two years, letters from Franklin Eugene were few. Since we were migrant workers, we kept moving from town to town in search of work in the fields. It is quite possible he may have written more letters that never reached us. The only sure thing was that he would have had to get help from others to write them. Ruby

Lee got one letter from him in which he had written, *"the river is wide and I can't step it. I love you a lot and I can't help it."*

His original thoughts that he had nothing to give to this war would prove to be wrong. He gave the ultimate gift anyone can give his country. He gave his life in Okinawa on May 09, 1945.

We were living back in Lindale in a small three-room house when the postmaster asked a young man in town to deliver the telegram to Daddy. The man, Angus Roberts, was about the same age as Franklin Eugene, and it pained him to deliver the bad news to Daddy. The telegram was dated May 16, 1945, informing my parents that Franklin Eugene Coomer had been killed. The telegram also stated that to prevent possible aid to the enemy they were not to divulge the name of his ship or station. These were two things Daddy and Mama didn't even know. Their oldest son had been due to come home in two months; however, they would never see or hold him again.

Ruby Lee, who had just turned twelve, remembered Mama taking off her shoes and hitting herself in the head with them. She didn't hit herself in the stomach though as she suspected she might be in the family way again.

Dollie E. (no middle name, just an initial) had been born on September 21, 1943, delivered by a midwife. She had blue eyes like Daddy. Mama thought that if she were going to have another baby, maybe it would be a boy; to replace the one she had lost.

Franklin Eugene was buried in the Philippines with hundreds of others who had lost their lives in this war. His body would never be returned to Lindale, Texas. Daddy received a letter from someone stating his son's personal belongings would be sent home. They never arrived.

Over the years my parents would sit and talk about Franklin's death. They wondered how he had been killed. *Did he really die instantly as one letter from a fellow Marine had indicated or did he suffer? What were his last thoughts? Did he think of them? Did he die a coward or a hero's death?* They felt they would never know just as they knew there would be no peace for them because of the not knowing.

In August of that same year tragedy struck again. The family was picking cotton in West Texas. Raymond Lewis, now sixteen, and girl crazy, was engaged. He was happy. He certainly was not going to enlist in any branch of the service. And they were not going to draft him either. He was going to get married and get rich. He was also going to have a big family like his parents. He was the oldest child at home, and the one Mama leaned on. He had his own car, and even though it was old, he kept it in good running condition. When it came to fixing cars he had talent, like his Grandpa Coomer. Inside his car he had pinned trinkets that he had collected on the sun visors. He was proud of that car. It was going to take him on a honeymoon.

He had been working hard all day. He washed his feet and hands and went to bed early. He thought about his girl friend and the wonderful life he was going to give her. He was going to get a regular job when he turned seventeen. The one thing he thought about most was sex. It was going to be nice to find out what that was all about. His brother, Franklin Eugene, had died without knowing, but it was not going to happen to him. He went to sleep on his pallet, smiling.

The next morning he woke up early and put on his boots that were placed next to his pallet on the floor. He felt a sting on his toe, the big toe on the right foot. He took the boot off and turned it upside down. A spider crawled out and he immediately killed it with the boot. Daddy came over and looked at the spider. He turned it over. It was a black widow. Neither one thought much about it, the spider was dead. It was time to eat and go to the field.

At lunchtime Daddy placed Dollie E. and me on a wagon bed that was being used as a table. Mama was putting food on the table and she felt the baby move in her. She smiled. Franklin Eugene's replacement was a boy. She just knew it. He could really kick.

Raymond Lewis and a friend, Hershel Lee May, were wrestling. Daddy said, "Boys, get up. One of you is going to get hurt." Hershel Lee, who was on top, got up. Raymond Lewis felt a sharp pain in his chest. He got to his knees and fell to the ground. He was dead. The doctor told Daddy the poison from the spider had reached his heart and had killed him. Hershel Lee lived the rest of his life feeling as if he, not the spider, had killed his best friend.

Soon after Franklin Eugene had been killed in the war, Daddy had taken out an insurance policy that would pay $150 toward a funeral. The funeral home in Lindale sent a hearse to West Texas and brought the body home. Daddy wondered how he would pay for all of this. To his surprise the $150 paid for the whole thing, including the long ride home.

Daddy sold Raymond Lewis' old car. Mama took out the trinkets and put them in a box along with his last pair of shoes. She would not throw them away until late in the 1980's. The girl who was engaged to Raymond Lewis went to California. She never married.

My parents were really grieving now. Two sons were dead. Another one was still in the war. Would he be killed also? They didn't hear from him much, and in their minds, he was probably in a prisoner of war camp in some foreign country. The family went back to West Texas. They had to. There was work in the cotton fields.

Mama handled her grief by working in the fields and taking care of her children. She talked to us and hugged us and told us she loved us and that nothing was ever going to separate us. Daddy, on the other hand, handled his grief by drinking beer and whiskey, staying drunk for weeks at a time. He also lashed out at Mama, sometimes striking her, as if losing his sons had been her fault, part of a plan she had concocted. He would leave the camp with anyone who would go with him. There were times when he didn't come home for days. Sometimes he left with a woman. If he had any money when he left, he was always broke when he returned.

Mama missed Thurman Harris something awful. She wished he would come home. He had been a lot of help to her before he had joined the Navy. He could cook and clean and sew. Once he had sewn sticks into the bottom of one of Ruby Lee's skirts making it stand out as though she had on a big petticoat underneath it. He would do anything he could for Ruby Lee so she would not feel too much of an outcast at school. At times when there was not any food to eat, Thurman Harris would boil sugar in water to make syrup. He then would make a piecrust from water and flour, put the syrup in it, cut the crust into a half moon and fry it. Daddy had let the older kids go to school only three or four months a year, and Thurman Harris always saw to it that they at least had the fried pie for lunch. Another good trait of his was his desire to have things as clean as possible. He made brooms out of corn shucks so he could sweep the floor. Sometimes after a rain he would sweep the dried mud away around the outside campsite. Mama grieved for her dead sons and for her living son whom she could not see. It was a terrible time for her.

Mama knew she would need him when the baby was born. She remembered the time when Thurman Harris had been much younger and Daddy was drunk, bragging about how he could break a person's neck by popping it with his foot. He had made Thurman Harris lie down on the ground and had proceeded to attempt to break his neck. Franklin Eugene had been a young boy himself and was very afraid of Daddy. Nonetheless, he would defy Daddy. The grown men in camp, probably all drunk, and all scared of Daddy, had done nothing to stop him from any of the abuse.

Franklin Eugene grabbed someone's gun, a .22 rifle. He told Daddy, when his foot was in midair, ready to strike, "You lower your foot one more inch and I will blow your head off!" After what seemed like an eternity, Daddy, red faced and mad as a hornet, put his foot on the ground. No one at the camp knew who was shaking the most—Mama, Thurman Harris, Franklin Eugene or Daddy. Later, when Daddy sobered up, he was secretly grateful to his son for standing up to him, but he never told him so.

Franklin Eugene did not know that you could not blow a man's head off with a .22 bullet. It would only make a small hole in a person. However, Daddy would still have been dead before his foot had hit Thurman Harris' neck.

Thurman Harris finally got to come home for a visit. We were living in an old house without any screens on the windows. I was sleeping in the bed next to him. He dreamed that he was playing baseball and he picked me up and threw me out the window. He thought I was the ball. I wasn't hurt, but Mama never put me in the bed with him again.

My family had bought a cow that Mama milked so that Dollie E. could have a good bottle. No one but Mama could milk her. Thurman Harris tried a few mornings to do just that. The cow kicked at him every time. One morning he put on one of Mama's dresses and a bonnet, went out and milked her. No animal was going to get the best of him.

Thurman Harris went off leave and back to the Navy. When his time in the Navy was up, he joined the Army. I cannot remember seeing him again until I was eleven- years old and in the sixth grade. I always wanted to see him and wondered, when I was hungry, why he didn't send us money to buy food, or why he didn't come home and stop Daddy from being so mean to us. I would not find out until I was grown that Daddy had been so mean to his older children that Thurman Harris had gotten away from him as soon as he had come of age. He did write, however, for Mama's sake. He loved her and wanted her to know that he was okay. When he finally did come home, he would have a new name. He didn't want to be called Thurman Harris. His new name would be Bud. To this day I still call him Thurman.

In February of 1946, Franklin Eugene's replacement was born. Sure enough it was a boy just as Mama had hoped. Daddy said to her. "The Lord giveth and the Lord taketh away." Mama wondered how he knew anything about the Lord. Mama did not have any more children. She didn't need anymore. After all, for twenty years, she had babies in diapers, and some without. She always worried if another child would die. The year would be 1998 before it would happen again. She would be ninety-four years old.

Four

Even as a very young girl I always had thoughts in my head. These were thoughts that would not go away, even in my sleep. For hours at night I would try to forget about things that had happened that day or what was coming tomorrow. I would dream things that would come true. It worried me as I felt that no one else on earth was capable of all this thinking. I hated it. I wanted peace and rest and not conflict. I was a combination of happy and sad.

My first recollection of life begins when I was five years old. It was August, 1947. I was on my first babysitting job. It was up to me to attend to Dollie E., not yet four, and Harvey Joe, the baby. All three of us were very dirty. Harvey Joe was sucking a dirty bottle. We had been left under a shade tree protected from the hot sun. I was hungry. The rest of my family was picking cotton in the field. They were so far away that I could hardly see them. I was scared. *Would they come back for us?*

Harvey Joe needed his diaper changed. He didn't have another one so I took it off, shook out the contents and put the wet, dirty thing back on him. A big pin in the middle of the three-cornered diaper held it together. Dollie E. was playing in the dirt.

I had just changed the diaper when I saw it coming toward us. "A snake!" In my young life I had seen a lot of them. Daddy had always been around to kill them. He was not afraid of them. I knew they were bad, and if they bit us we would die. The thing rattled, he was mad and he was going to get us. I would let him get me. He would then leave the other two alone. I got between him and the other two kids. In a split second I decided to kick at him with my bare feet. I hit the snake right in the middle. The snake made an awful sound, but he went off into the direction of the woods. Harvey Joe went to sleep. Dollie E. continued her play. I wet my pants.

Later that year we went to Roswell, New Mexico. The family found work there in the fields. On a trip to town Dollie E. and I got into a fight, pushing and shoving in the back seat of the car. The windows were down and our heads had been stuck outside. I believe we both wanted to be on the driver's side of the car, because when you rode on Mama's side of the car with your head out the window, you usually would end up with an eye full of snuff. Mama would spit into the wind.

Daddy said, "You girls stop that fighting or I am going to stop this car and give both of you a whipping." I knew he meant business, but I still wanted away from the snuff. Dollie said, "Get on your side of the car or I am going to push you out." I didn't. She opened the door on my side and pushed me out as she had warned. I landed in the middle of the road.

Daddy looked in the mirror of the car and there I lay. He stopped the car. Mama jumped out and screamed, "She is dead, another one of my babies is dead." Dollie E. started crying, "I didn't mean to kill her. We were just playing. She opened the door herself. I am not to blame. I think she killed herself."

Daddy picked up my unconscious body and carried me to the car. When we got to the hospital I was so dirty that the nurses had to clean me up before the doctor could examine me. I stayed in the hospital for a week. People I didn't know came to see me. My hair was washed and I had on clean hospital gowns. A preacher from a church brought me some clothes. I was getting food and regular meals. The farm workers took up money and bought me my first doll. Daddy brought it to me and acted like he had bought it. When I got out of the hospital, he had to buy Dollie E. one just like it. She also wanted my clothes. Our rivalry had begun. I had not seen her for days, and I sort of missed her, but I was jealous of her jealousy. I was mad that she had gotten a doll too. From then on when I had a birthday, she had one also, and when she had a birthday, I had one. If someone bought something for one of us, that person had to buy one for the other one of us.

One day all of us kids were playing around an old barn that was owned by the farmer we were picking cotton for. I stepped on a rusty, old nail. It went right through my bare, right foot. Daddy pulled it out, not listening to my screaming. Mama stood and watched, crying because she knew I was hurting, but she also knew Daddy would not take me into town to see a doctor. She put snuff from her mouth onto my wound and gave me an old sock to wear. I could hardly walk on my right foot for a few days. To my surprise the wound was healing fairly well, but one day while back in the car, Dollie E. stepped on top of it. The pain was so bad I almost passed out. She thought it was real funny. My foot swelled up and puss ran out of the wound. It took several weeks after that before my foot was healed. By that time, the sock was really filthy, so one day I just pulled it off and threw it away. It took several years before the scar finally faded out.

That year a movie was made in part at Lindale. The name of the movie was *Strike it Rich* with Rod Cameron. I was only five years old, but I was allowed to roam around the town. Every day I would watch as the actors acted out their parts. It was great fun. The movie was about striking oil. Men in the town were paid money to leave their old cars parked along the streets. One man in town bootlegged whiskey to the stars. I remember one scene where Rod Cameron kissed the leading lady right in front of the drug store. I thought that he was probably going to get arrested by our lawman. Everybody knew you could not kiss a woman in public view of other folks! Those movie stars were a bunch of fools. To my surprise no one went to jail, but when the movie came out, that scene was left out.

The next spring we moved to Lone Star, Texas, where we camped next to a big lake. We now owned a tent with a floor in it. The Hayley family owned the land we were camping on, and Daddy really liked them. They treated us better than anybody ever had.

Mama made lye soap in a big black pot. She washed our clothes with a rub board and hung them on the weeds to dry. She also washed her children with the lye soap. Every Saturday she put water in a #3 washtub and let it warm by the sun. Our hair, which had not been combed for a week, would get washed. We did not own a hairbrush but Mama had a big comb. Sometimes the comb would have several teeth missing. I hated having my hair combed because it really hurt. She usually put two kids at a time in the tub. The water would really be dirty after the day's washings. Our hair was washed and plaited until the next Saturday.

One afternoon Daddy, who sold his fish to just about anybody, had a stringer filled up with perch. He was looking for a buyer. Now it is against the law to sell perch in the state of Texas as they are considered to be fish bait. Daddy didn't think there was a law made that he couldn't or wouldn't break if given half a chance.

A man approached him and asked him how much he wanted for the fish. Daddy, who was very smart; he always thought so anyway, decided that he might just be looking at a plain clothes game warden. "Well, Daddy said, "these fish ain't for sale, but the stringer will cost you $2.00." The man bought the string of perch. Was he a game warden? Daddy didn't really know, but he was smart enough not to take the chance. He sure didn't want to have to whip a game warden over a string of fish bait.

Ruby Lee was fifteen. By now she was a seasoned smoker. She had started sneaking around stealing Daddy's cigarettes, usually when he was drunk, by the time she was nine years old. She also had started sneaking around with the boys. She was in love with H. L. "Bo" Paul. Bo was the boy who had helped Daddy deliver me. He was almost twenty. He loved Ruby Lee as much as she loved him. The first time he had seen her she had been nine years old and was licking a barber pole outside a barbershop in Lindale where he was getting a haircut. She had thought it was peppermint candy. Bo thought that if a girl could turn a barber pole into peppermint candy, she had to be really something.

There were two problems with the love affair. The first one was Ruby Lee was so young. The other one was that my sorry daddy, who was a drunk, lazy and chased women, thought Bo Paul was trash.

While living in Lone Star, to make some money, Daddy sold liquor. What he didn't sell he drank. He would hide the liquor in a tow sack and put the sack in the lake. He also had a favorite hiding place in the car. One day the law came calling. They searched but could not find the hidden whiskey. One of the lawmen told us kids that he would give anyone a quarter to tell him where our daddy had hidden his liquor. Now this was 1948 and a quarter was really a lot of money. William Henry, who was seven at the time, yodeled like a hound dog. Daddy was arrested, but he did make the lawman pay my brother the quarter. When Daddy got out of jail, my brother got a whipping.

We returned to Lindale and moved into a very small house. Ruby Lee would fix her bed like she was in it, and then she would leave the house to see Bo. Robert Lee, who slept close to her, was always afraid Daddy would discover what she was doing and whip the both of them. He would have whipped Robert too for not telling on her. Daddy never found out.

Every time Daddy got drunk he would be real mean to Mama and the rest of us. William Henry was his favorite target. Daddy loved to beat on that boy. William Henry was becoming mean too. He picked on us younger kids after Daddy picked on him. One day William Henry took a knife and cut a slice out of two of our old kitchen chairs. None of us would tell Daddy who had done it. Daddy told us he would give us a lick apiece until someone told him who had cut the chairs. We were lined up and each got a lick. I decided to lie and told Daddy I had cut the chairs. He had promised that if we would just confess he would not whip us. He had lied! I really took a beating from him. He made the other kids watch. Even the older kids were afraid to speak up and tell the truth, and the younger ones were not about to. I was put to bed without supper. Later in the night Ruth Evelyn brought me a cold biscuit. William Henry never even thanked me for taking his whipping.

The next day Daddy was sober and he tried to talk to me. He didn't apologize for the belt marks on my body. I hated him. He did tell me that he didn't think I was the one who had cut the chairs. I was too stubborn and too afraid of William Henry to confess the truth. For some reason, I knew it was bothering Daddy that I was giving him the cold shoulder. I was glad.

I decided that I would never take another whipping for my brother. I had learned the hard way that good deeds don't always go unpunished.

Daddy wasn't just mean to his wife and kids; he was mean to animals too. Once when I was about three years old, I had been playing with a small dog. I accidentally step on his foot and he bit my arm, his teeth tearing my skin some. Daddy had grabbed that dog and beat him to death with his fists. He always felt it was okay for him to be mean to us, but no animal was going to be that way.

The house we were living in was a few miles out in the country. We would walk to town with Mama on Saturday so she could buy groceries. The sun was hot, and so was the tar on the road. We would get a big stick, and roll the tar around the end of it. Then we would roll the stick and the tar in some gravel. We would then have a good rock to throw at the passing cars or anyone else for that matter. Mama would be getting on to us all the way to town and back. We were hard to control!

In August of that year we were living in Sinton, Texas, which is located in South Texas. The family was picking cotton. Ruby Lee and Bo decided to get married. The plan was for Bo to take her to the bus station in Odom, Texas, which was about seven miles from Sinton. From there she would catch a bus to Corpus Christi. Bo would meet her the next day. Bo did not own a car but he planned to take the bus himself the next day. He gave Ruby Lee $12, which would be enough money to get a room and something to eat.

Ruby Lee told Mama and Daddy that she was going to a party. Bo borrowed a car and took her to Odom to catch the bus. He came back to Sinton and hung around the camp. Daddy had only let Ruby Lee go to the party because the Paul boy was not going. She was to be back by 10 o'clock. Sometime during the night Daddy woke up and discovered that Ruby Lee had not returned from the party. He sent Mama to get her. Ruby Lee was not to be found. Mama came back to Daddy screaming, "Ruby Lee got kidnapped by the Mexicans." Daddy was sleeping off a drunk. Bo knew he had to tell them where she was. Daddy loaned Bo his truck and told him to go to Corpus Christi and get her.

Meanwhile in Corpus Christi, Ruby Lee had gotten off the bus and had taken a taxi to a hotel to get a room. She didn't weigh a 100 pounds, being only fifteen, and she was very young looking. The taxi driver asked her if she would be okay. She assured him she would be. She was very nervous. When she got to the lobby of the hotel there were two policemen sitting at a table drinking coffee. That scared her. She was shaking when she told the desk clerk she wanted a room for the night. The policemen hardly looked up at her. She went up to the room and lay down on the bed fully dressed. She couldn't sleep though. She knew Daddy would kill her if he ever saw her again. She comforted herself with the thought that now maybe she would never have to lay eyes on him again. She would miss the rest of the family though, especially Mama and the little ones.

She was so much in love. She thought about Bo and all the good years ahead. She had no idea that a girl had to be eighteen years old to get married in Texas without one of the parents signing. Around five o'clock the next morning she got up from the bed and decided to take a walk. She had never been to Corpus Christi before and didn't know it was a big town. She was sick to her stomach. *What had she done? Daddy would probably kill Bo too.* It was a chance she had to take. Now she was wondering where Bo was going to meet her. This was a fact they had overlooked in their planning. *What if Bo had decided not to come to for her? What would she do? He loves me, he* will *come!* She could not believe her eyes when right before her at a streetlight appeared the love of her life. She fell weeping into his arms.

The pair drove back to Sinton. They had no other choice. They had Mr. Coomer's truck. Bo may or may not have been a lot of things, but he was no thief. He would return the truck. He didn't want to return the girl. Ruby Lee was afraid. *Could Bo protect her from her Daddy?* They had no way of knowing that her Daddy, now sober, had decided he might as well let her marry that "sorry old Paul boy."

Bo was a few days away from his twentieth birthday. Ruby Lee was fifteen. Mrs. Paul would not sign for Bo to get married. It was unclear as to what she thought about Ruby Lee, but her being so young was probably the main reason for her not signing. Mama, however, went with the two of them, letting Bo drive the truck. Mama would sign for Ruby Lee. Daddy waited back at the camp. Mr. & Mrs. Paul waited too. The three of them did not talk. All of them were mad.

At the first Justice-of-the-Peace Bo told a lie. He said he was going to be twenty-one in a few days. He didn't think a few days would make any difference. Well it did. A man had to be twenty-one to get married in Texas in 1948 or he had to have one of his parents sign for him. The two were disappointed. Mr. or Mrs. Paul would never sign for him.

Mama decided to take them to another Justice-of-the-Peace in another town. Mama told Bo, "You lied a little bit back there, now you have to lie a whole lot." This time he told the Justice-of-the-Peace he was a few days away from his twenty-second birthday. The ceremony went off without a hitch.

That first night the newlyweds slept together for the first time on a pallet on the ground beside the highway in the camp. The parents didn't get any sleep at all. Daddy cussed and ranted all night, drunk as he was. The next morning the new couple got up at four o'clock and rode in the back of our truck to the cotton patch. Mama could not look at Ruby Lee. She felt ashamed, as she knew what had happened to Ruby Lee the night before. She had never discussed anything about sex with her, and she felt sure Ruby Lee didn't know a thing. Ruby Lee felt happy although she was a little bewildered about the sex.

That evening Ruby Lee took a bath in a small lake close to the camp. She wondered if the sex thing would happen again. If Bo wanted it to, it would happen. She felt safe as he lay down beside her on the pallet that night. Bo would take care of her. Ruby Lee decided then and there that she would never be hungry again. They would work hard and save their money. Three weeks later they had picked enough cotton to buy a mattress and an old car. They were good workers; it was true.

It didn't take Daddy very long to realize what a nice fellow Bo Paul really was. He did not drink beer or whiskey. He certainly was not a drunk like Daddy and Henry Paul, Bo's daddy. He worked harder than any man Daddy had ever known. They became real buddies. Bo became just like a son. If fact, from then on, if Daddy decided to do anything, like buy an old car, he would consult with Bo about it, and not his boys.

This was my first year to have to pick cotton. Mama and Daddy thought I was old enough now. I refused to work if they didn't make Dollie E. work too. She would be five in September and she was bigger than me anyway. Mama put straps on two tow sacks for us to put our cotton in. She pulled Harvey Joe on her cotton sack as she worked. This way no one had to baby-sit him. Mama had her three youngest children close. Sometimes Joe would go up the cotton row, pick some of the cotton and pile it up. Mama would pick it up and put it in her sack when she got to him. Most of the time he just rode on her sack sucking his bottle that was always close by. But, anyway one looked at it, we were all laborers in the field now.

Dollie E. and I soon got tired of picking cotton. We took a pair of scissors and cut the bottom of our tow sacks out thinking that if we didn't have anything to put the cotton in we would not have to pick it. We were wrong. When Daddy found out what we had done, he whipped both of us with a belt; he was drunk and mean. I didn't speak to him for a week. Mama fixed two more sacks for us. We were never unemployed again.

One night I had a terrible earache. We did not have any medicine to put in my ear. I was crying. Mama peed in a bucket, then took a spoon and filled it with her warm pee. She put the pee in my ear. In a few minutes I had hushed my crying and was sound asleep. The next morning I used that same spoon to eat my breakfast. Had she washed it? I doubt it.

Riding in our truck I started noticing Burma-Shave signs along the roadway. Mama would read them to us: "CAR IN DITCH…DRIVER IN TREE-MOON WAS FULL AND SO WAS HE." "DON'T LOSE YOUR HEAD…TO GAIN A MINUTE-YOU NEED YOUR HEAD…YOUR BRAINS ARE IN IT."

Five

August turned to September and then to October. We moved back to Lindale. I was six-years-old and I was going to start to school. I knew how to say my ABC's even though I had never actually seen any of them. I could count to twenty. I had never seen any numbers either.

School had been started six weeks when Mama took us to enroll. Right before this she had bought us a few clothes. We all had on brand new shoes. My feet that were not used to the shoes were hurting. I was nervous but excited. I really didn't know what it meant to go to school. I kind of figured I would meet up with those ABC's and maybe the numbers too. I handed my sack lunch to Miss Pruitt, the teacher. She told me to be seated at the back of one of the rows in an empty seat. I did what I was told to do. Well, wouldn't you know it; I sat down in an empty seat that someone was temporarily out of.

A girl said, "That is my seat, get out of it." I started to shake. I sat down in another seat across from her. I was a short girl and I couldn't see over anybody's head. All the kids turned around and stared at me. I began to cry. The teacher came back and hugged me. I liked her right away. I thought *I will whip that girl the first chance I get.*

To my surprise this girl looked at me and smiled, seemingly to say, "I am sorry." I regretted my decision to whip her, so I changed my mind. She was pretty and had really black hair. I touched my brown, thin, stringy hair and felt a little jealous, but I would like her; indeed I would.

Miss Pruitt sat us around in circles. There were three different sets of circles. She gave each of us a book. I was scared to death. This was my first time to ever hold a book. *Were the ABC's in here?*

The teacher, not knowing I didn't know anything about words, asked me to read the first sentence in the book. I stared at the word. I didn't know what it was. A girl in the group raised her hand and said, "Let me tell her." The word was "the." The kids laughed. I fought back tears. I wanted to go home. I knew I could not whip all of them.

During the first recess, the pretty black haired girl came over to play with me. Her name was Mary Shacklett. She showed me something to play on. It was swings. I had never seen swings before. I discovered I could really swing high. I stood up in the swings and pumped and almost went over the swings backwards.

Miss Pruitt signaled for us to come back into the building. I thought for a moment that I would just stay outside and play, but then I remembered Mama telling me that the teacher and the principal were the bosses. I got in line like all the rest of the kids. The boys got in one line and the girls were in another one.

We went into a room that had some doors inside it and some things lined up next to the wall. I had no idea as to what they could be. One by one the girls went behind the next available door. When it came my turn I did too. When I got behind the door I looked at the contraption in front of it. *What was this thing and what was I suppose to do with it?* I stayed in there just a few minutes and went back on the other side of the door.

I needed to relieve myself. I should have gone behind a tree in the schoolyard, but I had been having too much fun at recess to do it. Now the girls were washing their hands in the things that were lining the wall. I decided I had better wash mine too. As soon as I started washing them, I wet my new blue jeans.

During the second recess I asked my new friend what the contraptions were in the little room in the building. She told me about bathrooms. I could not believe my ears. She promised to show me how to use the commode to pee in and sinks to wash my hands in. I had my doubts that such a thing as a commode could work. *Where would it take my pee?* Sure enough after recess I used it for the first time. Mary showed me how to flush it. I jumped with surprise when the water rushed into it. I washed my hands; dried them and walked proudly back into the classroom. By now my pants had dried.

My skin was really dark from the summer in the sun and the fields. Some of the kids went home and told their parents that a Mexican had started to school. This caused a small stir, as there were no minorities in Lindale School in 1948. However, when the parents found out that I was one of the Coomer kids, everything was okay.

Within a few days things had settled down at school. The three reading groups we were in were classified high, medium and low readers. I had been placed in the low reading group the first day. Probably because of what had happened to me that first day, I was determined to learn and by the next six weeks I was in the high reading group. The ABC's were making sense and turning out to be my friends. I learned all about Dick, Jane, Sally and Spot, the dog. The girl who had made fun of me the first day was still in the low group.

I discovered I could beat everybody at jumping rope, could out run all of the girls and most of the boys. Shooting marbles, spinning tops and playing baseball were easy; I loved recess. First grade was turning out to be okay. I could tell that some of the kids liked me. One boy discovered that the initials for my name, Annie Bell Coomer, were ABC, so just about all of the kids started calling me Miss ABC. I would not have liked for my brothers and sisters to call me that, but I liked the kids at school to do it. It kind of made me special in some way, to my way of thinking.

The only sad thing about first grade was the fact that I began to notice most of the kids had better clothes and nicer shoes than I did. The girls' hair was washed and combed. Some of them had ribbons in their hair. I usually wore blue jeans and a shirt. I had only a couple of pairs. Blue jeans came in handy at recess. My hair was never combed and my face was usually dirty. However, because I was so good at recess, most of the kids took a liking to me.

I had my first boyfriend in first grade. He didn't know it though. I found myself wanting to be around him, especially at recess. One day when we were playing the game London Bridge he was holding hands with a girl to make the bridge that we were going under. I was jealous, and since she was a little taller than he was, I told him that it was against the law for a boy to marry any girl bigger than himself. I wound up with my first heartache. There would be many more.

One recess the teacher came and told us to get in line; we were going to get our pictures made. I had to get out of line to go to the bathroom. I could not get my pants buttoned up, and I couldn't find the teacher to do it for me. I got back in line and had my picture made. The picture came back, and sure enough, there were my pants, unzipped and unbuttoned. I was ashamed of that picture for a long time.

About two weeks before school was out, Daddy, who didn't care much about education, took all of us out. We went to Winnsboro, Texas, about thirty-five miles away to pick strawberries. It was spring and my shoes were worn out. I had been going to school barefooted for the last few weeks, so I was kind of glad to leave. I didn't get to see another book until I returned to school the coming fall, and I missed them.

In Winnsboro I met my second boyfriend. His name was Charles Frank Ragsdale. He was the son of the farmer we picked strawberries for. He wasn't good looking like my first boyfriend, but he was smart. He had a collection of funny books; however, he would not let any of us look at them. After I worked in the fields picking berries, Charles Frank and I would play. He was a year older than I. His parents did not make him work in the fields. He was an only child, and I thought that was pretty neat.

We called his parents Uncle Buck and Aunt Mandy. They were really good to my family. They furnished us an old house to live in while we gathered their crops. We had a Coleman stove and a lantern, and we always had a can of white gasoline to use in them. The can of gas sat outside the house.

Ruby Lee and Bo went to Winnsboro too. Uncle Buck and Aunt Mandy didn't have a house for them to live in, but they did have a chicken house they no longer used. Ruby Lee and Bo cleaned it up and moved in. They lived there until the strawberry picking ended.

Charles Frank taught me how to sniff the gasoline. It made us both pretty silly. One afternoon, after we had had our noses stuck to the can, he took my hand and led me to the woods. He pushed me down, pushed up my dress and pulled down my panties. I thought this was funny until he tried to put his "little thing" in me. He wasn't very strong, sort of sickly. I knocked him off me and kicked him hard. I ran back to the house as fast as I could. *What was he trying to do to me?* I didn't know, but I felt it wasn't right. From then on I avoided him as much as I could. I never told anyone what had happened. I continued to sniff the white gasoline, but always alone.

We worked hard in the strawberry fields. The kids would pick the berries in pints and take them to the parents who sat at a shed. The grown-ups would pack the pints, putting the best looking berries on top. The farmers would then take the berries to the market in town and sell them.

Before long the strawberry season ended, and we moved back to Lindale and picked blackberries before going to the Rio Grande Valley in South Texas to pick cotton.

Six

We started out on our trip to South Texas early one morning before daybreak. Daddy had purchased an old truck for us. In the back of the truck were clothes, bedding, cooking utensils, a water can, a Coleman stove and lantern, and cots for each of us to sleep on. Robert Lee, Ruth Evelyn and William Henry rode in the back. Daddy and Mama were in the cab along with Dollie E., Harvey Joe and me. Harvey Joe sat on Mama's lap while Dollie E. and I stood up in the seat between Mama and Daddy. Sometimes one of us would sit in the floor between Mama's feet.

We were on U. S. Highway 69 going through Tyler, a town about fifteen miles to the south of Lindale. Tyler is the county seat of Smith County. I saw the red light and knew it meant that we had to stop. Daddy didn't see any cars coming in any direction so it was nonsense to stop the truck. He ran the red light. In what seemed like just an instant the Tyler police pulled him over.

They didn't ask for his driver's license, but they asked him his name. He said, "Buford Coomer from Lindale, Texas. I'm practically your neighbor." "Mr. Coomer didn't you see the red light?" The policeman asked. "Yea, but I didn't see you," was Daddy's reply. "Well, Mr. Coomer, what's your hurry?" The other lawman asked. "I'm on my way to South Texas to pick cotton, and me and my family; we need to get on the damn road. Can we go now?" Daddy asked. I was scared. This was my first encounter with the law and I thought they would put us all in jail. Daddy wasn't afraid. I found out later it sure wasn't his first encounter with them. To my surprise they let us go, telling Daddy to slow down. As soon as the laws were out of sight, Daddy sped up, running all the red lights he came in contact with until we were out of town.

We got about two hundred miles that first day. We made our camp at a roadside park. Mama cooked our supper on the Coleman stove. Daddy got drunk, still cussing the laws for stopping him back in Tyler. He never needed much of a reason to get drunk.

Right before dark Mama fixed each of us a bed on our cots all close together. She got several ropes from inside the back of the truck and laid them all end to end. It looked like a long snake. Everyone knew that a real snake would think the rope was a snake, and one snake won't cross over another snake. We would sleep safe from them. During the night I needed to go the bathroom, but I also thought the ropes were snakes so I just peed in my pants. They were dry by the time morning came. Most of our bed coverings always smelled of pee.

On the road the next day Harvey Joe became very sick. Mama thought he was dead. Daddy pulled the truck off the road next to where some men were working on the highway. They came over to investigate. One of the men said that he would take Mama and the baby into the next town to the doctor's office. I was very sad. They were gone a long time. When they got back, Harvey Joe seemed to be all right. Mama said the doctor had told her he probably had something bad but wasn't quite sure what it could be. The doctor had wanted her to put the baby in a hospital as soon as possible. Mama knew that wasn't about to happen. Daddy would never go for that. The doctor had suggested that we all rest up for a couple of days at the next roadside park. He also had told her that the baby needed nourishment and should stay on the bottle for a long time. Mama took the doctor at his word. Her baby would suck the bottle until he was seven years old. We spent the night right there on the road. The next morning we continued our trip to the cotton patch.

Daddy's brother Harley and his sister Ellen lived in the Valley with their families. They had married brothers and sisters. Their kids were double first cousins. I didn't know what that meant at the time but I liked the sound of it. Uncle Harley had four children-Barbara, Larry, Judy (who was my age), and Tommy. Aunt Ellen had three girls-Patsy, Joyce and the baby sister they called Sissy. We camped out in Aunt Ellen's yard and went to work in the fields each day.

One Saturday morning Daddy took all of us to Reyonsa, Mexico, right across the border from McAllen. We went down into the markets. People tried to sell us all kinds of stuff. We didn't have any money. Meat was hung up and flies were buzzing all over the place. As we were going back across the border into the United States, our truck was stopped by the border patrol. One of the guards looked at me and said something to me in Spanish. He scared me to death. *What was he saying?*

The border patrol told Daddy in English that I needed to step out of the truck. *What was he going to do with me?* I didn't like Daddy very much but I liked that guard even less. I was not about to get out of the truck. Daddy told me to get out of the truck, but I told him no. "Damn it girl, get your ass out there and talk to these ignorant Mexicans. They must think you are one of them," Daddy ordered.

By now the guard was mad, after all Daddy had just said that he was ignorant. The guard began to open the truck door. I screamed, "Don't let them get me, Daddy please." The guard, realizing he had made a big mistake, shut the door. He explained to Daddy that he had thought I was a Mexican girl and was being kidnapped. I guess my East Texas accent had come in handy. Daddy was fighting mad by now. He got out of the truck, Mama begging him not to. Several more guards had come to the scene by now.

Daddy explained to them how he was going to get them all fired. They should be able to tell a white girl from a Mexican. We were all glad, including the guards, when Daddy got back into the truck and we drove off. The Mexicans knew after all that we were American citizens and we had our rights.

On the way back to Aunt Ellen's, Mama told us that a few years before any of us had been born Daddy and another man and his wife went across this very border. Once inside Mexico they got drunk, went to a Mexican graveyard and stole some bones and hid them in the car. What they intended to do with them was never made clear. They too had been stopped at the border and their car searched by the guards. When the guards found the bones, the trio was taken to jail and didn't get out for about a month. Mama told the story to try to cheer us up, especially me, but it didn't work. I was thinking how nice it would have been if they had kept Daddy in that jail.

Daddy also had a story to tell. He told us about the times he had gone into Mexico before they had paved their streets. When it rained and the streets were muddy, he would buy a lot of penny candy and throw it into the streets. He loved to see the Mexican kids run out there to pick it up, getting all muddy, sliding around in the mud and candy. Well, I believed him-that he would buy other kids candy but not his own. I plotted about his death while listening to this tale.

Mama, still trying to cheer me up, told us that when Franklin Eugene, Thurman Harris, Raymond Lewis and Ruby Lee were little, Daddy would give them a nickel a piece to buy candy with from time to time. Ruby Lee would not buy any candy, saving her money instead. When the kids got back home, she would bum candy from her brothers. Mama told us that she had had to stop Ruby Lee from taking the candy from the boys. I didn't think this was so funny, and was a little jealous, as I could never recall Daddy buying his present day kids any candy.

Mama continued with another story about Ruby Lee. Being small for her age, she would hide a lot and the whole family would have to look for her. One day when Mama could not find her, they all began to panic. Even Daddy was looking for her. They would call her name, and they could hear her answer, "Here I is", but they just could not locate her. When they finally found her, she was in a big tub filled with water and was about to drown. She had been unable to climb out of the tub and was weak from hollering, "Here I is." I smiled as I thought about my sister. She was probably just playing a trick on them all. We finally got back to the Valley.

Flour came in sacks made of cloth. A person could take the big sacks of flour and make dresses out of them. Mama made us several flour sack dresses sewed by hand. She stuffed cotton into two of the sacks that had the body and face of a doll on them and made dolls for Dollie E. and me. As she made the clothes and dolls she thought of Thurman Harris. If he were here he would help her sew. We slept with those dolls the rest of the summer, but by summer's end the dolls were dirty and torn up. We threw them away.

Uncle Earnest and his family came to the Valley to work. The oldest girl was named Betty Jo. She was two years older than I. Betty Jo was beautiful. She had blonde hair and pretty white teeth. Richard Earnest, the oldest boy, was my age. He was red complexioned and favored his Daddy. Mary Ann, Lillie Faye and John Henry were younger. Later on Becky would be born. One baby named Diana Kate had died.

Uncle Earnest's wife was named Kate. She was pretty. My Daddy must have thought so too, since he was always taking her with him in the truck. If that bothered Mama, she never let on. When Becky was born she favored Uncle Earnest more than any of the others did, even Richard Earnest. Mama was real glad about that. She was always saying, "Boy, that Becky sure looks like Earnest." She seemed real pleased like it meant something to her.

Uncle Earnest was as mean as Daddy. He drank whiskey all the time and chewed tobacco. He was never without a pint of whiskey and drank it straight from the bottle. He was handsome. I was afraid of him. He, like Daddy, treated his family bad and wouldn't hold down a real job. And, he didn't even have broken ribs. I believe he had been in some branch of the service and drew some type of disability check.

One day I noticed two of Aunt Kate's babies asleep on the bed, really sleeping sound. Now, I couldn't let that continue, could I? I went to the bed and pinched both of them, and they both woke up. So, I pinched them again to make them cry, and they did. I heard Aunt Kate say to Mama, "Now that is a mystery why those kids are crying, I just left them a minute ago and they were both fast asleep." I ran from the room, just escaping before she got in there. Aunt Kate never did figure out the mystery, as I am just now confessing about those howling babies.

That first summer in the Valley I noticed that Aunt Ellen and Uncle Harley were really good to their kids and to us as well. I would lie awake at night and wonder why Daddy and Uncle Earnest couldn't be like them. It was hard for me to believe that they were brothers and sisters.

When we left the Valley that year we went north to Sinton, Texas. We lived in a camp there in a small cabin. We were told that the camp had served as a labor camp during World War II. Whether it had been used as a labor camp during the war didn't matter, it sure was being used as one now.

We went to the fields early in the mornings. Work was hard. Daddy was always on us to pick more cotton, never letting up. The sun in South Texas seemed to be hotter than the one in Lindale. I believed back then that the sky held more than one sun. I was always tired and hungry. There was never enough to eat. I wanted to get back to school, to see my friends and to read. I wasn't cut out to be a cotton picker.

In the afternoons, a Mexican woman would come around selling snow cones for a nickel. Even though Daddy was mean, he would give us all a nickel, even Uncle Earnest's kids, so that we could get a snow cone. The Mexican woman was pretty. This was a fact not lost on Daddy. Several times that summer I noticed him going into her cabin and staying for over an hour. When he visited her, all her children came outside to play. I thought at the time that it was nice of my Daddy to visit them, as her husband had left her and she didn't know where he was. I had never known children before who didn't have a Daddy. I felt sorry for them. Anyway, I loved to hear the bell ringing on the woman's little wagon, and we would all run out to meet her.

I became very sick within a few days after we arrived in Sinton. It was the water. My stomach just could not adjust to it. I threw up quite a bit. I asked Mama to take me to the doctor, but Daddy wouldn't let her. I picked cotton in the tow sack, hardly able to walk. I was very sick, but as Daddy had said, I would get over it.

One day Aunt Kate, defying Daddy, took me to the doctor. I was afraid that Daddy would whip me when we got back. The doctor gave me some medicine to take, free of charge. Daddy didn't say a word to either one of us when we got back to the camp. Mama thanked Aunt Kate for what she had done. She would never have found the courage to take me. Uncle Earnest gave Aunt Kate a good cussing for minding another man's family business. That satisfied Daddy; Aunt Kate had it coming.

Sinton had a city park, and on the weekends Daddy would take us there to play. Mama would cook us something to eat. The Coleman stove was always in the back of the truck. We played on the swings. I felt like a different person during those times. I hated

South Texas, but I loved this park. I pretended to be a rich man's daughter on those days.

One afternoon in the park I was talking to a Mexican couple that had a nice looking car. I was jealous of their little girl who was about my age. She had on a pretty dress and her hair was combed. She didn't like me and made fun of me because she said I was a road tramp. I told her that at least I wasn't a Mexican. I would not always be a road tramp but that she would always be a Mexican, eating peppers. She started to cry. I had triumphed over her. But, for some reason, I wasn't happy about my victory. I was ashamed for having made her cry. I tried to apologize, but she wouldn't let me.

The parents of the little girl became mad and took me over to discuss the matter with Daddy. I knew I was in for it. For once Daddy let me tell my side of the story. He was drinking and got really mad when I told him she had called me a road tramp. The little girl's Daddy repeated that we were road tramps. Daddy hit him hard, and the man fell down. He took his wife and daughter and left the park. Daddy told them he never wanted to see them in the park again. I was proud of my Daddy. He had stood up for me. My happiness was short lived as Daddy shouted, "You kids get in the damn truck. You know that sorry Mexican will bring the laws out here." We loaded up and left. We never did see them in the park again.

Daddy's sister, Aunt Leona, lived in Taft, a town just a few miles from Sinton. She had one son, Orville. He was a very handsome blonde haired boy a year older than I. Well, I fell in love with my first cousin. They too would come to the park on the weekends.

Aunt Leona had at one time been married to a rich man who owned a big farm. He had been older than she. She had fallen in love with a ranch hand and had left the rich man for him. The ranch hand was Orville's daddy. I'm not sure if Aunt Leona ever married him or not. She was now married to Uncle Morton who was Orville's step-dad. He was real short and always had a cigar in his mouth. Aunt Leona wasn't all that nice to us, but Uncle Morton was a real pal.

Before Aunt Leona had been married to the rich man, she had had another husband who had died. The story goes that at his funeral, after viewing the body in the coffin for the last time, and crying over it, she went right out the side door into the cab of a truck and left with the truck driver who had been waiting for her. She was a character all right.

Aunt Peggy, who was Aunt Ellen's twin sister, lived in Corpus Christi. She would also come to see us on the weekends. She had a colorful past with several husbands, but she had now settled down with Uncle Eddie. He was short also. I remember how small his feet were. He wore size six shoes. Aunt Peggy had a son named Sonny, but he was older and we didn't see much of him. Uncle Eddie, who was a Navy Chief, and Aunt Peggy were really good to us. The Coomer girls seemed to be a better lot than the boys.

All the Coomers, however, both men and women, liked to drink alcohol. That is one reason they came to visit. Uncle Morton and Uncle Eddie drank too. Uncle Earnest would bring his family to the park. One of the reasons of course was so that he could get drunk with his siblings. I can't remember Aunt Kate ever drinking. Mama never touched the stuff.

Around dark, every Saturday at the park, the Coomer brothers and sisters would get into a fight. The fights usually started when Daddy or Uncle Earnest commenced telling their sisters that they were whores. Then the sisters' husbands would take up for them. It was awful how that bunch would cuss and hit at each other. Mama and Aunt Kate stayed out of it. They were too afraid to cross any of them. By Sunday morning, after sleeping it off, they would be sober and happy. They really loved each other. They had had a hard life growing up, and they were not going to let a few disagreements and fights come between them.

Concerning the park in Sinton, there were some monkey cages at that park. Some of the monkeys favored my brothers. All my brothers acted like the monkeys. We gave those monkeys a fit. We feed peanuts and popcorn to them which was against the rules. We threw sticks and small rocks at them. Sometimes they would throw the stuff back at us. We mocked them. You know if you have ever been to a monkey cage, that they pick things, like lice, off of each other. Then they eat the lice or whatever. We did that too. One of us would play like we were picking something off another one of us and play like we were eating it. We sometimes didn't have to play like we were picking lice off of someone's head, as most summers one of us would get head lice. The monkey cages were fun. Real monkeys on the inside and Coomer monkeys on the outside! Fun didn't get any better than that.

Sometimes Daddy and Uncle Earnest would get so drunk that their kids would pee into their beer bottles. They would then sell the homemade beer to their daddies for a nickel a bottle. The fun for the kids was watching the drunks enjoying the fruit of their labor.

Although Mama didn't drink, she had a bad habit. She dipped Levi Garrett snuff. She had to steal money from Daddy to buy it. She usually did this when he was passed out. She would then keep the money hidden in a tobacco pouch pinned inside her dress next to her bosom. Sometimes at night when everyone was asleep, I would think about trying to steal it off her, but I never got that brave.

During the week we went to the fields early. Daddy always thought ours had to be the first family to arrive at the cotton patch. Most of the time it wasn't daylight, and he would follow us down the cotton rows driving the truck with the lights on so that we could see the cotton.

We never got to eat breakfast, having to get to the field so early. If we didn't get up the first time Daddy called us, he would throw cold water all over us. If we didn't get up then, we got a whipping. I was always still sleepy in the mornings, but I never had to be called twice. Around nine o'clock, Daddy would go into town and would buy us something to eat. It was usually pressed ham and bread and sometimes a cold drink. He would let us take a thirty-minute break from work. Soon as we ate, we could lie down under a shade to rest. Daddy would soon holler to us, "Get back to work. Get your heads down and your tails up. If you get tired, I will rub your backs." He never picked cotton, just kept us working. But, of course, he kept all the money. I stayed away from him as much as I could.

We would all be tired at night. Mama would cook potatoes and usually some hamburger meat for supper and fry bread. After supper the girls had to wash the dishes. Most of our dishes were made out of tin. You didn't break as much that way. The boys never had to help with the chores. According to Daddy, this was not a manly thing to do. We would wash our feet in a wash pan and go to bed on our cots in our clothes. We only got clean clothes on Saturdays when we got our baths in the washtub.

After we left Sinton we moved farther north to Victoria to continue picking cotton. We moved into a small one-room house. There was never any indoor plumbing, so we stopped at a lot of gas stations. Most of owners didn't like to see a truck drive up loaded with kids to use their facilities. But they couldn't stop us. The first time I used the restroom at a gas station, I noticed that one had a sign on the door that read "Whites Only". I thought they were probably painting the inside of the restroom white. It was harder to figure out why sometimes this same sign was over a drinking fountain. I was just too young to understand man's inhumanity to man. Sometimes Daddy would buy us a coke just to please the folks who ran the stations.

We had a slop jar that we used at night. It had to be cleaned each day by one of us girls. I hated that smell. I wanted to get back to school to use the commodes. I decided that when we returned to Lindale I was only going to the bathroom at school. When school was out in the afternoons I would not pee again until the next day. I didn't know what I would do about the weekends however.

Ruby Lee and Bo caught up with us in Victoria. They had been pulling cotton all summer and had been saving their money. Bo's mama and daddy had been traveling with them. Ruby Lee decided they had enough money for a down payment to buy a trailer house to live in. She and Bo went to a bank to try to borrow the rest of the money.

As they were discussing the purchase with the banker, Mrs. Paul rushed in and said very excitedly, "Ruby Lee, hurry up. There is a really great rummage sale going on down the street." Ruby Lee turned red, from embarrassment and from becoming mad at her mother-in-law. She thought that she had impressed the banker up to this point. They were turned down on the loan. She and Bo went on to the rummage sale with his folks. They decided they would not buy a trailer house until they could pay cash for it.

When September came, I asked Daddy if we could go back to Lindale to go to school. He said, "You stupid girl, summer is not over, and the cotton is still good. We will go back to Lindale when I say so. I will whip your ass if you mention school to me again." I hung my head so that he would not be able to see my tears. Mama hugged me and told me that we would go back to Lindale in about six weeks and that I could start to school then. That night I lay on my cot, hating my daddy, loving my mother, and thinking about school and my friends in Lindale, Texas.

Even the Burma-Shave signs Mama read to us from the highway couldn't cheer me up: "PASSING SCHOOL ZONE...TAKE IT SLOW-LET OUR LITTLE...SHAVERS GROW." "IF NECKING ON THE HIGHWAY...IS YOUR SPORT-TRADE YOUR CAR IN...ON A DAVENPORT." I had no idea what that last one even meant.

We followed the cotton crops to West Texas. Bo and Ruby Lee went there too. In West Texas some of the farmers were defoliating their cotton fields so that the leaves would turn brown and fall off. This would make the cotton easier to pull by the cotton crews. Daddy hired Robert Lee out to an airplane pilot who was spraying the fields with this dust. Robert Lee would stand at the end of a cotton row, and that way the pilot would know which rows to spray. Then Robert Lee would move over a few rows so that the airplane could come down and spray. He would be white with this dust, and later in life, we found out how dangerous this could have been for him.

We returned to Lindale around the middle of October. School had been started for six weeks. Mama got a job at a rose nursery in a place called Owentown. All of us kids had acquired nicknames. Mine was Dotsie, Dollie E. was Dooter, William Henry was Nuse, Ruth Evelyn was Fats, Robert Lee was Buddy, and Harvey Joe was now just plain ole Joe. I hated my name Annie Bell. I hated Dotsie even more. Thank goodness, Nuse was the only one who kept his nickname forever. We also dropped the E. and called Dollie just Dollie.

Of course with the good news about going home to enroll in school, bad news was always around. Bo and Ruby Lee did not return to Lindale. They stayed in West Texas. We all missed them, even daddy. Hard to believe, isn't it?

Seven

It was the middle of October 1949 when I started second grade wearing my new shoes. I had on something I had never before worn-a skirt and a blouse. My Big Chief writing tablet was under my arms, and my sack lunch was in my hands.

Mama took all of us to the office and talked to the principal. I was happy. I was going to get to read books again. *Would there still be stories of Dick, Jane, Sally and Spot? Would I have to learn to read the words all over again? Would I have the same kids in my class? Would Miss Pruitt still be my teacher? Reckon she had gotten her a husband?* I didn't like it when the grown-ups called her an old maid.

The principal acted like he was mad at Mama. He told her that these kids should have been in school for six weeks. Mama didn't take anything off him. She told him that these kids belonged to her and Buford Coomer, and they would be the ones to decide if and when we went to school. We kids knew it was really Daddy, and not Mama, who had a say as to when we would start school. Daddy didn't care if we went at all, but since Mama had this job now during the day, he needed someplace to send us, or he would have to baby sit us. Dollie and Joe were still too young to go to school, and they were enough for him to be responsible for.

Finally a teacher came to the office and got me. Her name was Mrs. Pool. My heart fell. She was not Miss Pruitt. She was younger and a lot prettier. I wondered if any of the kids would remember me. I looked back and saw Mama going out the door. I wanted to run down the hall and beg her to take me home. As we walked into the room, Mama disappeared.

The kids, who had their heads down working on their lessons, looked up as we entered the room. I was relieved as I recognized some of them. Mrs. Pool asked me to have a seat in the back. As I walked down the aisle to find an empty desk, all the kids watched me, but no one said a word. I felt my knees would surely give way and I would fall before I reached an empty desk. I asked the boy sitting in front of the desk if anyone sat there, and he answered that they did not. I sure didn't want to make the same mistake I had made my first day of first grade; take a desk that belonged to someone else.

Mrs. Pool told us to get out a blank sheet of paper and a pencil. It was time to take our spelling test. *What was a spelling test?* In the first grade I had never heard the word spelling. As the teacher spoke each word I just sat there, tears falling down on my Big Chief tablet. *If Mama or Daddy really loved me, one of them would surely come for me.*

The teacher said that we should give our paper to the person in the front of us so that it could be graded. I handed the boy in front of me a blank sheet of paper, wet with tears. His name was William Jones, and he started laughing when he realized there were no words on the paper.

Mrs. Pool asked, "Why are you laughing William?" He told her the reason and some of the other kids began to laugh also. Mrs. Pool was not amused. She told the class that since this was my first day that I would not be expected to know how to spell the words, and they were not to laugh anymore. I felt relieved, but the damage had been done, and I was really mad at William.

What seemed like an eternity finally passed, and it was time for recess. This was something I excelled in. I ran to the swings. I was swinging really high when William walked real close to my swing. Now was my chance. I would teach him to laugh at me. I bailed out of the swing, right on top of him. On the way out my skirt caught on the swing and came off. I was glad I had my new panties on.

Mrs. Pool and the other teachers came running over to us. William was pretty shook up but was not hurt. Kids were all around us. Most of them were happy about the excitement. I was taken to the principal's office with nothing on but my panties and my new blouse. Both of them were dirty from the fall.

I was really scared now. Daddy had always told us if we got a whipping at school, we would get another one when we got home. The thought of the principal whipping didn't bother me. It was what was going to happen to me when I got home that was so upsetting. I wasn't going to cry though, not in front of that principal. To my surprise, Mrs. Pool was on my side. She told him that I must have fallen out of the swing onto William. That sounded good to me, so of course, I had to agree with her. The teacher was always right. I couldn't see any need to tell him anything other than what Mrs. Pool had told him. In fact he petted me and told me he was glad that neither of us was hurt. He wasn't as glad as I was.

Mrs. Pool sent Mama a note explaining about the fall and how my skirt had gotten torn and how she had pieced it back on me. I loved her. However, Mrs. Pool did make me stand in the corner for a while, explaining to me that I needed to learn to be more careful while I was swinging. I knew she didn't believe my story about the fall, but she felt sorry for me, this being my first day in school and the kids laughing at me. I loved her. She was my favorite teacher for the rest of my life. That is until I met my fourth grade teacher.

Spelling was not the only thing that was new for me in the second grade. We now had homework to do. I didn't mind doing it and thought it was easy. The only problem was, we didn't have electricity at our house. We would play outside until dark and then try to get our lessons. When we didn't have any money to buy white gas for the Coleman lantern, our lessons had to be done by flashlight. We would take turns holding the light for each other, shinning it down on the page we were working on at the time.

Daddy would not always give us money to buy paper and pencils at a little store that was located on the school ground. I developed a bad habit of stealing paper from the other kids. Once a week I would go inside the building at recess on the pretense of having to use the bathroom. Once inside I would go to a room and steal a page out of several students' tablets. The teachers always had recess duty, and I was never caught. I went into a different room each time, so apparently no one ever missed their paper. My heart would beat fast when I was doing the stealing. But I never felt bad about doing it. I had to have paper to do my work, didn't I? Sometimes I would take a pencil or two. All in all, the entire second grade turned out to be a pretty good year for me.

The second grade had a rhythm band. I was in it. Never mind that I had to play the sticks. I noticed the kids who wore the best looking clothes got to the play the other instruments. It had nothing to do with our musical talents. It didn't make any difference to me though. I was just glad to be a part of it. The girl who was the leader of the band was blue eyed and blonde headed. She was very pretty. At night, lying beside my sisters on our pallet on the floor that was our bed, I would think about how nice it would be to look like she looked.

After we had practiced for a long time, we finally got to invite our parents to see and hear us play. Mine didn't come. However, in my thoughts that night, they did come and sat on the front row. They were so proud of me.

One morning, when Mrs. Pool had left the room for a few minutes, I told the students that we should play a trick on her. Our desks were bigger than we were, so I suggested that we all hide behind them. When she returned to her classroom, we were nowhere in sight. Mrs. Pool ran out of the room screaming, "Something has happened to my kids, God help us all." Mrs. Pool's husband was a preacher, so she knew all about God. I sure didn't know anything about Him.

As soon as she left the room, we all got back into our seats with our heads down getting our lessons, but we were all laughing. The principal came running in along with several more teachers. There we sat, just like we were supposed to be. They were not laughing. The principal was a little smarter than the teacher, as he should be, and he figured out immediately what we had done. "Whose idea was this?" he asked. My heart was pounding. *Would anyone tell on me?* Well, of course, someone did.

I was escorted to his office. The thought of running out of there entered my mind. *What had I done wrong?* I thought Mrs. Pool would have enjoyed looking for us. How could I have guessed that she was going to pull a stunt like that, running out of the room screaming? *I* felt she had caused all the trouble, and I was going to tell the principal the real facts. *Would he send a note home to Mama to have her come to school? Well, I would tear it up; Mama could not miss a day's work.* I was really scared.

My body wanted to shake, but my mind would not let it. I was a Coomer, and no one was going to get the best of me. Once inside the principal's office he asked, "Annie Bell, was it your idea to hide from Mrs. Pool?" I started to lie and say no, but I saw the principal grin. "Yes sir," I answered in a sad, weak, little voice. "I just thought Mrs. Pool would think it was funny. I didn't mean to upset her." "Would you consider apologizing to her?" He asked. "I sure will," was my reply. "Okay, now go ask Mrs. Pool to come to my office."

Well, by now I was pretty sure I wasn't going to get a whipping from him. That also meant I would not get one from Daddy either. With a little luck Daddy would never find out about my little trick. Mrs. Pool went with me to the principal's office where I explained I didn't mean to upset her and apologized to her. She had calmed down by then and accepted my *sincere* apology.

When we got back to the room all the kids were still scared, after all, they had all hidden behind their desks. Mrs. Pool talked to us for a few moments explaining that we should not pull pranks on her and that she forgave all of us for it. I mentioned earlier that she was a wonderful person. I got off without being punished, but I could not let the snitch get off. I couldn't push the person down on the playground, but I saw nothing wrong with accidentally running into her and knocking her to the ground. One thing about it, she never told on me again.

Sometime, right before Christmas, one of my front teeth was loose. Earlier that year while living in Sinton I had lost my first one. I had been running and it just came out. I had promptly swallowed it, but as I ran, it came back up. I had given it to Mama, and that night the tooth fairy came and left me a nickel. I wiggled the latest loose tooth with my hands, but it would not come out. I wanted that tooth fairy to come see me again.

One night Daddy, who was drunk, decided that he would pull the tooth. He tied a piece of string to it and the other end of the string he tied to a doorknob. I was terrified and begged him not to do it. Mama tried to reason with him, but that just made him more determined. I shut my eyes. He slammed the door shut. As pain shot through my gums, the tooth came flying out. I was crying, but Dollie thought it was funny. I knew her day was coming.

I went to bed with the tooth close to my head. I didn't have a pillow to put it under. The tooth fairy was broke that night and didn't pay me a monetary visit, but she did collect the tooth. A few days later, when payday came, she came back and paid me for it. I never said anything about another loose tooth. The rest of my baby teeth came out naturally; the way God intended them to do.

Christmas was a sad time for me. I hated to see it roll around. The main reason-hardly any toys. The year before, the people from the welfare office came on Christmas Eve night and gave presents to Daddy for us. I remember seeing him cry. I had mixed feelings about the gifts. On the one hand I was glad to get one, but on the other hand I felt ashamed, especially when Daddy offered each one of the men who had brought the presents a drink of whiskey before they left.

This year Aunt Peggy, Daddy's sister who lived in Corpus Christi, sent each of us a present for Christmas. Nuse received a single shot cap gun and a lot of caps. We had cowboys and Indians dying all over the yard the next day. Dollie and I got dolls and Joe got a doctor's kit. That was all it took for Dollie and me to become doctors. Surgeons to be exact! We decided to operate on the owner of the doctor's kit.

Dollie and I took a pair of scissors and cut out the seat of Joe's new overalls. We were just about to start the surgery on his little rump when the head of the hospital, Mama, caught us. She was really mad that we had ruined the only pair of overalls that he had.

My doll had pretty blue eyes and long, shiny blonde hair. She had rosy cheeks and a face like none I had ever seen. The doll had on a pretty dress, lace panties, slip, and little white shoes and socks. I was really proud of her. She ate and slept with me.

By the time school started back in January, I decided I wasn't going to wait for Show and Tell day. She was definitely going to go to school with me. By then I had lost her shoes, and her face and dress were a little dirty, but she was still a little doll.

We had to walk to school, and ice was on the ground. Ruth Evelyn was supposed to hold my hand so I wouldn't slip and fall. She did, just long enough to get out of Mama's sight, and then she let go of me. I slipped and fell, my precious cargo falling too. I wasn't injured, but my doll lost three toes off one foot.

When we got to school, I set her in the window over the radiator so she could warm up some. She hadn't come with a coat, and she was real cold when we got there. I looked at her all day, wishing somehow I looked that good. The other kids felt sorry for her, having a crippled foot and all. She was definitely a conversation piece. In the spring I left her out in the rain and then the hot sun. Her face started peeling off and her hair was a mess. One day when I found her in the yard I remember thinking that she sure was aging fast. She went to an early grave, but I feel she is in doll heaven waiting for me to join her.

Our house did not have electricity, but we now had coal oil lamps, and when Daddy was low on matches, he would hold his cigarette over the lamp and catch the fire in it to light his smoke. We had an icebox that held a block of ice in the top of it. Daddy would get the ice at the icehouse in town. We kept margarine in the icebox. Margarine was a substitute for butter. The margarine did not have any color to it. You could buy packets of color to be mixed with the margarine to make it look good. Mama always kept a big bowl of it for us to eat with our biscuits and syrup.

Daddy had let Dollie and Joe get a little cat to play with while he babysat them during the day. Needing his rest after a morning of watching his two youngest kids, Daddy usually took a long nap after lunch. One day when he woke up from the nap, Dollie said, "Daddy I didn't do it." Joe said, "Well, I didn't do it either." "Do what?" Daddy asked. "Put the cat in the icebox," Dollie answered. Sure enough there the cat was, in the big bowl of margarine. He was squirming around, trying his best to climb out of the bowl. Daddy retrieved him and cleaned the cat hair out of the bowl and put it back inside the icebox. He didn't whip those two kids, but I thought they needed it.

That same week those two brats took his smoking tobacco, rolled them a cigarette and smoked it while he was napping. This time they did get their butts whipped. This would be the first of many times the two of them would sneak a cigarette. A whipping was rough, but cigarette smoking was great.

By now Joe was making his own bottles. Our house was located next to Rice's Grocery. Eb Rice, the owner, would let us kids come in and buy Kayro Syrup and Carnation Milk on the credit. Mama would settle up with him on the weekends. Joe would put the correct amount of each in his bottle, shake it up and suck it like he was two months old. A boy that was still sucking a bottle but also smoking cigarettes was a person one didn't meet to often. Coomer kids were capable of doing a lot of unusual things.

It was during this time that Daddy pulled a really bad drunk. He drank for several days. He started seeing pink elephants on the walls. He was really mean to all of us. One night he called Nuse over to his bed. When he got there, Daddy knocked him down for no reason. Nuse didn't cry, but he got really mad. We all stayed clear of that boy for a few days knowing he could take out his frustrations on some of us if he decided to.

Mama finally went to Doctor Kinzie's office and asked him to come by and check on Daddy. This was the first time that the doctor came out and gave Daddy a shot to help sober him up. There would be many more times.

I learned a lot in second grade. I was now reading everything I could find to read. Arithmetic was becoming my favorite subject. In reading, the vowels had different sounds, but two plus two was always four. For some reason arithmetic just made sense to me.

Spring came and we were taken out of school to go back to Winnsboro to pick strawberries. I knew I would miss school and all the friends that I now had. I would miss reading and arithmetic, but I would not miss stealing paper and pencils. I could put that part of my life on hold until the next school term.

We had all worn out our shoes and had been going bare foot to school. It's a good thing Mama made us all wash our feet at night and get that good bath in the washtub on Saturday. Our few clothes were worn out too, but I knew we would not get anymore until school started back in the fall.

The most wonderful thing that happened that summer was another baby was born into our family. It didn't belong to Mama and Daddy. Bo and Ruby Lee were the parents. She was seventeen now, and having being married almost two years, she was ready for this baby. She and Bo had rejoined the family in Winnsboro to pick strawberries. Bo always said that he could get along with her real good for a few months, but after that, he had to bring her home to see her Mama. We were all happy to see them, even Daddy.

None of us kids had ever heard the word "pregnancy." We knew she was in the family way. I thought she looked bigger. I didn't know at the time that gaining weight had anything to do with having a baby. I just felt like she was eating well. She no longer looked like a boy. Once, when Bo had stopped to buy gas for the car, Ruby Lee got out and got a cold drink from the drink box and drank it. As Bo was paying for the gas the attendant said to him, "Your little boy over there got a soda water." She always wore her hair rolled up during the week under a cap. On Saturday she would comb it out and go to town. Sunday morning she would wash it and roll it up again on bobby pins.

I knew the stork was going to pay them a visit, and only the stork could decide, right before she got to their door, if the baby would be a boy or a girl. I was hoping for a boy, as my sister Dollie was really getting on my nerves, and we sure didn't need another one like her. She thought the same thing about me.

The morning of May 08, 1950, was warm. We were in the field picking strawberries. Bo and Ruby Lee did not show up at the field to work. I felt this would be the day of the stork's visit. I could feel things that usually turned out to be right. It was hard to pick strawberries when all I could think about was the new baby.

Bo's old car came racing into the field. He had jumped out by the time he had gotten the car stopped. He told the first person on the first row he came to that the baby was a boy. That person in turn turned around and told the next person. This went on until the last person in the field had heard the news. That fellow just happened to be one of Bo's twin brothers, Pete. Pete didn't have anyone to tell, so he just turned his face to the woods behind him and shouted, "It's a boy!"

Bo's twin brothers were the babies of his big family. Their mother named them Perry and Jerry, but their nicknames were Nig and Pete. The midwife made a mistake on their birth certificates and wrote Clyde and Claude. I never knew of any more guys who had six names between the two of them. They probably held a world record.

All of us kids were so happy about the baby. We wanted to see him as soon as possible. When we finished picking all the strawberries in the field, we moved to another one. On the way, we went right by the house the new boy was in. Daddy stopped the truck and told us to run in for a minute to take a look. He even went inside.

The baby was asleep in my sister's arms. I got there first to see him. To this day I remember the excitement in the room, and how I felt looking down at him. She wouldn't let us hold him yet. Ruby Lee told us that Bo had been looking out the window when he saw the stork coming, and he had said, "Oh Ruby honey, it's a boy." I believed that stork story until I was at least twelve years old, and told it often. Joe, however, found some rubber things in the car pocket of Daddy's truck a few years later, and Joe's explanation of what they were put a little doubt in the stork delivery theory.

Billy Paul, another one of Bo's brothers, was at the house when the baby was born. He told us that the baby could talk. I didn't believe him. Well, I had seen newborn babies before. I wasn't a fool. Billy said to us, "Ask him what his name is." I did. The little boy replied, "Ronald Wayne Paul." Wow, it was unbelievable. I didn't realize that Billy was the one doing the talking for the baby. I told everyone I came in contact with for several days that my new nephew could talk. Nobody believed me. Imagine that! In fact, that baby didn't say any more words for several months. At the time I could not explain the reason why to myself.

It was almost Mother's Day, and in five days Ruby Lee would have a birthday. She told Mama that having a son was the best Mother's Day or birthday present a girl could have.

In a few days Ruby Lee was back in the field picking strawberries. All the workers in the field attended to the baby. He lay in one of the crates that we packed strawberries in between Mama and Daddy as they worked at the shed packing the berries, getting them ready for the market.

The Coomer kids were delighted with the birth of this baby. He had beautiful blue eyes and dark skin and was the prettiest baby ever born into the Coomer family. We carried him constantly. When someone put him down, another person would pick him up. Ruth Evelyn, now twelve years old, wanted to be with him all the time. She loved that boy. Ronald didn't learn to walk for several months. He didn't need to. We were his legs.

I had forgiven Charles Frank for what he had tried to do to me the summer before, and we became gas-sniffing buddies again. One day I smelled so much white gasoline that I felt I was going to pass out. I got up from the can and started walking across an old corn patch that belonged to Uncle Buck. I fell and couldn't get up. Ruby Lee found me. She had Bo pick me up, and he carried me to Daddy.

Daddy and Mama took me to the doctor. He washed my face and gave me some medicine. He also gave my parents a lecture. He told them to never let me sit at a gas can and smell the gas. It could cook my brain and probably would kill me. Daddy had to pay that doctor some money, and he was mad about that. I just knew that he would whip me for sure, but to my surprise, he was concerned about me and cried on the way back to the house. One could just never tell how he was going to react to something. I guess he thought I was going to be his third child to die.

When we got back to the house, there were a lot of people waiting there for some news on my condition. When they saw that I was all right, everyone was really happy. Dollie even seemed glad that I hadn't died. Uncle Buck and Aunt Mandy felt it was Charles Frank's fault for my gas sniffing habit, and they didn't let him come around us for several days. I continued to smell gasoline, but now I didn't do it in the open. I would sneak around when no one was about and put my nose on the can. The time I stayed at the can was always short. I felt that if I just smelled it for a little while nothing bad would come to me, and that I wouldn't get sick again. It worked.

That year one of kids from another family came down with the measles and didn't have to work in the field for three days. Boy, did I ever want to get the measles myself. One of my siblings got red bumps on him, so I slept beside that person that night. It didn't work; I didn't get them. One of the others did, so I slept in the bed with him. But, wouldn't you know it, I was the last one of the Coomer kids to take the measles, and by that time strawberry picking time was over.

When the strawberry season ended, we all returned to Lindale to begin picking blackberries. Ruby Lee and Bo could pick more berries than anybody, especially Bo. They worked really hard and Ruby Lee continued to save their money. Bo would pick blackberries in the morning and work at the canning factory at night. There were several canning factories in Lindale. The farmers would take the berries to the canneries during the day. They had to be canned quickly or they would ruin.

The sun was really hot in the berry fields, but we were accustomed to the hot sand. Daddy would get us to the fields before daylight. We would make us a bed out of blackberry lugs and sleep until we could see the blackberries on the vines. Sometimes a wasp would sting one of us. Mama would doctor us with the snuff from her mouth. Everybody worked except Daddy. He had to go into town and get ice or something for us to eat. He always had an excuse not to work. But, as always, he kept all the money we made.

When the blackberries played out, we loaded all our belongings into the truck and started back to the Valley to pick cotton. Bo and Ruby Lee loaded the baby and the rest of their stuff into their car and went with us.

Along the highway a Burma-Shave sign: "DROVE TOO LONG...DRIVER SNOOZING-WHAT HAPPENED NEXT...IS NOT AMUSING."

Eight

It took three days for us to make the trip to South Texas. We stopped and camped at a lot of roadside parks. Mama would cook our meals on the Coleman stove and spread the ropes around our cots at night so the snakes could not get us. If the kids in the back of the truck needed to use the bathroom, they would beat on the cab of the truck and Daddy would stop. Sometimes they would get into a fight with each other and Daddy would stop and give them a whipping. This year I got to ride in the car with Bo and Ruby Lee and the baby. I was happy about that.

Bo and Ruby Lee's car broke down one day, so we pulled off the road. Bo and Daddy went into town in the truck to get a part to fix the car. While we were waiting for them to return, I went across a barbwire fence to use the bathroom. I found some wild grapes growing in a field. They were Muscadine grapes. All the kids ate as many as we could hold. Dollie was allergic to them and broke out all over. I thought it was really funny. Every year after that, when we found these kind of grapes growing along the roadside, Nuse, Joe, and I would push her down in them and make her eat some. We knew of course that we would get a whipping from Daddy.

Daddy always kept us in watermelons. At the roadside parks, we would take the rinds, after we had eaten most of the insides, and put them on a table. In a few minutes, they would be covered with wasps and yellow jackets, fighting for the sweet juice of the melons. We would start fighting them, seeing who could kill the most. The loser was the person with the most stings. That was great fun. We knew Mama always had some medicine in her mouth, her snuff.

We didn't stay in the Valley very long that summer, only a few days. We did get to see the Coomer cousins. They didn't have to work in the fields, and I know that they felt sorry for us. We left the Valley and went north again to Sinton.

That summer in Sinton was like the summer before. We stayed in the labor camp. After working hard in the cotton fields, we ate and went to bed in our clothes. This way we would be ready to get right back up and go back to the field the next morning. On the weekends we went to the park. Our aunts would come to visit and we would get to play with our cousin Orville. The drinking and the fighting with Daddy's sisters continued.

That summer we met the Huey family. Bee Bee and Alma were the parents. They had two sons. The oldest boy's name was Billy Ray. He was six years older than I. The youngest son was Charles Roy (not to be confused with Charles Frank Ragsdale). The first time I laid eyes on him I knew he was the love of my life. I was eight-years-old, and that was old enough to know what love was. He was dark just like me, even more so. He had black eyes and was the best looking thing I had ever seen. I wanted to be around him all the time.

The Hueys actually lived in Sinton, but they picked cotton just like the rest of us. Mr. Huey was small and Mrs. Huey was big. She was the boss of the family. I wanted her to like me so that she would let Charles Roy marry me when we grew up. There was no doubt in my mind that this was going to happen. I would lie awake at night thinking about him, and could hardly wait until the next morning so I could see him again. I pulled cotton on the row next to him all day. He was two years older than I was and could pull more cotton than I could. When he got too far ahead of me, he would pull cotton in my row until I caught up with him. I knew he felt the same way about me.

We pulled cotton in several towns in South Texas that year. The Hueys traveled with us. They had a trailer house and lived in it. If we could not get a house to live in, we just lived under the shade of a tree. When it rained, we covered everything with a tarp and got into either the cab of the truck or underneath it to wait the rain out.

Mr. Huey would talk to the farmers and get jobs for us. We would pull the cotton, Mrs. Huey would weigh it, and then Mr. Huey would take the cotton to the gin. The cotton we pulled would be processed and turned into bales of cotton usually weighing about five hundred pounds. At the gin the seeds would be separated from the rest of the cotton. The ginning would get rid of the green boles, leaves and sticks that were in the cotton trailer. It took roughly two thousand pounds of pulled cotton to turn out a bale.

Mr. Huey got fifty cents for each hundred pounds of cotton that he took to the gin. He made good money doing this as he had several people (which we called hands) working for him, including us. They had a nice car and clean clothes.

Two bad things happened to me that summer. First I contracted the pinkeye from, Mama said, the Mexicans. For several days I was too embarrassed to pull cotton on the row next to Charles Roy. The kids made fun of me, including him. He was the only one I forgave for doing it.

The other bad thing was this: One Saturday while we were camped near a river and some of the kids were swimming, I wanted to get into the water too. Daddy would not let me go in. Charles Roy was swimming, and I just kept bugging Daddy about it. He was drinking and finally got mad at me. He grabbed me up, ran into the water, pushed me under, and then turned me loose, telling me to swim my way out of there. I had never been in a river before. I went down and couldn't come up. This was the worst thing that had ever happened to me. I couldn't breathe. I was dying and would never get to marry Charles Roy.

Then in an instant someone pulled me up. It was Mr. Huey. He carried me to the bank. To this day, I am afraid of water. Mr. Huey had a few words to say to Daddy. He was not afraid to take up for kids. Daddy didn't speak to either one of us the rest of the day. I hated him.

We found that a good place to camp was by the river under the bridge. We could stay out of the weather there. We left some of our belongings at the camp while we pulled the cotton during the day. Each evening we would return, and our stuff would still be there. *Who would want to steal junk?* When it rained, we would sit under the bridge on boxes and watch it come down. In the afternoons and on the weekends most of the kids would take a side of a pasteboard box, go to the top of the concrete wall under the bridge, get on the pasteboard and ride it down to the bottom. We did not realize at the time how dangerous that was. Fear was not part of our lives, except for the fear we had of our daddy.

Ruby Lee cooked supper for Bo every night. One afternoon I put a note inside their car asking her if I could eat with them. When I saw her going to her car, I was nervous, wondering if she would say yes. When she got out of the car, she came over and told me I could eat with them. She had fried hamburger meat and fried potatoes, the same meal that Mama cooked. For some reason, it just tasted better at Bo and Ruby Lee's. After that I ate a lot of meals with them. Bo was really good to all of us. His daddy had been mean to them, and he had been hungry a lot of times as a kid. Once his daddy had hung a piece of meat on a string from the ceiling just out of reach of him and his siblings. They were hungry, but could not reach the meat. Henry Paul, his daddy, thought that was really funny. As a grown up, Bo hated to see any child hungry and would feed one of us before he would eat himself.

I began to notice Ruby Lee was smoking a lot of cigarettes. Even though she was married, she was still afraid of Daddy, and she didn't smoke in front of him. His sisters could smoke, but his daughter couldn't. That didn't make much sense to me, but this was my daddy I am talking about. Several times Daddy would go into a room where she and Bo were, and Daddy would find Bo with two cigarettes in his mouth. All of us kids loved her and never told Daddy about her smoking habit. I was personally glad that one of us could defy him and get away with it.

We were pulling cotton at a town where the cotton was really bad. We called it "scrappy" cotton. It took a lot longer to pull one hundred pounds than it did when the cotton was good. But, Daddy told us that we all had to pull a certain amount or he was going to "beat the hell out of us". Well, we tried our best, but we just couldn't reach his goal. We knew we were in for it.

Daddy drove up, and as he was getting out, we all could tell that he was drunk. A lady, Viola May, told us to get into the lake and hide from Daddy. We all jumped in, clothes and all. When Daddy found out that we hadn't pulled as much cotton as he wanted us to, he began to pitch a "fit", yelling for us to come to him. Viola would not let us out of the water.

She tried to reason with him, say, "Mr. Coomer these kids worked as hard as they could, the cotton is just not any good." "That doesn't make any difference," he said. "These kids are good workers and they could have gotten what I told them to do. I am going to whip every one of them." "You are not going to do it," Viola defied him. "These kids will stay in this lake all night if they have to." We were in a pickle, not knowing what to do. We knew Daddy was going to about kill us and maybe Viola too, but she stood her ground and would not let him come into the lake. Everyone was watching from the bank.

What seemed like an eternity passed. I was scared of that water, but I was scared of Daddy more. What was going to happen to all of us? Well, thank goodness, Daddy still drinking his whiskey, passed out. It was dark. Slowly, we all climbed out of the water, walked past Daddy's drunken body and went to bed. The next day he was sober and didn't mention a word about that before. He probably didn't remember it, but I can tell you, I never forgot it.

Around the middle of October we moved back to Lindale. Mama was going back to work at the rose nursery. We were going back to school. The Hueys moved back to Sinton so the boys could start to school also. I was heartsick, as I felt I would never see Charles Roy again. There was hope though, as Daddy shook hands with Mr. Huey and told him we would see him next summer when the cotton crops were ready. If Daddy were glad that Mr. Huey had stopped him from drowning me, he never told him.

Bo and Ruby Lee went on to West Texas so that Bo could go to work in the oil fields. I cried when they left Lindale. *Would I ever see them again?* I felt life was really bad, to lose your sister and brother-in-law, and their baby boy, your three favorite kinfolks in the whole world.

Going back to school for the first day of my third year, I was not afraid. The same principal as last year enrolled us, but he did not ask my Mama where we had been for the first six weeks of school. I guess she had got it across to him the year before that it wasn't any of his business. I did wonder who my teacher would be, and if we would have anything different to learn this year. I didn't want any surprises like the spelling had been the year before.

Well, of course, there was something new. The kids had stopped printing their letters and had started writing them in cursive. I didn't have a hard time reading the ABC's but I sure had a hard time trying to write them. I had a lot of catching up to do, but I really never did. To this day my handwriting is bad. Sometimes I write myself a note and later cannot even read it myself. My writing looks like chickens have walked across the page.

Mrs. Era Mae Brazil was my third grade teacher. She was very pleased when I worked really hard, and before long had caught up with the rest of the class with my learning. I loved to read books, and she kept me supplied with them. When I read, I pretended I was the main character in the book. It didn't matter if that person was a boy or a girl.

One day, not long after I started third grade, I was on the playground seesawing with another girl. A girl, who was a bigger than me, walked up. "Get off and let me seesaw," she said. She scared me. "What grade are you in," I asked. "In the first," was her answer. I was no longer afraid of her. She was just a first grader. I could handle her. "I am not going to get down," I told her. "I am in the third grade." This seemed to scare her. "I know what we can do," I said. "Let me go and get on the other end with the other girl, and you can seesaw both of us." "Okay," she smiled. We became good friends.

We rented a house from an old couple. Mr. and Mrs. Tucker were nice to us, and I visited them often. They lived down the road from us. Their son lived across the road from the school. He was married with a family. He and the rest of his family were good to us, just like his parents were. His name was Henry Clay and his wife's name was Verita. They had three children: Joy, who was older than I; Barbara, who was a year younger than I; and Jimmy, who was younger than Barbara. The Tuckers would let their children come and play with us. Once they took me to Tyler with them and bought me a Coke Float. That was the best tasting thing I had ever eaten in all my life.

Across the road from us is where the Shacklett family lived. They had a big family like ours. One of their sons had been murdered. The murder was never solved. Mary was my age. She was my friend at school, with the pretty black hair. The youngest girl, Joe's age, was named Betty Jo. The other kids were all older than I was.

Mr. and Mrs. Shacklett were large people. They were bootleggers (beer and whiskey). Daddy, who had once been in the same business, decided he would be their competition. If Daddy felt the Shacklett's were getting too much of the business, he would turn them into the law. They in turn would do the same thing to him.

Mrs. Shacklett always kept a couple of pints of whiskey in her bosom. After the laws had searched her bedroom, she would go in there and take the whiskey out of her bosom and hide it under the mattress of the bed. When she got to the jailhouse and was searched by a woman, they never found whiskey on her.

Bootleggers never stayed too long in jail. They usually paid a fine and were let out, so they could get back to work. All in all it was a friendly competition, and the Shackletts were good friends with Mama and Daddy.

Mr. Shacklett was a mean man sometimes. One day in the strawberry patch, he got mad at one of his sons. He went to the woods and came back with a big tree limb. The boy was about ten years old. Mr. Shacklett began to beat him with the limb. Everyone just watched as the boy was screaming and begging his daddy to stop. Daddy finally went out there. The boy was on the ground, not moving. Daddy said, "Lidge, that boy of yours is dead." Only then did the beating stop. Thank goodness the boy was not dead, probably just unconscious. Was he taken to the doctor? Of course not! He was back picking strawberries the next day.

The house we rented from the Tuckers had three rooms in it. Mama and Daddy bought a real bed for them to sleep in. It was in the front room. The only other thing in the room was a wood-burning stove in the middle. One room served as a bedroom for us kids to sleep in. We slept on two mattresses, boys on one side of the room and girls on the other. In the kitchen there was a table and benches for us to sit while we ate. There was not a cook stove; therefore, Mama used her Coleman stove. She also did some cooking on the wood-burning stove in the front room. In the corner of the kitchen there was a stand with a pan and a water pitcher on it. We used these to wash our feet before going to bed each night and to wash our face in when we got up in the morning, usually in the same water. In the back yard were a well and an outdoor toilet. This was a good set up for us.

At school I had to go back to my old habit of stealing paper and pencils. I really didn't like to do this, but it was a necessity. *What was a girl to do? I had to have school supplies, didn't I?*

When winter came, it was Robert Lee's job to get up early and build a fire in the wood-burning stove. The house would be warm by the time the rest of us got up. There was electricity in the house, but we did not have any light bulbs, so we used the Coleman lantern and candles for lights.

Mama was still making lye soap and giving us the Saturday morning baths. In the winter she heated water on the wood-burning stove, and the baths were taken indoors in the front room in the washtub. She did her wash outside on the rub board using the lye soap. She still hung the clothes on a barbed-wire fence to dry.

I was happy and content. School was easy and everyone accepted me. I was better at recess than anybody. No one cared that my hair was always a mess or that I wore the same two dresses all week, and most days had a dirty face.

It was while in the third grade that I got a very special, new friend. Her name was Carol. She was an only child. She was blond haired, blue eyed, and very pretty. She was new in Lindale. On the weekends I would walk to her house, and we played with her dolls in her room. Her mother and daddy were nice and seemed glad that I came over so that Carol could have company. I never went there without taking my Saturday bath first.

Carol and I had many secrets. We discussed what we would be when we grew up. I envied her because she had clothes, a room of her own, and since she was an only child, she had all the love from both parents. She lived in a nice white house with a living room, two bedrooms, a kitchen and a bathroom. The thing that really struck me as being really neat was the fact that they had light bulbs in every room. Carol envied me because I had a lot of brothers and sisters to play with. That was something I could not figure out. I loved her and she loved me. She also had a dog that I liked, which was unusual for me, as I ordinarily didn't take a shine to animals. I looked forward to the weekends.

Carol didn't get to roam around town like I did, so she had never been to my house with the three rooms. We had gotten a lamp with a book of green stamps. It had taken us two months to save them. We had placed the lamp in the window in the front room on top of an apple box. Daddy even bought a light bulb. We now could get our lessons by a good light. We still didn't have light bulbs for the rest of the house. Only rich people had enough light bulbs to use in every room in the house. Anyway, I was as proud of the lamp as a peacock is over its feathers.

One Saturday afternoon, after having visited Carol, I went home to find Daddy drunk, sitting in the yard with a fifth of whiskey at his side. I was glad that Carol could not see him. I had been home about an hour when Carol and her mother pulled up in the yard in their car.

I had just had a boxing match with Joe in which I had lost. He had boxed my skirt off, and I was trying to get it back on. Carol said that they could not find her dog, and she wanted to know if he had followed me home. I was ashamed of our place and especially of Daddy's condition. But I was proud that they could see our lamp from their car. The dog had not followed me home. I didn't know where he could be.

That night lying on the pallet I had mixed emotions about their visit. I felt bad about our house, but I was glad that they had seen the lamp. I could hardly wait until their church was over the next day so that I could go to her house to see what she had to say about the lamp.

I didn't realize I was about to have the beginning of the biggest heartache in my entire life, something that would stay with me forever. When I knocked on the door, Carol's mother opened it. She said that I could not come in and that I could no longer be Carol's friend. I was in disbelief and asked, "Why?" She told me that she had not realized that I came from such a bad family. They were dirty and vulgar. I didn't know what vulgar meant. She told me that Carol could not see me again on weekends, and I could no longer play with her at school. She told me not to come visit them again. She also accused me of stealing Carol's dog.

Tears were running down my face as she asked me to leave. As I looked back, I saw Carol's face in the window. I could tell she was crying too, but her mother pulled her away from the window.

I went home and down into the woods behind our house. I lay down on the ground and cried until I fell asleep. Ruth Evelyn came about dark to find me. They were all looking for me, even the Shackletts. I told no one about my heartache, just that I had fallen asleep. I trembled and cried all night. Ruth Evelyn hugged me most of the night knowing I was hurting for some reason that she could not figure out. I knew if I told her then she would tell Daddy, and I knew Daddy would blow his top and show his ass. He would most certainly whip Carol's daddy. He could be mean to us, but he didn't want anyone else to be. It made no sense to me.

At school the next day Carol minded her mother. She had nothing to do with me. I was as low as a human could get. At recess I sat and cried, trying hard for the other kids not to notice. At night I just could not sleep. I could hardly eat. The pain would not go away. In a few days Carol had a new best friend at school. I watched them play, and it hurt so badly.

I was really glad when it was time to move to Winnsboro to pick strawberries a few weeks before school ended. I would no longer have to see Carol and her new friend playing. I never forgot though. Through the years I would think about her and wonder if she still remembered the fun that we had had together. *Did she hurt as much as I did because her mother had stopped our seeing each other, or did she care at all?*

I decided that if someone could hurt me this much, then I could hurt other things. That summer I became kind of mean. Nuse, Joe and Dollie joined me in my antics. We tore up a lot of red ant beds, gave cigarettes to horned toads knowing they could inhale but could not exhale, and they would die. We decided that dogs and cats were our natural enemies, so we tried to be as mean to them as we could. We stirred up a lot of wasp nests, and poured salt on snails' tails.

We were mean to our friends, and a lot of our buddies were on the wrong end of our rock throwing and snake-in-pants kind of things. If we caught someone in an outdoor toilet, we pushed it over. Well, we were mean to each other too. We engaged in grass burr and bull nettle fights, as well as plain old fistfights. After giving someone some bull nettle kernels to eat, we will tell them that they had poison in them. That was always good for a reaction from them.

We liked coming across empty houses with perfectly good windows. If we came to an empty house where the lights had not been cut off, as was the custom in those days, we went inside and turned them on and left them that way. Some of the empty houses still had a phone connected. We would tell the operator to connect us with a number pulled out of the air. When the person answered, we would curse at them and then hang up. Lying came easy, so we lied on each other, as well as other kids, just to get them into trouble.

Even Ruth Evelyn got into the action. She wrapped the steering wheel in Daddy's truck with black sticky tape. When he got into the truck, he started screaming, "Someone has tried to steal my damn truck. I'll whip someone's ass for this!" Later, he accused Nuse of doing it, and Ruth Evelyn didn't confess. That boy finally got the whipping he deserved from cutting the hole in the chair.

Being mean didn't stop the heartache, but it sure masked the pain. I had a really wonderful, but awful summer!

Nine

After the strawberries played out, we moved back to Lindale into the Tucker house we had left a few weeks before. The blackberries were ready, and so were we. Bo, Ruby Lee and the baby moved back to Lindale too. I rode in the car with them, holding Ronald Wayne all the way. I knew that he would never hurt me like Carol had. He would never leave me for a new friend. I just knew it!

Bo and Ruby Lee rented a small apartment from Henry Clay Tucker. They didn't have any furniture, so Ruby Lee, not wanting to spend money for frills, took empty apple boxes and made furniture. She made a couch and a chair for the front room. She did buy a bed for them and one for Ronald Wayne. She bought some material and sewed some curtains for the windows. Ruby Lee had always believed that only rich people could afford a mirror to comb one's hair by. She bought an old dresser at a rummage sale with a good mirror on it. She was rich now herself. She was married to the handsome Bo Paul and had a beautiful baby boy. There was something else too that was very important to her. They had money saved. She was happy, happy, happy.

Work in the field was getting harder for me and the rest of the kids. Daddy felt that since we were older now that we ought to work harder. We were bare footed for the most part, and the sand in East Texas was very hot. Our feet were tough. They had to be. We went to work as soon as it was daylight enough to see the blackberries. Usually by 1:00 p.m. we would get to quit, as most of the berries would have been picked, and it was too hot in the afternoons to work.

I would play with the baby and rest. I was always hungry. Daddy was playing poker with our money and drinking whiskey instead of buying enough groceries to keep us fed. Ruby Lee and Bo had plenty of food. Sometimes I thought I would have starved if they had not let me come to their house to eat. Bo was working in the blackberry patch in the mornings and working again at the canning factories at night. Ruby Lee was saving a lot of the money they were making. She wanted to buy a house trailer and was determined to save enough money to pay cash for one.

Robert Lee, who was fifteen, started acting silly when girls about his age came around. Ruth Evelyn was developing into a very pretty girl. She was now a teenager. Nuse was fighting everyone he felt needed a whipping. Dollie and I were friends one day and enemies the next. Joe, the baby, was spoiled, but for some reason, didn't mind the attention that was being shown to Ronald Wayne. Daddy, it seemed, was always mean to us and gave us a lot of whippings. Mama still loved him, even after he had slapped her for no reason at all. *One day I would be big and I would stop him from doing that!*

One day Robert Lee decided he would make some blackberry wine. He didn't mind his brothers and sisters knowing about it. He knew we wouldn't tell on him. Common sense and fear of death kept our mouths shut. However, he didn't want Mama and Daddy to find out. He knew Mama would be mad at him and that Daddy would just drink it up. He put his brew in a jar and dug a big hole in the ground and buried it so that it would ferment. Well, the weather was really hot that summer. In fact, it got so hot that his brew blew off the lid of the jar. It also caused a huge hole in the ground with blackberry juice all over the yard.

Daddy knew right away that one of those Shacklett boys across the street had been in our yard and hid that blackberry wine making business from their own family. Well, as you know, our daddy was always right, so we just agreed with him, especially Robert Lee.

Sometimes, on the weekends, Daddy would take us to see our Uncle Earnest and his family who had settled down in Daingerfield, a town not too far from Lindale. Aunt Kate's family lived there, and they owned several acres of land.

On one of these visits all the kids were told to clean up the kitchen after lunch. Someone came up with the brainy idea to hide the dishes in the oven of the stove. We could go outside and play, coming back later to really wash them. All the kids agreed this was a good idea. The only thing though, is that we forgot to come back and wash them. When Aunt Kate and Mama went into the kitchen to cook supper, they found all the dirty dishes. Oh boy, we all got a whipping, and still had to wash the dishes.

On this same visit Betty Jo let me play with her doll. When I was through playing with her; I threw the doll down in the weeds. Later I could not find her, but I didn't tell Betty Jo. She thought I had put her back in the house. About a week later she found her doll that had been ruined by the hot sun and the rain. It was a long time before she forgave me for that little stunt.

Other weekends we went to Dekalb to see Uncle Jean and our Sikes cousins. I loved this family. One of the girls was my age and two others were close. Dollie and I had a lot of fun playing with them. They were pretty. I envied them because they all had lots of hair on their heads. They also had huge, pretty eyes. Aunt Pearl saw to it that they all worked, and they always had a clean house. Uncle Jean was a kind man. He loved Aunt Pearl and his kids. I cannot remember him ever speaking harsh to any of them. He was good to all of us as well.

The pain I had that spring of thinking about Carol, and the way I had lost her as a friend, was replaced by a warm feeling inside me when I thought about the possibility of seeing Charles Roy Huey later in the summer. I knew that we would be going to South Texas to pick cotton. Picking cotton on a row beside him would take some of the sting out of the hard work.

Sure enough, around the first part of July, we loaded up the old truck and left the berry fields for the more lucrative cotton fields. Daddy had placed a tarp over the top of the truck so we would have shelter when it rained on us on our trip South. Everything we owned was in the back of that truck. Mr. Tucker had promised Daddy that he would not rent our house to anybody while we were gone, so we knew we had a place to come home to in the fall. Mama also had been promised her job back at the rose nursery processing plant in Owentown the next winter. We sure had a plan for survival.

The trip to Sinton took us three days to make. Daddy thought it was a good idea to stop at nearly every roadside park on the way to eat, rest or spend the night. He, of course, would get drunk and tell us how sorry and lazy all of us were. Mama would just listen and never defend herself or us. I lay awake at night thinking about Carol, Charles Roy, and Ronald Wayne. I tried not to think about the way our daddy mistreated us, especially the way he treated Mama. She loved us, and every once in a while she would tell us so.

One evening right after supper Mama cleaned up the dishes and made our beds in the back of the truck. Nuse, Joe, and I earlier that day had rolled Dollie in the muscadine grapes, knowing that she was going to break out and swell up. Daddy had given us a whipping, but it had been worth it. We had just gone to bed when a car pulled up. When the men got out, one could tell that they were the law. One of the men said, "This looks like the bunch we have been looking for." I know my heart stopped for an instant. I had not realized it was against the law to push your sister down in grapevines. A whipping was one thing, but going to jail was something else.

My daddy was defensive and said, "What are you looking for us for?" The lawman answered, "For stealing." I was relieved. I had not stolen anything that day. Daddy said, "Well, if you think we have stolen anything, get up in the truck and look for it." One by one the kids' heads starting popping up, as they were getting curious. A third lawman got out of the car and said, "Would you look at all these damn kids. Jesus Christ. Is this all these tramps do, make babies?" I thought, *he sure is stupid; tramps didn't make babies, storks did.* I was just about to tell him so when Daddy told him, "Hell man, I have four more kids. Two of them are dead. One got shot by them crazy ass Japs overseas. Another boy of mine is in the Army. You two best get out of here before I get the Army on your asses."

One of the lawmen started laughing and stated that he felt we had not stolen anything. I felt proud of my drunken daddy. He was not going to take anything off these fellows. I was kind of hoping though that they would take him to jail and keep him there until I was grown. Daddy asked them, "Do you have a drink of whiskey you could spare? After all, you have woke up my whole damn family for no reason at all."

One of the men went to the car, got something in a paper bag, and brought it back. Daddy took a drink from the bag. For some reason the men shook his hand and wished him luck. Daddy thought they had been touched by his story about his two dead sons. I thought they probably didn't even believe him.

After they left, Daddy cursed them and got the axe ready. He would take care of them if they decided to come back and give us any more trouble. I worried all night thinking they might come back to get him, even though I wanted them to. After Daddy went to sleep, I got up and hid the axe. I had to catch up on my sleep the next day on a pallet, in the back of the truck, while going down the road with the rest of the kids arguing and fighting around me.

The day I had been looking forward to since last summer finally came. I saw Charles Roy. I had recently had a birthday, and I was nine. All of a sudden the memory of Carol was gone, at least for now. Charles Roy would be my best buddy for the rest of the summer. I began to wash my face more often and combed my hair myself, instead of waiting on the Saturday bath day. I became aware of the fact that I needed to wear clean clothes and wished that we had an iron.

We picked cotton on Saturday morning, quitting at noon. For some reason Daddy began letting us have one half of the money that we made on that day. I think it was because Mr. Huey let his two sons have all of the money they made. I worked harder on Saturday than I did the rest of the week. I wanted as much money as I could get.

The first Saturday afternoon that I had my own money, Mama took me to a rummage sale, and I bought a pair of shoes, a pair of blue jeans and a shirt. They were second hand, but I didn't care. They were new to me. I went back to the camp, washed up, and put them on. *Where was Charles Roy?* I wanted to show him my new clothes. He was always clean and had nice clothes. His mother saw to that. I felt it was because she just had two kids and she could afford to do it.

That evening the kids in the camp starting playing a game called "Post Office". The postmaster would ask you have many letters you wanted. If you answered that you would like three, you could kiss someone that many times. My heart was really beating when it came Charles Roy's time to get letters. *Would he want to kiss me?* He told the postmaster that he wanted one letter. He went directly and kissed my brother, Nuse, on the cheek. I had no other choice when it came my time to get letters; I had to go kiss a girl on the cheek. The game wasn't working out like I thought it should.

The next Saturday afternoon we decided to play the same game. Charles Roy had a girl cousin playing the game. Her name was Frances. I knew that Nuse liked her a lot, but he didn't have the guts to kiss her. *What stupid boys* I thought. This could go on until I was old enough for the stork to pay me a visit. I heard Nuse say to Charles, "If you will kiss Annie Bell, I will kiss Frances." How I loved that brother of mine!

Would Charles do it though? He just had to! I wanted him to kiss me so bad. He did. He asked the postmaster for three letters. He kissed me on the cheek three times. The feeling inside my body was indescribable. When it came my time to get letters, I gave them to him on his cheek. He liked them; I could tell. The awful feeling I had felt when Carol's mother told me I could no longer play with Carol was replaced with a feeling of sheer joy and happiness.

That night, as I lay in bed thinking about the wonder of it all, I thought that maybe this is what started all that stork business. I didn't know, and I sure wasn't about to ask anybody. A kid could get into a lot of trouble asking questions about how a stork could visit someone's house and leave a baby.

The weeks that we lived in Sinton our aunts and uncles would visit us on the weekends, mostly on Sundays at the park. Just like the years before, they would all get drunk and fuss, fight and make up. Uncle Earnest and his family did not come this year to pick cotton. He was helping his in-laws farm their land. My good-looking cousin, Orville, would come with his mother, and we all enjoyed playing with him. If I hadn't been so in love with Charles Roy, I probably would have delivered some of my letters to him. I knew back then that it was against the law for you to deliver letters to a cousin. It was a dumb law. Later in life it would be a law that I would break.

After most of the cotton had been pulled in Sinton, we moved on to several towns to find work. We found cotton in Refugio, Victoria, Edna, El Campo, Wharton and the twin cities of Richmond and Rosenberg. Later we moved back toward East Texas camping at such places as Rockdale, Cameron and Hearne.

Daddy hired a man and his family to pick cotton who had never worked with us before. The first night in the camp he began to brag to daddy that his kids could pull more cotton than the Coomer kids could. We were living at Three Rivers, Texas, at the time. Daddy said, "Man, you have got to be crazy, no kids can pull more cotton than these kids of mine." The bet was on. The man told daddy, "If your kids pull more cotton than mine in the morning, we will leave camp and move someplace else to work.

The next morning, we were at the field early, both families. Well, the Coomer kids were working on their third sack of cotton (I may be stretching the truth a little here) before those kids even emptied up their first sack full. The man, good to his word, pulled his kids out of the filed and left. We never saw them again. If we would have thought daddy would have pulled us from the field, we would have slowed down and let that bunch of kids beat us. That may have been what those kids had done. They were probably a little smarter than the Coomer bunch. However, daddy most likely would not have left with us; he probably would have beaten the living day lights out of us. Maybe we were not that dumb after all.

We had not gone all the way to the Valley that July, since we had stopped in Sinton. We did not see our Valley cousins and would have to wait a whole year before we saw them again.

The Hueys were still traveling with us, as were Bo, Ruby Lee and Ronald Wayne. I was pretty content. Charles Roy and I were still delivering letters to each other, still on the cheeks. I was staying clear of Daddy, especially when he was drunk and disorderly. The other kids were not so lucky and were the recipients of unearned whippings that summer. I just could not figure out why Mama stayed with him. We didn't need him. He didn't work. We could make a living without him.

At Hearne I came down with tonsillitis. It was the worst pain imaginable. Knowing that Mama would not have the courage, I asked Daddy to take me to the doctor. He said no, that all I needed was to work it out. It rained on us, and I got very wet which made the pain worse. I continued to work in the field, barely able to drag my cotton sack. I was very hot and knew I was burning up with fever.

That afternoon I just couldn't go back to the field after lunch. I didn't care what Daddy would do to me. I climbed into the back of the truck and cried. The other kids could hear my crying, but they could do nothing. They watched in terror as Daddy came up into the truck to get me. He had his belt in his hands. I saw him coming toward me, but I felt too bad to care. He would whip me, I knew. All of a sudden Robert Lee climbed into the back of the truck. He told Daddy that Mama had said that we needed to go back to the camp, as she had a plan that might get me well. Daddy was really mad, but Robert Lee, who was now taller than Daddy, stood his ground. Daddy said, "Well, hell, Mama might take her back to the camp, but the rest of you kids are going to stay in this field and work." Robert Lee picked me up took me out of the back of the truck and placed me in someone's car for the trip back to the camp. Everyone was proud of Robert Lee, especially Mama, but no one told him so. They were still too afraid of Daddy. I love Robert Lee to this day. He was always Mama's favorite son and my favorite brother.

The person who owned the car took Mama and me to our camp. We were living under a shed. Mama browned salt in a skillet, getting it very hot. She poured the salt into an old towel and wrapped it around my neck, directly on my tonsils. I was lying in the back seat of the car. I felt as if I was dying, but I didn't care, as death would take me away from the pain I was feeling. All afternoon Mama kept the hot towel with the hot salt in it wrapped around my neck. She kept reheating the salt in the skillet. By the end of the day my pain was gone. Mama put the salt up so that it could be used in her cooking. I didn't have any more trouble with my tonsils.

We followed the cotton crops north to Paris, Texas. I wanted to go back to Lindale to go to school. Daddy said that too much school was not good for kids. October came and the mornings were cold. Daddy would build a fire near the cotton trailer so each time we brought in some cotton to be weighed; we could warm by the fire.

One day a big car stopped at the cotton patch. A man got out with a movie camera and asked mama if he would take pictures of us working. I was embarrassed. There were a couple of kids in that big car and they stared at us like we were monkeys at a zoo. I just knew she would tell him, "No!" But she didn't. He stayed over thirty minutes talking to us and making pictures. Daddy was mad when he came back to the field and found out about it. He told Mama that the man was probably the law and would come back and arrest them because the kids were not in school.

Daddy and the other men talked it over and agreed that the best thing to do was to get the kids out of the field for the rest of the day. That made all of us happy, and I was no longer mad at Mama for letting the man take the pictures. The grown-ups stayed in the field and worked the rest of the day. The man did not return. Daddy told Mama he would "kick her ass," if she let that happen again.

Bo and Ruby Lee had saved enough money to buy a trailer house and pay cash for it. I was very proud of them. Mama always said that Ruby Lee could smell a dollar bill walking up the road. She was lucky too. If all of us bought a nickel box of peanuts, she would be the one to get the box with a prize it in, usually a quarter. The same thing would happen if we all got a box of crackerjacks; her box would have a better prize in it than ours. I wanted to volunteer to go live with them and baby sit, but I knew that I would miss my brothers and sisters, even Nuse and Dollie. They returned to West Texas and Bo went to work in the oil fields.

Around the middle of October, Daddy finally decided we could go back to our house in Lindale, and Mama could go back to her job. School was in its seventh week when the Coomer kids got to start.

Ten

The morning was cool on the day we walked with Mama to start to school that year. Joe, although not old enough to go to school, walked with us. He was sucking his bottle that was always present. I was excited about being able to get books and to start my reading again. I had not seen a book since last spring. We all had on new clothes and new shoes bought mostly with the money we had made on Saturday mornings in the field. Thinking about my new clothes on our way to school, I silently made a promise to myself to take care of them from here on out. It was a promise I couldn't keep.

The principal assigned me to Mrs. Saunders room. She was a new teacher in Lindale, and it was also her first year to teach. When I entered the room with the principal, she turned and smiled at me. As I smiled back I noticed how pretty she was, prettier than Mrs. Pool, my second grade teacher. I liked her immediately and felt this was going to be a good year.

My happiness lasted only a few minutes. I was at Mrs. Saunders desk, and she was checking out my books to me, when in she walked. Carol! She came right up to me and said, "I wondered if they would let you go to school here this year. Where have you been?" I started to tell her it was none of her business, but in an instant I decided to say nothing. She went to her seat and sat down. I did not want to be in the same class with her, but what could I do. After I was assigned my place, I sat down also. I looked across the room and Carol smiled at me. I did not smile back. She was my enemy, and I was not going to be her friend.

When I had been in the first grade at Christmas time, I had drawn a girl's name for whom I had to buy a Christmas present. She had also drawn mine. I had gotten her a Santa Claus that had some type of light in him. She had given me a set of play dishes. I still had them. The year of my fourth grade Ernestine became my best friend. I also got another good friend. Her name was Helen. Both girls were very smart. Of course another buddy of mine was Mary. She walked to and from school with me each day. She lived right across the road from us, and our families were still in the same kind of business, bootlegging, and trying to stay one step ahead of the law. Before long Carol and her family moved from Lindale, and I never saw her again. However, it was years before the pain of what happened between us went away.

Daddy's drinking was becoming worse. He was selling whiskey to make money, and he could not resist the temptation to drink it. When he wasn't drinking, he could be nice to us. I began to feel that he was really sorry for the way he acted when he was drunk. I just could not understand why he didn't stay sober all the time. I wanted my daddy to be right and good. *Why didn't he get a regular job so that we could have money to buy food and clothes and be like other people were?* The reason for his behavior was not clear to me. He would treat Mama and us nice, but when the drinking began, this other person, the monster came out, and life was a living hell for us.

Men started coming to our house to play poker with Daddy. I hated to come home and to find that bunch there after school. They would have cigarette ashes and empty beer and whiskey bottles all over the place. When I came into the house I just stared at Daddy like I could kill him, but I was too afraid to say anything to him and the rest of the drunks.

Ruth Evelyn had to cook supper and have it ready by the time Mama got home. I tried to help her as much as I could. I drew water from the well outside and peeled potatoes. She hated the dirty house as much as I did, but nothing could be done.

One afternoon one of the men asked me if I would make him a cup of coffee. I said, "No sir." One thing Daddy and Mama had taught us was to say, "Yes sir," "no sir," "yes ma'm" and "no ma'm." It didn't matter if they were black or white. If they were older, we had manners and showed respect.

Daddy grabbed me by the shoulder and said, "Make him some coffee or I will whip your ass." The man said, "Mr. Coomer, it's all right, I really don't need any coffee." I was already on my way into the kitchen to get the coffee pot on. First I had to pump the

Coleman stove to get it going. I was mad. As I was making the pot of coffee I decided that I was going to go in there and pour it all over that bunch of men. Of course that was just a thought; I knew I didn't have the nerve to do such a thing

I sat the cup of coffee in front of the man who had asked for it. He felt ashamed for me and sorry that he had nearly caused me to get a whipping. To my surprise he gave me a quarter for the coffee. Some of the other men, wanting to sober up some before going home, asked for some coffee. Each of them gave me from a nickel to a quarter for a cup of it.

From then on the Coomer kids had a business to run when we got home from school if a poker game were going on. It got so that I would be glad to see cars in our yard. I still hated the way the cigarettes and booze stunk, but I loved the smell of money. I no longer had to steal paper and pencils from other kids. I was glad about this since I kind of figured that, because we were getting older now, one of them was going to catch on to what I was doing.

Down the street from us back toward the school is where the Warren family lived. C. B. and Floy Ella had at least ten kids by now. Before they divorced years later, sixteen children would be born unto them. Like the Coomers and the Shackletts, the Warrens were poor, but Mr. Warren didn't resort to selling whiskey. On the weekends the Coomer, Shacklett and Warren kids would play down behind our house near a stream. There were grapevines in the trees. Tarzan had nothing on us. When we got tired of playing, we would get into arguments and be mad at each other for a few days. Sometimes it would be the Coomers and Shackletts mad at the Warrens, the Warrens and Shackletts mad at the Coomers, or the Coomers and Warrens mad at the Shackletts. Other times it would be a mixture of our own family members mad at each other.

We were all great friends though, and we all looked forward to the weekends when there would be no lessons to get and we could all just play. I made up a little saying about our three families: *It is Warren's town, Shacklett's street, Coomer's hotel and nothing to eat.* We all knew we were poor, but when we were playing together, we didn't dwell on this fact and felt lucky to have each other.

The night watchman in town stole bent cans of peas from the local canning factory and would sell the food to Daddy. Other times Daddy would get the bent cans out of the garbage behind the canning factory himself, cutting out the middleman. Daddy would only do that when money was especially tight. He wasn't a natural born thief, not like a night watchman, anyway.

Dollie, Joe, and I tried to catch birds. We took a pasteboard box, cut a hole in it, and tied a string through the hole. We propped the box up with a big stick, and ran the string back into the house through a window. Food was spread out on the ground, starting a little way from the opening of the box right up to the inside of it. After that we sat inside the house, waiting on the unsuspecting birds. When one of them got inside the box, we pulled the string, thus making the box fall over the bird. We would then take the bird out of the box and pet it some. We always turned them loose, just to see if they would be dumb enough to eat our food again. We would know who the second timers were, since the Coomer kids could tell the difference between one blackbird and another. It's a talent, you see.

Mama had talked to us some about God and the devil. I knew God didn't want a bad person like myself, and, *what if Daddy were* right *that the devil was too afraid of me to let me down there? What was going to happen to my body when I died?* I spent a lot of sleepless nights worrying about my future corpse.

The Central Baptist Church in Lindale decided to hold a revival. Mama took us to church on opening night. Daddy wouldn't go and said that he wouldn't take us or pick us up. We had to walk. Big deal, I didn't care. I walked almost everywhere I went around town anyway. We all did. He thought he was getting our goat. We paid no attention to him.

The preacher started talking about burning in hell, and I really got scared. *What was a person like me going to do?* Right out of that preacher's mouth came the solution to my problems. He told us that if we would join the church, God would forgive us of all the bad things we had done in the past, namely our sins, and when we died, we could all go to live with Him.

That was a deal I could not pass up. I knew it would be a lot better living with God than it would be with Daddy or the devil. When it came time for the altar call, I was one of the first ones to walk down the aisle. Sleeping was a lot easier after that. I was really happy and wanted to show my appreciation to that preacher, so I went back to church every night of that revival and laid down on the front pew so that God and the preacher could see how easy they had made it for me to go to sleep.

The Sunday after the revival was over, the church sponsored a dinner on the ground. I had never seen so much food in all my life. I ate until I could hold no more. I also got baptized. Mama took me to the lake in our truck. Daddy decided to go too. He wanted to see this bad daughter of his put under the water. The preacher led one person after another into the lake, baptizing them in the name of the Father, the Son and the Holy Ghost. Then it was my turn.

I was remembering the time Daddy had almost let me drown. I began to tremble. *Maybe this had not been such a good idea.* I wanted to go to Heaven, but I didn't want to go today. I heard the preacher say, "Do not be afraid my child, God is walking with us." *He'd better be and he better have good legs!* Before I could cut out of there and run, I felt myself going under the water. Before I had time to stop breathing, the preacher pulled me up from the water. I was happy to still be alive. I decided right then and there that it was going to be a long time before I got saved again.

I remember seeing Mama crying when I was led out of the water. To my surprise, my daddy was crying too. *What had I done to make them cry?* I felt they should have been happy about the occasion. Man, grown-ups were something that I just couldn't figure out.

As we left, riding in the back of the truck, I looked back at the lake. The water that had been clean and blue when we first pulled up was as dirty as Mama's wash water was on washday. A week or two later another church in town had a revival. I went each night just so I could go the Sunday dinner on the ground. I didn't walk down the aisle again, as I wasn't about to get back in that lake. There were more revivals at other churches in town each year. I was always in attendance.

We started going to Sunday school on Sunday mornings. I began to learn a lot about the Bible. Memorizing things came easy for me, and I got all kinds of little prizes and stars by my name. I looked forward to Sundays.

The first thing I memorized was the Ten Commandments. I thought about them quite a bit and wondered about them too. Several things I didn't understand at all. God said not to commit adultery. *Well, what was that?* He said not to covet thy neighbor's house. Sometimes I lived around neighbors who didn't even have a house. God commanded us to honor thy father and thy mother. *Surely he wasn't talking about my father.* God didn't want us to take His name in vain. Daddy did that all the time, and *if I honored my daddy, would I be okay taking God's name in vain*? It was really confusing. God commanded us to work six days a week and rest on the Sabbath. Daddy didn't work one day a week must less six. *Was it okay then for me not to go to church?*

I felt that most of the Ten Commandments must be for adults anyway. Kids didn't kill. I didn't know how old Cain was when he killed his brother Abel, but he had killed him before God commanded him not to; therefore, I felt Cain had gotten away with the first murder ever committed.

God didn't actually come right out and say, "Thou shalt not lie." He did say not to bear false witness against thy neighbor. *Did that mean not to lie*? I didn't know. Since it wasn't clear to me about lying being really wrong, the only Commandment I felt I could break, other than honoring thy father and thy mother, was the one about stealing. Usually the things I stole were things I really needed, like notebook paper, pencils and crayons. God would surely have to overlook those things.

God commanded us not to do all these things, but yet I guessed it must be okay to do just that because He said He would forgive us if we asked Him to. This was a way I figured to keep Him busy. If *no one broke any of the Commandments, then God would have nothing to do and He sure would get bored in Heaven.* One reason He didn't make it crystal clear about lying being a sin was that He knew so much of it would go on that He wouldn't have enough time to get around to forgiving everyone who asked forgiveness for it. I didn't worry too much about breaking any of the Commandments because I knew I wouldn't hesitate to ask God to forgive me.

I missed Bo, Ruby Lee and the baby. At night I would wonder if he had grown and what he had learned since I last saw him. I hoped that they would come soon for a visit. I waited, and I waited; we all did.

Daddy and Mama started taking us to see Daddy's sister, our Aunt Bessie and her husband Uncle Jack. They lived in a small, cute house in the country between Longview and Gilmer, Texas. They did not have any children and treated us really good. Uncle Jack worked for a supermarket in Longview, and they always had plenty of food. When we left their house to return to Lindale, Uncle Jack always had groceries to give us.

Aunt Bessie was red headed and had a really big bosom and she was very pretty. I didn't understand what people meant when they told Daddy that his sister was really stacked. Sometimes Daddy wouldn't take Mama with him when he went to see Aunt Bessie. Those times he would take one of his men friends to visit her. Sometimes he would take a friend and a kid or two along. I didn't know why we would have to stay outside with Daddy while the friend was in the house with Aunt Bessie. Daddy told us that his friend was showing her his respect. It wasn't always the same friend either.

I really liked going to see Aunt Bessie and Uncle Jack. However, there was a drawback. They liked to drink whiskey, and Daddy always got drunk with them, and then he would be mean to us and usually stayed drunk for a few days. I really had mixed feelings about visiting my favorite aunt.

Uncle Earnest had moved his family to Gilmer. Aunt Kate was working, and I assumed that Uncle Earnest was too. Betty Jo, the oldest girl, had to take care of her younger brothers and sisters, clean house, and do the cooking. She was in school, had to get her lessons and help the others get theirs too. The responsibility was overwhelming to her. She became very unhappy and decided to end her life. Betty Jo took a gun and shot herself. She aimed for her stomach. Luckily, she missed and hit one of her legs.

My pretty cousin was taken to the hospital in Gilmer. When we received the news, Daddy took Ruth Evelyn over there to stay with her. After I found out that she was going to be okay, I hoped that Uncle Earnest would become a better man. It was his fault that she had become so unhappy. *Maybe Daddy too would see how bad both of them were and would mend his ways also.* It didn't happen. In fact, the near death experience for Betty Jo just added fuel to Uncle Earnest's bad personality.

Unlike my cousin, the fourth grade was really a good year for me. There were two boys who were really cute, and I enjoyed being around them. They were Norvell and Billy Frank. Another guy I liked was Whan, and he was the smartest person in the entire fourth grade. None of these boys had a crush on me. I didn't really care because I knew I had a boyfriend living in South Texas who outshined them all. I never told my Lindale friends about my summer friends. There was no need. None of them could have ever understood about love like I did. I needed to keep these two worlds apart. I liked them both.

At recess we played softball. Everyday someone was a captain for two teams and took turns choosing who they wanted to be on their team. I was always one of the first ones to be chosen. Two other girls, Johnnie Sue and Marilyn, were picked early too. Johnnie Sue was strong and a fast runner. One day she was playing on the opposing team. I was playing shortstop. She hit the ball way out to centerfield. Around the bases she came. I was standing in the baseline figuring to slow her down some and make her go around me. She hollered for me to get out of her way. I didn't.

She ran right over me, knocking me down. I pretended to be knocked out cold. I could hear a teacher say, "Back up, you kids, and give her some air to breathe." One of the kids was screaming, "Go get the principal, I think she is dead." I was really enjoying this. I had a hard time keeping my eyes and mouth shut, not smiling.

The principal came and picked me up and took me to his office. He washed my face and I slowly came to. The first question I asked in my low, weak voice was, "Did she make a home run?" The principal answered, "Yes, she did, she didn't slow down." That was the last time I ever played shortstop standing in the baseline.

Another game we played was Red Rover. Two lines of kids holding hands would face each other and one group would say, "Red Rover, Red Rover, let so-and-so come over (they would call someone's name here)." The person called would run as fast and as hard as he/she could go trying to break through the line at any place he/she chose to crash through. If the calling line held, then that person had to join that line. If the person broke through the line, he or she could chose someone from the line to take back to join his or her line. There was never a winner or loser line, but that game was a lot of fun.

The odor in our outdoor toilet got pretty strong. It would almost make me sick going in there. It didn't bother me to go into the bushes to pee, but I just didn't like doing the other thing in the weeds. One day Daddy went to town and came back with some lime. He went into the outdoor toilet and spread the lime into the mess in each hole. In no time at all one could smell the odor. Daddy got to where he put lime in our toilet pretty often. You might say we had the cleanest outdoor toilet in town.

Two weeks before school was to let out for the summer, Daddy took us out so we could go to Winnsboro to pick strawberries. Charles Frank Ragsdale was glad to see us. I played with him a lot that summer. He had a lot of comic books that I could read, but I never entertained the thought of letting him play Post Office with me. I hoped and prayed that Bo, Ruby Lee and Ronald Wayne would show up, but they didn't. Bo was making good money in the oil fields.

After the strawberry season was over, we returned to Lindale to begin picking blackberries. The sun was really hot. If a person looked just right he could see the heat in the air. We, of course, were all barefooted. To complain to Daddy about not having any shoes was useless. He had to have the money to drink, play poker and chase women. He did not give us half of what we made on Saturday like he did in the cotton patch.

I decided I would steal some money to buy me a pair of shoes. Daddy always left quarters in a box at the middle of the field at the end of the row. When he had to go into town, the honor system was in place. When a person brought up a lug of blackberries, they would pay themselves from the box. If berries were paying fifty-cents a lug, a person would take out two quarters, and if the pay were seventy-five cents a lug, three quarter were taken. Everyone was honest. We did not get paid for our work. That was not fair; so one morning, when Daddy was gone, I paid myself for a lug of berries. I didn't get caught. The next Saturday I went to a rummage sale and got me a pretty decent pair of shoes for twenty-five cents. I had money left over. No body questioned me as to where I had gotten the shoes, but I had a big lie ready just in case. I was going to tell them that someone I knew from school gave them to me. It was nice to realize I could steal and didn't have to lie about it, as no one seemed to care about me and my new shoes.

Every day the next week I stole some money. I put the money in my socks in the shoes. I had to walk real careful so not to make any noise when I walked. I was real nervous about that. There was no question in my mind what Daddy would do if he caught me.

At the end of the week, I decided my crime wave had to come to an end. If I started spending the money, somebody would tell on me. My siblings would have delighted in that.

On Sunday, after church, I took my stolen money to the schoolyard. I had in my possession an empty coffee can. Beside one of the large trees in the schoolyard I dug a big hole. The money was placed in the can and buried. I knew that I would dig it up later, maybe after I was grown. *This life of crime just couldn't go on.* When I got home no one asked me where I had been. I felt relieved. I truly didn't think about the money again for a long time. *If I put it out of my mind, then the crime never happened.*

When Daddy didn't have whiskey or beer to drink, he would buy a product called Beef, Iron & Wine from the local drug store. He also drank vanilla flavoring or hair tonic. All of them had alcohol in them. Daddy had a bad habit of sending some of us into town to get these items. The Beef, Iron & Wine cost $1.00 a bottle. The druggist finally told me to tell Daddy that he would no longer sell it to him or his kids. When I gave him the news, Daddy, about half drunk and needing another fix, got really mad. He grabbed me and took me to town. Nuse, Dollie, and Joe jumped into the back of the truck.

I know that he thought I was lying to him. I was mad too, at both of these men. The kids were caught in the middle. Daddy confronted the druggist, "Didn't my gal have the money to pay for what I told her to buy me?" He shouted. "Now Mr. Coomer, just calm down. I know this stuff should not be taken the way you drink it. It is medicine and is not to be used as alcohol," the druggist countered. Daddy took a knife out of his pocket and opened it. Someone in the drug store ran to get the city marshal. I was hoping he would not be somewhere shooting dice.

"Are you telling me that I can't buy something in this store that is legal for anyone of any age to buy?" Daddy asked. "That's right Mr. Coomer, I will no longer sell it to you, your kids or any of your friends if I think it will end up in your hands," the owner said. Daddy, knowing the law was on his way in, put the knife back in his pocket. "Get in the truck kids before I have to whip this son-of-a-bitch. He knows he ain't a real druggist anyway. I should report him to the laws," Daddy hollered on our way out of the store, almost knocking the city marshal down as he was coming into the store. I had no idea what the druggist said to the law, but he didn't come looking for Daddy. The rest of the day we all stayed away from Daddy. He was still mad, but he never asked us to go buy anymore of the Beef, Iron & Wine.

One Saturday Daddy got really drunk. All the older kids were gone from the house. Dollie, Joe, and I were the only ones at home with him except Mama. Daddy started hollering and cussing her. He then proceeded to start hitting her. The three of us huddled together in a corner of a room. We were crying but afraid to try to help Mama. All of a sudden she ran from the house. She didn't come back that day.

None of the older children came home either. I was the oldest one there, and Daddy took turns cussing and hitting us. He finally passed out. I decided then that I had to do it. I had to kill him! I went outside to get the axe that was used to cut wood. I could not find it. I wanted my mama to come and get us. It was getting dark now. I had never been this afraid in my life.

There were three cold biscuits on the table left over from breakfast. I gave one each to Dollie and Joe. However, I didn't eat one, since Daddy would need it when he came to. Darkness came to the house. Daddy had refused to pay the electricity bill, and our lights had been turned off. We had coal oil lamps to use. I was afraid to try to light one with a match. I thought I might catch the house on fire. Darkness not only filled the house, it filled my soul. Dollie and Joe went to sleep huddled together. Tired, hungry and afraid, I put my arms around those poor souls and cried myself to sleep.

Sometime during the night I felt someone covering us with a quilt. Mama had come home! But terror welled up inside me as I realized it was Daddy and not Mama tending to us. I felt his tears as he sat close to us, but I pretended to be asleep. "What have I done?" Daddy cried. "Where has these kids' mama gone? She has got to come back. I love her, and I love these kids. She took all the money. How will I feed them?" *To whom was he talking? Was it to God? Well, too bad. The Lord would know that he was just* telling *a lie.* He didn't love anyone. But, I was happy that he had said it. I was also afraid that we would never see Mama again and cried silently.

The sun had come up before we awoke. No one was around. Not Mama, not Daddy or any of the older kids. I was shaking. *What were we going to do?* Dollie and Joe were hungry now. Out of the blue I remembered what a preacher had said about praying. God would help me. It was worth a try. I went into the outdoor toilet, and I prayed to God asking him to let Mama come home. I told him how afraid I was and that we were hungry. I also promised God a lot of things that day. I would be good, would never tell another lie, or steal. I would go to church each Sunday and not sleep on the front pew. However, I stopped short of telling Him that I would quit playing Post Office. That promise could be saved for later if I needed it. As I prayed I cried, and my voice got louder and louder. I finally stopped so that I could check up on the little ones.

Just as soon as I got out the toilet door, I saw her. Mama! She was sitting in the grass in the field next to the house. That preacher sure knew what he was talking about when it came to praying. I ran to her; she picked me up and carried me to the house. She didn't ask any questions like, "Where is your daddy?"

Mama cooked some biscuits and gravy for us. After we ate, she washed us up, stopping ever so often to hug us. She had come back for us. I just knew we would be going away. I wanted her to wait for the older kids to come home so we could take them too, but I didn't say a word. I would miss them, but I sure would not miss my daddy.

In the early afternoon all the kids came home. My thoughts that they had all run away were false. They had just gone to friends' homes to spend the night. Later in the day Daddy came home too. He told Mama he was sorry, and that he had been out looking for her. We all knew he had been out looking for something to drink. He also told her that she had better never leave us again or he would whip her ass. She did not respond to him.

He was not drinking. He had no money. All my family was home. For some reason I thanked God that he had sent Daddy back to us. But I didn't really understand why I did. He let me sleep at the foot of their bed that night. I slept like a baby, even though I was always mindful of Daddy's smelly feet. The next day we all went to work in the blackberry patch, all except Daddy of course.

That summer the folks who ran the town decided to have a blackberry festival. They declared that Lindale was the Blackberry

Capital of the World. Excitement was everywhere. People came from all around to join in the activities. Ruth Evelyn won a bubble-blowing contest and got a dollar bill for her efforts. I decided to enter a singing contest. I got up in front of the local people and sang a song about meeting a blue-eyed stranger. Before I was finished, the whole audience was laughing. I didn't realize it at the time but I could not carry a tune. I just had a lot of nerve. Having nerve paid off as some stranger gave me a dollar bill and said just that, "Girl you sure have a lot of nerve." The dollar spent just as well as it would have if I had had a lot of talent.

There was also a blackberry-picking contest. What seemed like hundreds of people, including myself, went to a field outside the city limits. The contestants picked berries for fifteen minutes. When the judges weighed the berries, a black lady was the winner. That didn't sit too well with some people. Some of them declared that black people should be barred from the competition.

I knew it didn't matter, for next year I was going to make sure that my brother-in-law, Bo Paul, knew about the contest. Nobody would be able to pick more blackberries than he could. He was the fastest worker I had ever known. He and Ruby Lee just happened to be in Hobbs, New Mexico, at the present time. Bo was still working as a roughneck in the oil fields.

A person could buy a Blackberry Derby to wear on his/her head. Everyone was getting one. They cost one dollar a piece. I sure wanted one of them. The problem was that I could not come up with the dollar to buy it. I decided to take matters into my own hands; I would steal one. Sure enough, the opportunity for me to do this happened at the drug store. Several men were sitting at a table and drinking coffee. They had all been wearing the hats when they first came in and sat down. Being gentlemen, they had removed them when they came into the building. Noticing that they were not paying any attention to me, or the derbies, I grabbed one and left the store. The promise I had made to God about never stealing again was already gone from my mind.

After I got home with it, I didn't know what to do with the thing. If any of my family members saw it, I would not be able to explain where I had gotten it. Daddy would not put up with stealing. I hid it in a box and forgot about it. I was not about to be seen in town wearing a stolen hat. Although all the derbies were identical, I began to think that maybe the man I stole it from might be able to recognize his. *Why is it that when a person commits a crime, nothing good ever comes from it?* I asked God to forgive me, and He did.

I wasn't the only kid in the Coomer family stealing. Robert Lee and Nuse took two dimes from Ruth Evelyn's penny loafers, went to a dice game and came back home with fifty dollars. Those two crooks did not share the money with anyone; in fact, they would not even return Ruth Evelyn's two dimes. I thought they were sorrier than I was; at least I didn't steal from a family member. Don't you agree with me? And besides, they would not have let a girl get into a dice game back in those days.

Daddy stayed sober until the blackberry season was over and we went to South Texas to pick cotton. We first went to the Valley. We camped out in Aunt Ellen's yard again. Everyday she would have lunch fixed for us. I always thought that if she didn't drink she would be the best person that I had ever known. She wasn't mean though when she drank. All in all, she was okay.

In the Valley we picked the cotton, but when we moved back to Sinton we pulled it, boles and all. We got into a bad habit of having green bole fights. Before the cotton opened up enough to be picked or pulled, it started out as a hard green bole. A kid could take one of them and hit someone up side the head and it would really hurt. We fought each other as well as other kids.

Daddy had started back to drinking by now. His sisters would come over on the weekends and drink with him. But, I didn't pay much attention to his drinking that summer. I was with Charles Roy and we were playing Post Office again. This was the summer that I fell in love. Really in love! One night while playing Post Office, Charles Roy turned my head with his hands and kissed my lips with his. The stars fell out of the sky and hit me. I was ten years old, and this was the man I would marry.

The next day the work in the field didn't seem too hard. Charles Roy and I shared a secret. That night we delivered more letters to each other right smack on the lips, and every night for the rest of the summer it was the same.

One Saturday Nuse, Frances, Charles Roy and I went to a movie. It was a scary one. I was happy. It was hard for me to believe that I was actually sitting by him at the show. The boys wanted us to sit in the balcony. That was okay with me. I would have gone to the moon with him if he had asked me to. While we were up there, the boys peed over the rail onto the people sitting below. We got down from there as quickly as possible. Before the show was over, the two guys were hiding under the seats; they were so scared. I didn't care that I had selected a sissy for a boyfriend, but I sure didn't figure Nuse for one.

My heart ached when we left the Hueys in October and moved back to Lindale. When we waved good-bye, I cried. It would be a long time before we would go back to South Texas to pick cotton, but I knew the thoughts of him would never go away. And they didn't.

A couple of Burma-Shave signs cheered me up: "BROTHER SPEEDERS...LET'S REHEARSE-ALL TOGETHER...GOOD MORINING NURSE."

"CAUTIOUS RIDER...TO HER RECKLESS DEAR-LET'S HAVE LESS BULL...AND A LOT MORE STEER."

Eleven

We arrived back in Lindale in October as usual six weeks late to start to school. It was cold now. The winter was going to be long and hard. Robert went to the woods and cut firewood. He would surely need it to start the fire in the wood-burning stove in bad weather.

Mama took us to Tyler in our old truck. We were going to buy school clothes. I was very excited. I made another promise to myself to take better care of my clothes. When we got to the first store, I found a pretty dress on the rack in just my size. It was red with lace around the sleeves and neck. I asked Mama if I could try it on. She looked at the price tag and said, "No." I put it back on the rack and I began to cry silently. I would not show Mama how disappointed I was. She did not have a lot of money to spend on our clothes.

The other kids were looking at clothes they wanted to buy, but Mama said they were all too high. She complained to the sales clerk that everything in the store was too high and that she should be ashamed of herself for trying to sell stuff for that much money. The store clerk became angry and went to the manager with her anger. The store manager, a man, of course, came to her rescue. He told Mama to take her brood of kids and get out of the store. I was embarrassed to death. We left, but not before Nuse and Joe pushed over about half the clothes racks in the store. As I left the store I noticed the manager was on the phone. He was calling the police! I just knew it.

We never found out if the police came; we loaded up into the truck and went to another part of town to buy our school clothes. We each got a new pair of shoes, which we tried on, with dirty feet.

We left each store with sales clerks glad to see us go. I was heartsick about the red dress because the three dresses I got were all very plain and cheap.

The morning finally came for us to get up and go to school. We all washed our hands and feet in the pan of water Mama had warmed on the Coleman stove in the kitchen. We put on our new clothes and our new shoes. Mama combed our hair with a comb that had several of its teeth missing. It really hurt.

When we all started our walk to school, tears were streaming down my face from the hair combing. Six kids and one Mama were walking down the road. We looked like we might be part of a circus. Mama scolded us as we pushed and shoved each other. We walked onto the schoolyard into the principal's office. The principal wasn't surprised that the Coomer kids were starting to school late. Baby Joe was in the first grade. Daddy would no longer have a babysitting job during the day. It would give him more time to chase women and play poker. Nuse had failed the sixth grade and would now have to repeat it. It sure didn't make him any difference.

My teacher in the fifth grade was named Mrs. Giles. She was heavier than any of my other teachers, and I took an instant dislike to her. I felt like the feeling was mutual. Right on the spot I decided I would not worry about lessons or learning anything. I was going to be a bad girl this year. That teacher would soon see that I wasn't afraid of her because she was big. It meant nothing to me.

The girl sitting behind me was named Barbara. She was kind of blond headed and pretty. I wasn't going to like her either. One reason was that she had to grade all my homework and spelling test papers. We had to pass this work to the person that sat behind us. For the first four weeks of my fifth grade the teacher gave our spelling words out just like they were in the book. I would just copy them down before the test, in order, and then hand the paper back to Barbara to be graded. Of course I always made a 100 on the test, without studying one bit. I was a genius at cheating. I saw no reason to study.

On the fifth spelling test as usual I pretended to be writing down the words as the teacher was giving them out. When she was through, I pulled out the paper with all the words spelled just exactly right from under the page I had been pretending to write on. I handed it back to Barbara to grade. As I was grading the paper of the person in front of me, I realized that Mrs. Giles had not gone right down the book but had skipped around giving out the words for us to spell.

I was doomed. I turned around and told Barbara in a very threatening tone that she better not tell the teacher what I had done. It worked too. Barbara passed my paper back up to me. It had a 100 written on top. When Mrs. Giles called out my name for my grade, I proudly said 100. At recess Barbara told me she was not afraid of me, and that I was not to pull that stunt again. I told her I would do it again if I wanted to and that she had better not tell Mrs. Giles.

Barbara must have scared me some because I decided to actually learn how to spell the words as I had done in the lower grades. I began to study them at night. Arithmetic was a favorite subject of mine, so I decided I would do all my homework for it also. I discovered that the answers to all the Arithmetic problems were in the back of the book. I would just simply work on the problem until my answers matched the ones in the book.

After I had changed my ways about my schoolwork, I noticed that Mrs. Giles was acting a little better to me, so I decided to give her a second chance. Sometimes I would actually speak to her in the mornings when she said good morning to her students.

Mrs. Giles decided that she was going to teach us how to tell time. Only one person in our class had a watch to wear. So I decided I was not going to pay any attention to her in this endeavor. I felt this would just be a waste of time. Mrs. Giles had a bear with a big stomach. The watch was located on the bear's stomach. The teacher would move the big and little hands explaining to us how it worked.

Well, I was determined not to learn how to tell time. Mrs. Giles taught us a little each day about time. Then one day I decided I might as well pay attention and learn it as some of the kids had begun picking up on it. I discovered that I just did not understand it, and I really tried too. I was the last student in the class for the light to come on in my head and understand about the big and little hands on a clock.

One morning I came to school after I had slept in my dress all night and had not washed up after breakfast. Mrs. Giles took note of the way I looked, hair not combed. That day she told our class that we should take baths more often, brush our teeth and put perfume on so that we would smell good. She was looking straight at me. This was the first time I had ever heard the word perfume, but I couldn't believe that it would smell better than sweat, dirt and home-made lye soap.

That teacher really hurt my feelings. I had to hurt hers. The next morning I spotted her key chain lying on her desk. When she was out of the room, taking them was easy. I threw them in the burn barrel on the playground. On the key chain were her car keys, school keys, house key, freezer key and goodness knows what other kind of keys. All the doors to the schoolhouse had to have the locks changed.

Several people, including myself, helped her look for them, but to no avail. I was happy as a lark. After the keys had been missing about a week, I told Mrs. Giles that I had had this dream where I saw the keys in the burn barrel. We found them! All the kids thought I was really something to be able to have a dream that was true. I may not have been too clean, but I was popular.

There was a boy in our class who was always in some kind of trouble, so I told the teacher that in my dream he was at the burn barrel. The principal had a good talk with that young man. Later in the year his family moved. There was a rumor that went around that he had left to go to reform school. Now my memory fails me a little here, but if I look in the mirror real close, I think I would recognize the one who started that rumor.

That winter was brutally cold. Robert Lee would get up each morning and start the fire in the wood-burning stove that stood in the middle of the front room. Daddy and Mama had a bed set up in the room for them to sleep on, but the rest of us had to sleep on the floor on pallets. The mattresses that we had previously owned had been sold so Daddy could have money to buy beer. The house was very cold in the night so we snuggled up to each other as much as possible. The three boys slept on one pallet and the three girls slept on the other one. The fire had to be put out at night because we had to conserve as much wood as possible

After Robert Lee got the fire going in the mornings, the rooms in the little house would heat up and we would get up. Mama would cook breakfast usually consisting of biscuits and gravy. She then would leave for her job. She and several other women paid a man fifty-cents a day for a ride to work. We would then wash up, put on our shoes, comb our hair and walk to school. We didn't have coats to wear, since the school clothes money did not include enough for them. It was always nice to get to school so we could warm up at the heaters in the building. We usually arrived at school about an hour before school started.

Around Christmas time Daddy did something really remarkable. He got a job of sorts. He opened a fruit business in an empty building downtown. He sold bananas, apples, oranges, nuts, grapefruits and other items. He had gone to the Valley to visit his brother and sister, and when he came back he had a truckload of that stuff. All of us kids started going down to the fruit stand after school to help him out. To our surprise Daddy was actually making some money.

Daddy began to give us money on Saturday to go to the movie. It cost nine cents to get in if you were under twelve. I stayed under twelve until I was at least fourteen. Every week there would be a new western to see, a cartoon, and a serial, usually Superman. He would be left, almost dead, every time, and we could hardly wait until the next weekend rolled around so we could see how he would get out of the mess he was in. He always did. In the main movie the good guys would always win, the posse showing up just in time to kill all the bad guys. The six shooters that they used would fire twenty-five times when necessary. That kind of stuff only happened in the movies. I fell in love with Gene Autry, Roy Rogers, the Cisco Kid, the Lone Ranger and all the rest of them. My favorite cowboy was Rex Allen. I never missed one of his movies on Saturday.

There was an old heater in the back of the fruit stand and Daddy always had a fire going. The crates that the apples came packed in had a lot of paper in them. Dollie and I started to pin the paper on our heads pretending we had very long, beautiful hair. One night I got too close to the stove with the paper flowing down my back, and the paper caught fire. Dollie and I both started screaming. My clothes were on fire! Daddy rushed to the back. He grabbed my clothes with his bare hands and pulled them off me. My whole head was singed, but fortunately I was not burned in any way. Daddy hugged me for the longest time and cried. Dollie did too. To my surprise he did not cuss or slap us for being so foolish for standing that close to the open fire. I can tell you right now, I never got close to the fire again.

There was an old man who lived at a boarding house, which was located next door to the fruit stand. He would come over every day to visit us. We really liked him. Daddy enjoyed his company too. They drank whiskey together. I would sit on his lap, and he would hug me, and tell us funny stories, and give us money every once in a while. One day he asked me to go up to his room. He wanted to show me something he had up there. Up to his room with him I went. Well, he was nice and I sure wasn't afraid of him.

As soon as we got into his room, he picked me up and laid me down on the bed. He began to unzip his pants and said to me. "You show me your thing and I will show you my thing." I said, "I don't have anything to show you." "Oh, yes you do," he stated. Suddenly I realized what he was meaning about "his thing". I started to scream, but he put his hands over my mouth. He smelled like whiskey. I could not breath.

I began to kick at him. He began to pull off my panties. I remembered my church training and began to pray silently, promising God the same things I had promised Him in the outdoor toilet the time Mama had left us. It worked. The door burst open and Daddy pulled the old man off me, cussing at him. Daddy hit him hard with his fists. The old man fell to the floor. Daddy told him to leave town, and he meant today.

I was still lying on the bed. I knew I was in for it now. Daddy would surely think I had done something wrong. To my surprise he came and picked me up, held me close to him and cried. I smelled the whiskey on Daddy's breath. I was shaking, not understanding exactly what had happened.

We never saw the old man again. I felt bad about him though and would think about him at night, especially when it was so cold. I wondered if he had any place to live or if he had frozen to death. *Had I done something to cause the old man to do what he had done? If I were as bad as Daddy sometimes said I was, then surely what had happened had been my fault.* Mama was not told about my being in the hotel room. Daddy said it would be better if she never found out.

We had gotten a big, old, German Sheppard dog that had just starting hanging around our house. We named him Stormy King. We never had any food to feed him, so I guess he got it elsewhere. In the mornings he would walk to school with us, then go back to the house or roam around looking for food. When it was time for school to let out, he was always waiting for us outside the schoolhouse. We could not figure out how he knew what time it was. Sometimes I would ask him if he had one of Mrs. Giles' bear clocks in his head. We loved that animal, even me.

One afternoon at the fruit stand the dog came in foaming at the mouth. Daddy said that someone had poisoned him and that he would die. We all started crying. Daddy said that if he had a gun he would shoot him to get him out of his pain. Instead of shooting him, Daddy put him in the truck and took him several miles out in the country to let him die. That night I prayed for him. We had lost a member of the family.

I decided I would never like another dog. It was too hard on one's heart. About a week later, what do you think showed up at the schoolhouse after school to walk us to the fruit stand? It was Stormy King! What a miracle. He had not died. The dog had survived the cold, the hunger and found his way back to our house and to our hearts. He would die for real later, in Vernon, Texas. He walked to the grocery store with Robert Lee and Ruth Evelyn. On the way back, a car hit him. We dug a big hole and buried him in the ground. I kind of thought that maybe he would climb his way out of that hole, but he didn't.

Dr. Kinzie, the doctor who had taken credit for my birth, was building up a good practice. It had been a slow start for him. He had been in Lindale now for ten plus years, and some folks still thought he might be one of them Yankees or even worse, one of them Republicans. He was originally from Kansas, a state directly north and on top of the state of Oklahoma; therefore, he had to be one or maybe both of them, but he was a doctor and Lindale needed one, so like I said, his practice was growing.

Daddy had gotten to be good friends with Dr. Kinzie. He made house calls and came ever so often to help Mama get Daddy sober after he had been on a drunk for two or three weeks. Daddy decided that he would call upon that friendship to help him borrow some money from the bank. Dr. Kinzie assured Daddy that he would talk to the bank president about it.

One Saturday afternoon Daddy, Dr. Kinzie, and the bank president were standing on a street corner in town discussing the possibility of the loan. A truck pulled up at the four way stop in the middle of town and stopped. A lady Daddy knew was standing up in the back of the truck. She had on a see through dress with no under clothes on. She waved and hollered real loud, "Hey Coomer, borrow some money for me too." The truck took off, throwing her down in the back. It was obvious she was a white trash tramp.

Daddy was embarrassed and felt that he would not get the loan. He didn't want Dr. Kinzie and the bank president to know that he knew trash like her. They both just laughed though and the bank president said, "Mr. Coomer you can socialize with the best and worst of people. Come over to the bank Monday morning and get your loan." Daddy didn't know what he had meant by "socializing" and he didn't care; he was going to get the money. That Monday night, with the money in his pocket, he and the white trash tramp shared a pint of whiskey to celebrate. The doctor and the bank president didn't have to know trash like her, but he sure didn't see anything wrong with it.

That was the beginning of a long friendship with the bank president. Daddy paid back the money with interest before the note came due. That same day he borrowed some more money, a little more than last time. Before long Daddy could get any amount that he asked for just by signing his name. He began to realize that a man's good word was worth something, so when he told someone he would pay them back, he did. It didn't matter how hard his children had to work to make the payback happen.

Daddy and I started a little side business at the fruit stand. He would bet a man a quarter that his daughter was so smart that she could guess just about anything. He could show them too if they didn't believe him. It was a bet that no man could turn down. Daddy would throw a quarter against the wall. I would have my head turned. After the quarter hit the wall, Daddy and the guy would walk over to it to see if it had landed as heads or tails. My job was to guess which way it had landed. I would stay back away from the quarter. When Daddy leaned his head over to see what it was, I would make my guess. If Daddy kept his right foot flat on the floor, the quarter had landed on heads. If his right foot was raised just a little, the quarter had landed on tails. I never made a mistake. Daddy kept all the quarters.

Daddy did several embarrassing things. One such thing was this: he would blow his nose and the snot would land on the floor in the fruit stand. Daddy would then take his shoes and rub the snot into the floor. I got on to him just once about it. He told me to mind my own damn business that I was not his boss. The way his fists were curled up, I thought it would be in my best interest to do what he told me to do.

Back at school, things were going pretty well. Mama tried to get all of us to study and get our lessons. She had her hands full talking to Nuse about them. He didn't see any reason to study. Reading and arithmetic were the only things a person should know how to do, and he could do them both. Going to school was fun for him though because he could whip anybody in his present grade and the grade he had just left. Getting licks from the principal didn't bother him even though he knew he was going to get one when he got home if any of us told Daddy about it. Well, I made that mistake just once. After he got his whipping from Daddy, Nuse gave me one. He made me believe whatever went on in that principal's office was just between him and the principal. A girl can learn to mind her own business, you know.

Nuse did have one bright spot that year. His teacher made a scene on a bulletin board in the hall about the country Mexico. She put a school bus on the scene. It appeared the kids in the bus were touring there. Inside the school bus she put Nuse's picture from the past year. His teacher thought it was appropriate since he was the only student in the sixth grade that had actually been to Mexico. Some of the students told him that they thought he lied about that. They only accused him one time. How dare that they think he would ever lie about something! Every day for six weeks, until the scene was changed, the students could see Nuse smiling at them from Mexico. It was pretty neat. I was proud of him and glad he was my brother.

At recess I was still able to beat anybody in jump rope, and I usually wound up with all the boys' marbles. I could still spin a top as well as the next fellow. Since Daddy was working at the fruit stand, he was not playing as much poker, and I wasn't making any money with my coffee business. I began to steal paper and pencils every once in a while. A girl had to get her lessons if she wanted to pass on to the sixth grade. That was my reasoning about the stealing.

Every time I had to steal, I asked God to forgive me. I knew He was doing it too because I never got caught. I was going to

Sunday school regularly now. It was a place to go on Sunday. I was good at learning Bible verses. Our Sunday school teacher and the preacher always said the Lord would forgive us of anything if we would ask for forgiveness. I can tell you I worked the Lord overtime as I talked to him on a regular basis. I was doing a lot of lying. Sometimes I would feel guilty about it but never felt guilty about the stealing. Stealing was necessary.

Ruth Evelyn, who was fourteen, was beginning to have boys coming around. She was acting as silly as Robert Lee did when he was around girls. I couldn't figure out why anyone would want more than one boyfriend. One was all I needed. I would lie awake at night and think about playing Post Office and the fun Charles Roy and I were going to have when summer came and it would be time to go back to South Texas to pick cotton. I was actually looking forward to all the hard work in the fields.

Robert Lee was old enough to drive. He was girl crazy. I thought he was mostly just crazy. One day he had borrowed a car from somebody to have a date. He took the girl to the Saturday western. Dollie and I got as close to them as he would let us. We had to keep an eye on that boy. No telling what might happen if he got out of our sight. He might just hold that girl's hand. We could not let that happen, now could we? When the movie ended Robert Lee told us to get on home; he and the girl were going to ride around for a while. "Ride around where?" I wanted to know. "None of your business," he answered. "Now go home."

I sure didn't want to go home. "We want to ride around too, and we are going to get into the car." I dared him. Dollie and I tried to get in. He pushed me, and I went down like a terd in a well. The girl jumped into the car and closed the door in Dollie's face. Robert Lee jumped into the driver's seat and thought he was going to start the car. He did not know that I had gone outside during the movie and gotten the keys out of the ignition.

I got up from the ground, keys in my pocket. Robert Lee realized that I probably had the keys as other kids began to gather around the car. Robert Lee was really mad. I thought if he hits me, I will play dead and get him arrested. He wasn't about to hit me though, and I knew it. I sure wanted to go riding in that car. *Why was he so set against our going?* When he pulled out a couple of quarters from his pocket and gave them to Dollie and me, we decided to go get us some ice cream. He could take that girl for a ride.

Later in life we learned that Robert Lee had taken her parking at a place called Huckleberry Thicket. This was the place where most of the dice games were held and the place where Robert Lee and Nuse had won the fifty dollars after stealing Ruth Evelyn's two dimes. Going in there he met Daddy coming out in our truck. In the truck was a woman who was not Mama. Robert Lee just waved. He never discussed the incident with Daddy.

In January, it snowed. Daddy decided it would be best to keep the fire burning in the wood-burning stove all night. Snow blew in through the cracks in the house. It was so cold that water left in a pan or a bucket at night would be frozen in the morning. We did not dare go outside to use the outdoor toilet, so a lot of nights, I just peed in my clothes. Dollie and Joe did the same. School was turned out for several days because the school buses could not run on the icy roads. We played in the snow during the day throwing snowballs at each other. Nuse did not care if he hit us in the face and made us cry. I picked up a rock, wrapped it in snow and let him have it on the right side of his face. He was surely going to kill me, but Robert Lee stopped him. In the evenings Mama made us something we had never had before, snow ice cream. She put milk, vanilla flavoring and sugar with the snow. It was some treat.

Mrs. Giles and I had become better friends ever since I had had the dream and found all her keys. She asked me to be in a play about a girl who had gotten three wishes. I was to play the girl. One of the wishes was that she would have a stick of bologna on her nose. The good fairy that was granting the wishes came out and pinned a balloon on my nose. I was excited. Some pretty girl in the class was playing the beautiful fairy. I would have liked to have had the main role, but I was glad just to be in the play. I had asked Mama to come to see me in the play. When I got up on stage I looked for her in the audience, but she was not there. I was sad. Parents of the other kids had come. Mama was working at the rose nursery, and she had not entertained any ideas about taking off from work. In my thoughts lying on the pallet that night, she was at the play, smiling at me from the front row.

Mrs. Giles, who really liked to put on these plays, let me be in another one. It was about one of the fairy tales, the one where the king opens up a pie and blackbirds fly out of it. I was one of the blackbirds. The teacher, with the help of some of the parents, made costumes for us. One would almost think we were actually birds. To my surprise and happiness Mama actually came to this play. The only way she could tell which of the birds was me was by looking at the old boots that I was wearing. I cannot remember my lines in the play, but I remember the lines of one of the birds, Gary, who had been my first boyfriend. That was a fact he was never made aware of. He said, "We will go just as soon as we have a little fun with the cook." She laughed and said, "goody, goody," when the hunter brought us into the maid. "Come, blackbirds, away to the forest to find the good fairy." With that we exited the stage.

It was in the fifth grade that I learned my multiplication tables. Mrs. Giles worked really hard helping all of us on this. One day she told us that multiplication was actually just an easy way of adding. After that, they became clear to me. I think kids start this in the second grade now. I would later realize what a wonderful teacher Mrs. Giles had been, and that I had learned quite a lot in her class. I never did have the nerve to tell her that I was the one who had stolen her keys, and I saw her a lot during the years to come.

By the first week in May our shoes were worn out. Nuse, Dollie, Joe, and I were glad to get out of those things and go barefoot to school. Robert Lee and Ruth Evelyn were too ashamed and continued to wear their worn out shoes. Two weeks before school was out Daddy had Mama checked us out of school. We were moving to Winnsboro to pick strawberries.

Mrs. Giles hugged me that last day of school and told me she would miss me but that she would see me next year. She also did something so very special that it still warms my heart when I think about it now. She loaned me five books to take with me to read that summer. She did ask me to take care of them and to bring them back in the fall. I promised. One of the books was *Emily of Deep Valley*. It was about a girl whose mother was dead, and her grandfather was rearing her. She had two snooty first cousins who were sisters. A boy came into their lives, and Emily won his heart in spite of the cousins. They liked him too. I read the book over and over that summer. I kept my promise and returned the books to her in good condition the next fall.

Another thing Mrs. Giles told me that last day of school was to be a good girl. I didn't know what she was talking about. I was always a good girl.

Twelve

We loaded up all our belongings into the old truck. Daddy put the tent onto the top of it for our move to Winnsboro. It took us two hours to get there, as Daddy had to stop every few minutes to let one of us pee. We stood on the bed Daddy had set up in the front part of the truck. We could stick our heads out the tent openings. That way we could catch all the bugs that flew into our mouths.

At Winnsboro Uncle Buck did not have a house available for us to live in that year. Daddy said that was okay. We would live in the open spaces. Daddy had bought new cots for us to sleep on. Mama set up the bed that she and Daddy slept on, putting a mattress and cover on it. She took one of the apple boxes and made a table for the Coleman stove.

The strawberries were plentiful that year. I was getting older now and Daddy expected me to do a lot more work. Picking strawberries is very hard. A person has to be on their knees most of the time because the vines grow on the ground. I wanted to please Daddy, so I worked as hard as I could. It was never enough though. If he saw us standing up, he would holler out for us to get back to work. I hated him most of the time.

If a person had to go to the bathroom, he/she would just go into the woods and dig a hole with their hands. One was expected to cover it up when you finished your business. I was defiant and usually just left things uncovered; hoping someone without shoes might just walk into the middle of it. Sometimes I would later step into it myself. I wasn't the only Coomer kid to do this. We were all a bunch of rebels.

Charles Frank Ragsdale would come to the field and watch us work. He had turned out to be a pretty neat boy. He was still reading quite a bit. He never had to work though. It was really nice being an only child. I figured that Charles Roy Huey and I would have just one kid. Then he would not have to work. Right now I was enjoying Charles Frank's company. In the evenings he would read to me. We would play in his room at his house, but he never again tried to pull the wool over my eyes about anything.

Joe was still sucking the bottle even though he had made it through the first grade. Daddy told him that if he would quit sucking the bottle he could go to town with him every time he went if he wanted to. This was an offer Joe could not pass up. The next morning when Joe woke up he said, "Mama, fix me a bottle." "What did you say?" Mama asked. Joe replied, "I mean a sandwich." From that day forward, Joe got to go with Daddy just like he promised him he could do. Daddy was a man of his word, as everyone knew.

Every Saturday, Daddy would take the older kids, Robert Lee, Ruth Evelyn, and Nuse to town with him. Joe got to go too. Dollie and I had to stay with Mama. We would be so mad about it that we took our anger out on each other. We usually would pick fights and more than likely would get a whipping from Mama before the rest of the family got back. It wasn't fair, but what could we do about it? Daddy would let them go to the show in town. Ruth Evelyn would tell Dollie and me about the story when she returned.

That summer in Winnsboro a person could buy a pint of ice cream for 19 cents and get another pint for a penny. One Saturday Robert Lee decided he would buy a pint of ice cream apiece for Dollie and me. He had the pints in a paper sack. By the time they got back to us the ice cream had melted. I sat down and cried. It seemed that the Lord just didn't want me to enjoy anything. *Was he punishing me for telling so many lies?* Sometimes at night when I talked to Him, I would try to get Him to show me his face, if He wanted me to believe that He really existed. It seemed I just never made much headway with Him or my daddy.

When the strawberry season was over, we moved back to Lindale. Daddy pulled the worst drunk I had seen to date. For two weeks he lay flat of his back and did nothing but drink whiskey. When he needed to go to the bathroom, he either just peed in his pants or he made Mama take his thing out of his pants so he could pee in a can. Several times his bowels moved, but he didn't. Each time Mama just cleaned him up.

The second weekend of his drunk Mama asked the bootleggers not to bring any more whiskey to the house. Daddy was really mad, slapping her once when she got close to the bed to try to feed him. He knocked her across the room cussing her and calling her all sorts of ugly names. All of us kids stayed outside as much as possible. Daddy had drunk up all the rubbing alcohol and vanilla cake flavoring. He knew he could not buy any more Beef, Iron & Wine from the drug store. Mama finally called Dr. Kinzie to come to the house to sober Daddy up.

After Daddy got back on his feet, Mr. Tucker told him that he had rented the house to another family. We had to find another place to live. Daddy asked around and sure enough he found another house for us. The house belonged to a family named Clinton. They had three sons, Ashley, James and Thomas. They were all older than we were. Mr. Clinton was known as "Duck Clinton" and he was the local barber.

This was the most wonderful family I had ever known. The Clintons treated us really well. Mr. Clinton would give us haircuts and would not let Daddy pay for them. Daddy saved money, since haircuts were fifty cents back then, and Daddy had six kids with hair. Mrs. Clinton would give us ice cream just for the asking. There was a yard at the side of the house where we could play cowboys and Indians. We rolled our old tires with someone inside them. A Chinaberry tree was located in the front of the yard. We had good times throwing the Chinaberries at each other.

A game I loved to play was when one of us got on another person's back and fought another team of kids. The object was to try to knock the person off the back of the opposing team. Since I was small, I usually was the one riding on the shoulder. I got knocked off a lot myself, but I also knocked a lot of kids off, trying to take their heads off their bodies.

The house they rented us sat to the side of their house, just back a little bit. It had four rooms and electricity. We only had two light bulbs, however, so Mama put one in the kitchen and the other one in the front room. Daddy bought us two more beds, mattresses and slats to go under them. He also bought a coal oil stove for the kitchen, and ironing board and an iron that we could heat up on the stove. There was a fireplace in the front room. We still didn't have a mirror to look into to see how to comb our hair, but things were getting better. Mama and Daddy slept in the middle room. One bed for the girls was set up in the front room and the other bed was put in another room. That was all the furniture we had, but we were happy. There was an outdoor toilet outside in the pasture.

It turned out that Thomas Clinton had known Ruby Lee in the years before she had gotten married. The few times that Daddy had let her go to school, always after school had started, Thomas had tried to help her get caught up. He had always known that he was going to be a schoolteacher. He saw potential in her and liked to help her. He was very smart. I believe that he graduated first in his class.

I had run out of shoes to wear. Mrs. Clinton went to town one day and came back with me a pair of shoes. I think I was her favorite. Mama cried and hugged Mrs. Clinton's neck. I told you this was a wonderful family.

Daddy, who seemed really sorry for being on the three-week drunk, rented a building and put in a café. We picked blackberries in the early mornings and ran the café in the afternoons. Nuse and I washed dishes and waited on the colored trade in the back. Robert Lee and Ruth Evelyn waited on the customers out front. Mama was the cook, and since Daddy was the boss, he got to take the money and put it in the cash register. That cash register was off limits to us, but I eyeballed it a lot. I don't remember if Dollie and Joe had to do anything. Being young, they probably just hung out.

Nuse got him a Lindale girl friend. She was not bad looking, but she was real dirty all the time. He nicknamed her Cigar Annie. Nuse said that he raised her dress up one day and cockroaches ran out from under it. He also said that they were so dirty that their own hogs wouldn't eat their slop. I actually believed him. She had a cousin Nuse named Cigarette Susie. I believe Robert Lee was sweet on her. I always wondered if she was full of roaches too. She probably was, as things like that usually run in a family.

The temperature was really hot, and because one of the blackberry pickers, a lady, had died one day in the field, Mama made Dollie and me a bonnet to wear on our heads to pick blackberries in. She made it by hand since she did not have a sewing machine. Slats for the bonnet were made from old shoeboxes she had gotten from a store in town. I tried mine on. It looked as if I had a mailbox on my head. She said that I had to wear it anyway, as the sun was really hot on my head. *She had never cared about my hot head before.* I did try it, but the bonnet got caught in the berry vines, so she let us throw them away. She never made us anything else.

The town was in the middle of another blackberry festival. It seemed as if everybody in Smith County was in Lindale for it. Bo and Ruby Lee came home for the blackberry-picking contest. I knew Bo was going to win. I wanted to go see him do it. Mama told me that I could not go because we were too busy at the café. *Well, good grief,* I thought, *let old Nuse wash dishes and wait on the customers a little while by himself-just until I get back.*

I hitched a ride to the berry patch. Just as I got out of the car at the field, I saw him. Nuse! That brother of mine had had the same idea I had. There we were, both out in the field with no way to get back into town until after the contest.

Bo won first place, just as I had predicted. A man named Bud Whitehurst won second, Ruby Lee won third and Robert Lee won fourth. I was proud of my family members. They could do anything if they set their minds to it. When the man from the newspaper wanted to take their picture, Robert Lee said, "I need to comb my hair first." The man replied, "Now, son, you weren't worrying about your hair when you were picking those berries. Everyone laughed. I didn't though, as reality had set in, and I knew I had to return to town to get what was coming to me. The consolation prize, a whipping! I got one, and so did Nuse.

Ruth Evelyn didn't win the bubble gum blowing contest that year. I decided not to enter the singing contest, probably would not have won anyway. Ruby Lee, always the lucky Coomer, won a set of dishes. All she did was put her name in one of the bowls that was part of the set, and her name was pulled out. I always wondered why Ruby Lee's luck didn't rub off on me; as some folks said I did look like her.

Officials of the festival were giving away a television. Anyone could put his or her name in the pot, so to speak, and whoever's name was pulled from the pot would win the television. There was only one family in Lindale at that time that had a television, and it sure wasn't ours.

I signed up, feeling really confident. *Well, hadn't I been going to church regularly?* I was nervous when the name was pulled out. It wasn't mine. The Lord had let me down. Mary Alice Hilburn, a girl in my grade at school, won the television. I was happy for her though. Her daddy told her she could not keep it, as it would use too much electricity. However, his wife overruled, him and the television went home with the wrong family, to my way of thinking.

Bo Paul got a letter from Lyndon B. Johnson, who was at the time, a United States Senator from Texas, and a future President of the United States. The letter congratulated him for being the world's Blackberry Picking Champion. It did have a misspelled word or two in it. I did mention that he was from Texas, didn't I?

Later that night the whole town was celebrating the festival. There was dancing in the street. I was right in the middle of things doing the Charleston. Out of the blue, my Mama stood with her hands on her hips, shaking her head and saying to me, "Get in the car. You are going home. You have disgraced us. Your daddy is mad as a hornet." I said, "Well, Nuse is dancing, hasn't he disgraced you too?" "No, of course not, he is a boy," was her reply.

I got another whipping, and I had to listen to Daddy all night as he raved about what a bad girl I was and how I was "going to hell in a hand basket." If they hadn't stopped me from dancing that night, who knows-I might have become a Rockette or a Las Vegas show girl.

Two days after that disastrous night when I thought my family was going to get run out of town because I danced the Charleston, I passed the open off-limits cash register in our café. I just had to peek in there, and I saw several rolls of dimes. No one was looking. Surely Daddy wouldn't miss just one little roll. I took one. There was a carnival in town so I decided to go to it. I didn't think anyone would miss me. All the rides cost a dime, as did most of the food such as cotton candy and candied apples.

I was having a ball with money to spare. I rode the rides and ate the food. It was my second ride on the merry-go-round when Mama appeared again, out of the blue, and I knew that she knew I had taken the dimes. Since I had cotton candy all over my face and hands, I could not deny anything.

The result was another spanking and another lecture from Daddy about what an evil little girl I was and how I would never amount to anything. What he didn't know was that I knew that God was going to forgive me for the stealing. I didn't feel too bad about it, since Daddy didn't pay us anything for working in the café.

Besides, I had had too much fun at the carnival. The bad, in reality, was much better than the good, and it was a lot more interesting. I even considered joining up with those carnival people and leaving town with them.

Ruth Evelyn also got into trouble at that café. It was for something that she did not do. Robert Lee was stealing money from the cash register. He had a secret hiding place where he kept the loot. He had placed a jar inside a wall, and had punched a hole in the wall, just big enough for the money to fall through right into the jar. One day, while Daddy was drunk, he fell into the wall, and found the money.

Ruth Evelyn was the only kid there at the present time, so Daddy immediately blamed her for stealing the money. He beat her almost to death for something she had not done. She knew nothing about the money, and had no idea how the money had come to be in the jar. She begged Daddy to listen to her, but to no avail. The next day when she went to school, she had a black eye. The teachers assumed, incorrectly, that Ruth Evelyn had been into a fight with one of her siblings. It was several years later before Daddy found out who had actually stolen the money, as Robert Lee was not about to confess. There was no reason for two kids to get a whipping for something only one of them had done. Daddy had a knack for whipping the wrong kid for things that one of the other kids had done. I guess it evened out in the end.

Back at the house Mama was still making lye soap in a black pot that was set up in the front yard. Dollie, Joe, and I still took our Saturday baths in it. Mama also used the pot to wash clothes and scald chickens. She would ring a chicken's neck off with her hands. The headless chicken would jump around the yard. We would close our eyes and jump around also. Most of the time the chicken would sling blood all over us. It was great fun. We would hold the chicken by its feet and put its body into the scalding hot water. After that we would pluck the chicken's feathers, hold its legs and singe it over a fire in the yard. Mama would then cook the chicken.

One of the handsome boys in my grade, Norvell, lived near us now. Several times I thought about teaching him how to play Post Office. It gave me something to think about at night. We played hide-in-seek almost every afternoon with other kids from the neighborhood.

As time drew close for us to go back to South Texas, Daddy decided not to be in the café business. Two Yankee ladies bought the business. They hired two colored boys to wait on customers in the back and wash dishes. These two ladies made a bad mistake by letting the guys come out front to be busboys. One has to remember that this was in a Southern state in 1953. City officials paid the two women a visit and discussed the situation. The ladies refused to stop the two young men from working up front. The city shut the café down. A short time later a man bought the building and put in a washateria.

When we left to go to South Texas to pick cotton, Mr. Clinton told Daddy we could leave our furniture in the house, he would not rent it, and we could live there when we returned in the fall. I was really happy to be going to see Charles Roy, but I was going to miss Norvell. I could only hope he would still be there when we returned.

The trip to South Texas was awful. Daddy began to drink whiskey that he had purchased just before we left. He whipped us for no reason. Mama would cook a meal for him on the Coleman stove; he would just throw it at her, telling her she was the worst cook he knew. He would continue to hurt her feelings by telling her that all his women except her were good cooks. Hitler was alive and well, disguised as my daddy. I plotted ways to kill him.

We stopped at every roadside park between Lindale and Sinton, and there were plenty of them. Nuse, Joe, and I rolled Dollie in the grape vines so that we could see her itch and cry. We got our yearly whippings for this. We had a lot of flats on the old truck. Daddy knocked Robert Lee and Nuse around when they couldn't fix the flats. Several times Robert Lee had to walk into the next town to have a flat fixed. I began to suspect that Robert Lee had had just about all the knocking around that he was going to take. I also felt that if he did not love Mama and us so much that he would leave. I was impatient about all the delays. I wanted to see my Charles Roy.

When we arrived in Sinton, it was raining very hard. Even though we were under the tarp in the back of the truck, we still got soaking wet. We spent the first night sleeping on the ground. The rain had stopped, but our cots were wet. The next morning Mama hung everything on the weeds or fences to dry.

Daddy went to find Mr. Huey. I asked him if I could go with him, but he said no. Joe asked the same question. Remember Daddy had promised Joe that if he would quit sucking the bottle that he would always get to go with him. Daddy told Joe to get into the truck. As Joe was getting in, I pushed him hard, and he fell into the front seat, hitting his head on Daddy's whiskey bottle. Joe didn't need to go, I did! I needed to see Charles Roy.

When Daddy and Joe returned, Joe jumped out of the truck and hit me, knocking me to the ground. Daddy said, "You kids stop that fighting or I am going to whip both of your asses." I didn't retaliate for two reasons: my fear of Daddy and knowing that Joe had news of Charles Roy. My heart sank when I heard Daddy telling Mama that Mr. Huey had told him that the cotton was not ready to harvest. We were going to the Valley to pick cotton there for a couple of weeks and see our kinfolks. I lay down on a pallet on the ground and cried. I would have to wait a while before I would be able to see Charles Roy.

We began our trip to the Valley the next morning, after our things had dried. Sinton was about half way between Lindale and the Valley, and I figured it would take us more than a week to get there. However, to my surprise, Daddy didn't drink, and we didn't have any more trouble with the truck. Our kinfolks didn't have any knowledge if we would be there this summer or not, but our Aunt Ellen seemed happy to see us when we pulled into her yard. She knew we would be living there until we left the Valley.

I could tell Aunt Ellen's three daughters didn't appreciate our being there. I know our living in their yard embarrassed them. However, these girls loved their parents so they treated us decently enough. I tried to stay out of their house as much as possible. We did go into their house to take a bath every few days. Every day at lunchtime Daddy would take us from the field, and we would go to their house. Aunt Ellen always had a good meal cooked for us. I believed her daughters helped her. I loved Aunt Ellen for this, and later in life, I would wonder why I never told her so. She would die before I ever got the chance to express my feelings to her. I can only hope that maybe she knew.

Daddy's brother, Harley, got work for us in the cotton fields. I think that he worked for a gin or some farmer who had hundreds of acres of cotton. Uncle Harley would come to Aunt Ellen's house in the afternoons, and sometimes he would bring his children with him for us to play with.

The grown-ups would all drink beer together. I hated that part of the visit. Aunt Ellen and Uncle Harley didn't get mean like Daddy did when they drank. That was something I couldn't figure out. If Daddy had been happy like the other two were while drinking, I probably would not have cared about his drinking. But, because of his meanness, I hated him. For some reason I wanted to blame Aunt Ellen and Uncle Harley for his drinking, but in my heart I knew he would drink with or without them.

Our first Saturday in McAllen, Robert Lee and the rest of us were walking down the street. A car drove up beside us, and a lady asked Robert Lee if he knew where the library was located. That lying Robert Lee said, "Yes ma'm, go to the next street, turn left, go one block, and you will see the Sears-Roebuck Store on the right, on the corner. You will turn by the store. The library is the second building on the right." Ruth Evelyn was shocked, she had no idea that he knew where the library was, and neither did the rest of us. "How did you know where the library is?" Ruth Evelyn asked him. "I don't know," Robert Lee confessed. "Now let's get out of here before they come back". We ran all the way back to the truck.

After about three weeks Daddy got mad at Uncle Harley and decided we were going back to Sinton, since the cotton there would be ready to harvest. Daddy stated that since we would pull the cotton in Sinton instead of picking it like we did in the Valley that we would make more money. I knew this to be true.

After we got the truck loaded up and were saying our good-byes to our cousins, Aunt Ellen brought out a big box of clothes for Dollie and me. I had suspected that they were kind of rich, and now I knew it for sure. The clothes were beautiful. She and her daughters had no idea how happy they had made us. After that, giving us clothes each summer became a tradition with them. Later I would find out that they were not rich. They owned a dairy, but Aunt Ellen and her husband, Uncle Edgar, worked very hard and tried to give their girls nice things.

On the return trip to Sinton, I was about as happy as a person could be. I was going to see my boyfriend, and I had some new clothes to wear. The next morning after we arrived back in Sinton, Daddy got us to the cotton fields about 4:30 a.m. We could not see the cotton, but we got our cotton sacks around our necks and started to work. Daddy followed down the rows behind us using the truck lights for us to see to pull the cotton.

About 7:00 Mr. Huey and his family drove up. I had been waiting almost a year for this. When my future husband got out of their car, my heart just about burst. He was as handsome as ever. He did not speak to me right away, but I could tell he was anxious to play Post Office again. We did that very thing that night. This time we got right down to business, not kissing on the cheeks. Life was great. I began to study ways for me to not have to go back to Lindale in the fall. *Maybe the Hueys would let me stay with them; after all I was their future daughter-in-law.*

The days and nights fell into a routine for me. I got up early with the rest of the family, went to the fields and worked hard all day. Because it got so hot in the afternoons and the fact that we went to work so early, Daddy usually let us quit working about 1:00 p.m. Then I would go to the camp, wash up, eat supper and get ready for the games with the other kids at night.

Besides Post Office, we were playing a game called "Pleased or Displeased," in which a person were asked if he/she was pleased or displeased. If a person were pleased, the question would be asked to the person to the right. If a person were displeased, he/she would be asked what it would take to please him or her. That was when the person would say something like, "I would like to go for a walk with so and so," or "I would like to get three kisses from so and so."

We also played Spin-the-Bottle. When the person spun the bottle (usually a Coke bottle), he/she would have to kiss the girl or boy that the bottle stopped spinning in front of. If the bottle stopped at a person of the same sex as the spinner, then the spinner would loose his or her turn. By now, there was no such thing as a person kissing someone of the same sex among the cotton pickers as we had done back when these games had first begun. Nightlife was wonderful!

I believe it was this summer that Daddy's brother, Henry, who lived in Oklahoma died with a heart attack. I had never seen him. Daddy was drunk when he got the news, but by the time his two siblings got to Sinton from the Valley, having stopped in Corpus Christi to pick up two more of his sisters, Daddy was sober as a judge. He did cry about his brother dying, and I almost felt sorry for him. They drove in two cars, one borrowed from a family in the camp with us. When they got to East Texas, they stopped and picked up Aunt Bessie. Uncle Earnest traveled to Oklahoma by himself. Now I am not sure how long this took as they did drive almost nonstop. I don't think any of them drank at all on their way to the funeral. The kinfolks in Oklahoma knew that they were on their way and did not bury Uncle Henry until they arrived.

Life with Daddy gone was great. I did not worry about his drinking and being mean to us. They were gone for several days, and I began to hope that maybe he would not come back. The man who loaned them his car was beginning to worry, wondering why he had let them take it. But as my luck went, one day they pulled back into the camp, all of them drinking. Daddy was drunk.

I was sad. Mama was happy, but I could not figure out why. She ran to Daddy and tried to hug his neck. He pushed her backwards. I picked up a big rock and threw it at him, hitting him in the back of the head. He was so drunk that he apparently didn't feel the rock. In a couple of days, when he sobered up, he could not figure out why he had a knot on his head. I was the only one who knew, and I wasn't about to tell him.

I hated the work in the field. Daddy had bought me a longer cotton sack. It was hard to get it upon my shoulder when I got it filled up. Someone else had to help me. I then had to walk with it on my shoulder to the trailer to get it weighed and emptied. Sometimes one of the boys would empty the sack for me.

Daddy came up with the idea to put a plank across the top of the trailer and a ladder on either side. A person could walk up one ladder with his sack full of cotton, go out on the plank, get someone to untie the end of his sack and let cotton fall out of both ends. The person could then walk to the other side of the trailer and down the other ladder. This saved a lot of time when emptying the cotton sack, and made it a lot easier. Before long all the cotton contractors were using his idea. I was proud of my Daddy. Too bad one could not have received a patent for this idea.

Daddy's sisters came to see us on the weekends as usual at the park. Uncle Earnest was not there that year so they didn't seem to fuss so much. Orville was there to play with us. He was getting better looking each year. Not as handsome as Charles Roy of course, but pretty close. I couldn't let myself think about him, my cousin. It was against the law, as you well know. At least I thought it was.

On a Saturday afternoon, Robert Lee, Ruth Evelyn, Nuse, and Joe were at the show seeing a movie. The name of the movie was "Calamity Jane" starring Doris Day. Dollie and I had not gone. Out of the blue, Daddy decided that we would load up our stuff and move to another town to work. He let me out in front of the show. My job was to go in and retrieve the kids. They were going to drive around the block and come back around to pick all of us up.

When I got into the show, Doris Day was singing "Secret Love." It was a beautiful song. Because I had just come inside from the sun, I couldn't see anything, much less my brothers and sister. I had to sit down a minute and wait for my eyesight to come back. *It wouldn't hurt me to hear this good song, now would it?* I got so interested in the movie that I forgot what I had gone in there for. In the meantime, Mama, Daddy, and Dollie were making a block, and then making another block. Daddy was getting increasingly mad.

Daddy finally stopped the truck and told Mama to go in that damn show and to get those damn kids of his. He also told her to tell me that I had a whipping coming. When she walked in, I saw her immediately. Her hands were on her hips. She didn't have to tell me that I had a whipping coming. I knew it! This would be one of the few times that I had actually deserved it. Mama found the others, and we all left the show with her. We climbed in the back of the truck.

All the way to our next stop, I worried about the whipping that I knew was coming. *I needed a plan to get out of it.* Nuse came to my rescue. When we stopped at a roadside park, he jumped out of the truck and told Daddy that we were all going to look for wood, so that we could build a fire that night. Daddy was so shocked that we had offered to do something without being told to do it, he just forgot about my whipping. I sure didn't remind him!

We were getting paid half what we made on Saturday. We were also getting to go to the shows and going to carnivals that seemed to be everywhere we went. It was as if the carnivals were following the cotton pickers from town to town. I tried to save some of my money for clothes, but it was hard. It took a lot of money for entertainment, especially at the carnivals. On the weekends I was usually happy and tried to get rested up for work in the field on Monday morning.

Ruby Lee and Bo were still in New Mexico. I wanted to see the baby. I thought about him a lot. *Why couldn't they just pick cotton like us?* It wasn't fair that Ronald Wayne was learning to do things, and we were not there to help him along.

We finished picking cotton in South Texas and began our trek north. It was time for school to start again. I had been reading the books Mrs. Giles had loaned to me, being very careful not to damage them or let anyone else read them. I began to realize why Charles Frank Ragsdale didn't want to lend his funny books to anyone. My question to Daddy at this time of the year was always the same, "why couldn't we go to Lindale to start to school?" His answer was always the same, "shut your mouth or I may not let you go to school ever again."

October came and the weather was getting cold. Daddy built fires in the cotton patch for us to warm up to. Finally he announced it was time to go home, back to the Clinton house, so Mama could go to work in the rose nursery.

As always I was both happy and sad. I said good-bye to Charles Roy and told him not to be playing Post Office with any girls. He made the promise. I hoped he would keep it. I promised him I would do the same, but I had my fingers crossed behind my back. *Well, I was moving back into the neighborhood where Norvell was living, and I didn't know if I could keep myself from playing Post Office with him.*

The Burma-Shave sign on the highway read: "THE MIDNIGHT RIDE...OF PAUL FOR BEER-LED TO A...WARMER HEMISPHERE."

Thirteen

We were going back to Lindale to go to school. As we were approaching town on a Friday afternoon, I was standing up in the back of the truck with my head on the outside of the tarp. A little tune was on my mind, and I was humming it: *Lindale will shine tonight, Lindale will shine. When the sun goes down and the moon comes up, Lindale will shine.* I was thrilled that I was going to get back in school and see all my Lindale buddies and all the guys, especially Norvell Alvey.

As we pulled into our yard at the Clinton house, Mrs. Clinton came out the door and gave all of us a big hug. I loved that lady. We unloaded all our stuff onto the yard. It was probably several days before we got it all into the house. When Mr. Clinton came home from work, he shook Daddy's hand. He looked at all of us and said, "B. F., all these kids need a hair cut. Bring them by tomorrow and I will fix them up."

When we started school the following Monday, we all had new haircuts. We had on new clothes too, and shoes. Mama had bought the clothes for us this year before we came back to Lindale. Dollie and I had the clothes that our cousins had given us too. I knew it was going to be a good year for me. However the year turned out not to be so great. You will understand as you read on.

As soon as we landed in the Clinton's yard, I ran across the street to see Norvell Alvey. He seemed pleased that we were back and he would have someone to play with. He only had one older brother. He told me he was in Mrs. Barbee's room at school. I just knew he was telling me this, hoping I would get into her class too. Well, you know my luck. I was put in Miss Forrest's room. She was an old maid. Talk about disappointment! However all was not lost,

Whan Boaz, the smart boy, was in my class. I thought *I would like him during the day and Norvell during the evenings.* It always pays to have a plan.

Mama got her coal oil stove back in operation. The stove had an oven on the side of it. Mama put the coal oil in a globe-like container and then turned it upside down. The coal oil would flow onto a wick, and the wick would let the coal oil flow into the burners and the oven. Cooking was easier for Mama on this stove than it was on the Coleman stove, but the food tasted like coal oil. Mama made biscuits from scratch. She would just take some flour, put in some water and mix it together. If it had not been for the coal oil taste, those things would have been really good.

Mama decided we would get back into church and Sunday school. We lived a little closer to the Central Baptist Church than we had when I first joined. I fit right back in with the kids in my class. Nuse and Dollie were also in this same class.

The Saturday after we started to school, Daddy gave us the money to go the show. I wanted my friend, Barbara Tucker, to go with me. She could no longer go to the movies, however. Her Daddy had gone to Oklahoma to visit his family, and while he was there, he was saved into the Assembly of God Church. Their congregation believed it was a sin to go to the movies. I felt sorry for their kids, but they didn't seem to mind. Kids back in those days had respect for their parents, especially the Tucker kids. So I went to the show with Dollie, Joe, and Nuse. It was the usual Saturday western. I felt good about being home, being able to roam around town in familiar territory.

About the third week of school, Nuse came to the door of my room, and he just came right on in. He told Miss Forrest that I had to go home; there was a surprise for us at the house. He said Daddy had sent word to him. This was in 1953, and a teacher believed that all the students told the truth. I got my books and left the room. We had to collect the other kids as well. Nuse would not tell us what the surprise was. I didn't have to wait long, however, as we lived about two minutes from the school.

When we went into the front door, there he sat, some man. He was really handsome. Daddy was sitting beside him, looking proud. Both of them were grinning at us. "Who are you"? I asked. "Well, goddam it girl, don't you recognize your own brother,

Thurman Harris?" Daddy asked. I was skeptical. I had never seen a Coomer who looked this good, him being clean and all. One could tell instantly that this person had not recently been in a cotton patch. Daddy made all of us hug him. I had a hundred questions for him. Where had he been, why hadn't he sent us money to eat on and how long was he going to stay?

He told us he was in the Army, had been in Germany and had been a POW during the war. Wow! Most of the stuff he told us, I didn't believe. One thing I remember him telling was this: after the war was over and he had gotten out of the POW camp, he was on a plane ride home. (Imagine that, my brother, on a plane). He was the best poker player that ever was and just happened to get in a game on the plane. Riding on the plane were several officers who had on nice watches. Before the plane landed, he had won all their watches and had them on both arms. The stories were something I could brag about the next week at school.

When Mama got home from her job at the rose nursery, she had no way of knowing that her son was in the house. When she saw him, I thought she was going to pass out. She patted her hands together and danced around. "Thurman Harris! Thurman Harris!" she screamed. After she got her bearings back, Thurman Harris reminded us that he still had his new name, Bud, and that we could call him that. Daddy let him know right quick that he had named him Thurman Harris and that he was not about to change it. He was not going to call him Bud or anything else. I wasn't going to call him Bud either. After some soul searching, Daddy and Mama decided they would compromise and call him Thurman, dropping the Harris. I could live with that.

Thurman stayed for about two weeks. He cleaned our house and cooked good meals for us. Mama really enjoyed his visit. He told us that he was married and that he would bring his wife to see us soon. I think that by now he had a son too. His name was Stephen Douglas. He would send us some pictures. Thurman told us he was living close to Denver, Colorado, working at an Army hospital and that he was a Master Sergeant. Something else I could brag about at school.

While he was visiting, he decided that Dollie and I needed to have a permanent in our hair. He would pay for it, as he knew Daddy wouldn't. Our permanents turned out just awful, hair frizzed. This was because after the permanents were given, the person had to sit under a big machine. Our hair was just too thin to take the permanent and the heat of the machine.

Too soon he was gone, and our life went back to the way it was before. Dollie and I went to Mr. Clinton and got him to cut our permanents off. Daddy started drinking again. Mama acted like she didn't care about the drinking, she had seen her son and she knew for sure that he was still alive.

Robert Lee was taking Agriculture at school and was in the Future Farmers of America, better known as the FFA. Now he did not have any desire to be a farmer, working in the field the rest of his life. However, this seemed like an easy course for him so he had signed up for it. The teacher, Mr. Arthur, told Robert Lee he had to have a project pertaining to farming. The Clinton's had an old school bus in the back yard, and they told Robert Lee that he could raise some baby chickens in it.

Daddy didn't much like having to pay for the chickens, but he let Mrs. Clinton order them for Robert Lee. They came into the post office in town. Daddy took all of us, even Mama, to town that day. When we went into the post office, we heard the chickens chirping. They were in boxes in the lobby. A lot of people were in there discussing them. I felt proud that they were ours. We helped Robert Lee load them into our truck.

Robert Lee's project became a family project. All of us helped water and feed the chickens. It was getting to be cold weather, so Mr. Clinton put lights in the bus and left them on so the chicks could stay warm. I enjoyed taking care of them. I felt pretty good about myself. Robert Lee had to write up his progress, and he did, like he was the only one seeing after them.

As you know, baby chickens become bigger chickens. I lost my interest in them as we all did, even Robert Lee. Finally though he got to sell them. You know a person needs to sell his chickens before they die. He kept most of the money. I've often wondered if Robert Lee ever gave Mr. Clinton any money to help pay the electric bill. Heck, I know he didn't.

According to a country and western song concerning chickens is this: One needs to sell their eggs before they hatch. Well, he got rid of those chickens before they even started laying eggs. A good thing too as they would not have lasted much longer under our care.

Things at school were going pretty well. One bad thing though was this: we had to take an Art class. We had never had this requirement before, and I was no good at it. I hated to go into that class each day. Miss Forrest, our teacher, was an Art major in college, and this was her favorite time of the day.

On Friday we had Arithmetic races. Two of us would go to the blackboard at a time. Miss Forrest would give us a problem to do. The first one to get it right would put their name on the board. This would go on until everyone had had a chance at the blackboard. Then we would start with the winners and keep going until we eventually had a final winner. Unlike art, this was my calling. Miss Forrest always let the first student that asked on Friday if he/she could go against the last person in the class if there were an uneven number of us at school that day. Since I lived right at the school, I was usually the first to ask. Most Fridays I had my name on the blackboard more than once and had two chances at winning. I won the Arithmetic race almost every Friday.

Now, when we had Spelling bees, that was a horse of a different color. I could spell pretty good and sometimes would win, but it was not important to me. I didn't care one way or the other. I felt as if I had to win the Arithmetic races. It was my right and my responsibility.

There was a home for troubled boys located near Lindale. It was a big, beautiful house with a lake in front of it. One of the troubled boys was in my class and sat right behind me. He worried me almost to death. He would take a pencil and act as if he was a radio announcer, announcing things right in my ear. I told him several times to stop, but he did not listen. One day, I stood up, took his make believe microphone and broke it like it was a twig. It scared him so bad; he didn't talk for several days. I guess he thought that I was going to break him next. His D. J. days were over.

I was playing with the kids in the neighborhood in the afternoons and on the weekends. I got to see Norvell a lot, but I just could not entertain the notion of playing Post Office with him. I was too much in love with Charles Roy. I even wrote Charles Roy a letter, telling him "Don't let the stars get in your eyes, don't let the moon break your heart." I never got an answer back.

One Saturday afternoon I had an invitation to a birthday party. Daddy said I could either go to the show or take the money and buy a birthday gift. It was an agonizing decision, since I surely wanted to see how Superman got out of his near death experience the Saturday before. I decided that one of my siblings could tell me about Superman. I bought a little gift and went to the party.

At the party they had cake and home made ice cream. This was a bonus I had not thought about. The girl's mother had a game for us to play. She told us she was going to give each of a piece of paper with two words all scrambled up on it. The first person to figure out their two words would win a prize. Bring it on! I figured I was probably the smartest kid in the room. I got my two words, and try as I might, I could not figure out what they were. One of the kids eventually figured out their words and got the prize. When the mother told me what my two words were, I was really embarrassed. The words were *Lindale, Texas.* I was mad at myself for years to come about that.

During December, our Art class got really hard for me. Miss Forrest had us cut out a reindeer's head from some pieces of wood she had. We were to paint a face on the animal. My reindeer looked like a horse by the time I had finished cutting him out. He looked awful. She also had us bring some paper plates to class so that we could paint a Christmas scene on it. I don't remember how many plates I ruined. Miss Forrest finally told me to paint a plate blue. She then cut out a beautiful snowflake and pasted it in the plate.

She hung all the paper plates on the wall. She didn't put any names on them. At open house right before Christmas, she let the parents vote on the plate that they liked the best. My plate won! She never told any of the other students that she had done it for me. I really liked her after that. I finally realized that not all people can do art, and it is nothing to be ashamed of.

It was getting really close to Christmas. I missed Bo, Ruby Lee and Ronald Wayne something awful! One Saturday afternoon I got this gut feeling that they were on their way to see us. I told Mama, Daddy, and all the kids in the neighborhood that they would be in today. No one believed me. Ruby Lee had not written that they were coming home, and we did not have a telephone.

Nighttime came, Daddy told us to come in and go to bed. I said, "No, I am going to wait outside until they get here." "You stupid, hard headed girl," Daddy said, "Stay out there until morning if you want to." I knew they were coming. I lay down in the yard, cried some and dozed off. About 10 o'clock I saw the car lights coming. I jumped up and watched the car lights come right into our yard. It was them! To this day I don't know how I knew they were coming home, but I did.

Bo and Ruby Lee had good news for us. They were moving back to Lindale. Bo was going to leave Ruby Lee and Ronald Wayne with us, and he was going to go back to get their trailer house. This was going to turn out to be the best Christmas I had ever had, having the baby around us. When Bo left to go back to Hobbs, New Mexico, to get their things, I secretly wondered if he would come back. I can't explain why I thought that. I was hoping that he would return.

In three days Bo and the trailer house came pulling up. Mr. Clinton let him park the trailer house to the right of our house. We could see the baby all we wanted to. I don't remember where Bo went to work, but I know that he did.

Ruth Evelyn was as crazy about the baby as anyone could ever be about a child, except for me, of course. She took him everywhere with her. One afternoon, Ruby Lee came into our house, and she was mad. Why? Because Ruth Evelyn had given Ronald Wayne lice! Ruth Evelyn had long hair and kept it platted most of the time. You could actually see the lice in her plats. They also could be seen in the baby's hair.

Mama went to town and bought medicine for both of them. The medicine turned Ruth Evelyn's hair purple, but in a few days the lice were gone. By now, Mama had to use the medicine on all of us.

Daddy had put in a firecracker stand in Mineola, a town about ten miles north of Lindale. He was going to sell firecrackers during the Christmas holidays. He figured this was a way to keep us busy, helping him.

We knew that Ruby Lee had bought us something for Christmas. I really wanted to know what the gifts were. I finally found them hidden in a closet in her trailer house. Dollie and I each had a baton. I was happy. Now I couldn't tell anyone about sneaking into the trailer, but I could have a dream about what the gifts were, couldn't I? The kids would believe anything I told them, since I was the one that knew the family was coming to see us in the first place. I told each of them about their gift that I had dreamed about. They promised not to tell Ruby Lee about the dream. I was worried that they would, but no one did. Ruby Lee was older and would not fall for that dream business. She would know that I had found the presents.

We still kind of believed in Santa Claus, even though we were getting older now. On Christmas morning, sure enough, there in the front room were the things that Santa had left, the things that dreams were made of. Daddy, who had profited from the firecracker business, also had paid Santa for toys for us. He had left for me a dollhouse and a chemistry set. I learned to make ink with the set. The kids were really impressed with my knowledge, but one of them must have told Ruby Lee about my dreams. In the years to come I was never able to find any presents to dream about. She always bought us something though.

Santa Claus had left Joe a Roy Rogers's gun and holster set. It was really nice. I tried to trade him my dollhouse for it, but he wasn't having any of that. He did let me wear it though. I put it on a lot; impressing Norvell by the way I could twirl the guns around in my hands. When we played cowboy and Indians, I killed every bad guy in the neighborhood.

Mama, who had been so thrilled about her children moving back to Lindale, decided we would have a really good meal on Christmas day. She made a combination of twenty cakes and pies. I had never known of her making anything like this before. She sat outside and watched us play while she beat the egg whites with a fork. She did not have a beater of any kind. She let us do some of this, and I was excited about this holiday. I had never cared about Christmas before.

Mama killed a lot of chickens and cooked chicken and dumplings. Ruby Lee also cooked various things, including dressing for the chicken. On Christmas day I had never seen so much food at one time except on the day I had been baptized in the lake. We were enjoying each other so much that I thought that this might be the way it would be from now on. I, of course, was wrong.

Daddy would be the reason for things to go bad for us. Right after Christmas my parents received a package from the Veterans Administration. Inside it were a Purple Heart in Franklin Eugene's memory and a book about the Sixth Marine Division that he had been in when he had been killed. This brought back memories of their son, and the only way Daddy could deal with it was to drink whiskey.

Mama put the book and the Purple Heart in the box that held the trinkets from Raymond Eugene's car and his shoes. Also in the box was the telegram that had announced Franklin Eugene's death. Mama dealt with her grief by telling us kids how much she loved us. Through the years I would take out the book and look at all the pictures, trying to find a Marine that I thought might be my brother. I never found him. His name was in the back of the book.

One Saturday Daddy went to Gladewater, a town to the east of us. He took Nuse with him. We lived in a "dry" county where alcohol could not be sold except by the bootleggers. Gladewater was the place they got it. This city was located in what was known as a "wet" county. One of the honky tonks in Gladewater was the Green Frog. There was a light outside on top of the building where a green frog jumped back and forth.

Daddy drank all day and into the night. When he got ready to come home, he was so drunk that he suggested that Nuse drive the truck. Nuse was game for anything and jumped right in behind the steering wheel. He had never driven a truck before! Coming down the country road toward Lindale, Daddy spotted a soldier that was hitchhiking. "Pull over Nuse," Daddy said, "Lets pick up this damn soldier." Nuse obeyed. The boy came running. When he opened the truck door and spotted the drunk and the kid driving, he declined to get in. He said, "Thanks anyway, but I think I will just wait for another ride." "Suit yourself," Daddy stated, and Nuse drove off.

Between our house and the Clinton house was a storm cellar. If we lived close to one, Daddy had always made us get into it when a storm came up. I was scared of those places. I felt they were full of snakes and spiders and rats. Daddy would make us stay down there until the clouds went over before he would let us come out. Every time I went down into one I wondered if we would live through the storm. The next morning after Nuse's drive, Daddy found the truck parked on top of the Clinton's storm cellar. We could never figure out why the storm cellar didn't cave in. I was hoping that it would, as I wouldn't have to go down there again.

On a cool Saturday afternoon not long after this incident, Daddy took Mama, Dollie, Joe, and me over to the Green Frog. It was against the law for kids to go into a honky tonk, at least that's what Daddy told Mama. She would just have to stay outside with us. She stayed in the car, but we got outside and played. After about three hours, I grew tired of playing. I was also hungry. Daddy had lied when he had said that he would just be in there for a few minutes.

I decided to take it upon myself to get him out of there. I snuck up to one of the windows and looked in. Daddy was drunk, and an old bar fly, a woman, was sitting in his lap. I could see money lying on the table. I also saw red. I burst through the door, telling my daddy that we were ready to go home. I also knocked the chair from under the bar fly, and she went crashing to the floor. The bar tender hollered, "Get those damn kids out of here. You know they are not allowed."

Fear went through me as Daddy hit at me, but was so drunk that he missed. By now Mama was in the room. She was scared too. Dollie and Joe had also joined the group. They were gathering up the money on the table. We needed it for groceries. Two of the men in the room helped Mama get Daddy to the car. We all jumped in with Mama behind the wheel and Daddy in the back seat cussing up a storm. Before we got home he had passed out. Sleep didn't come easy that night. I knew we would be in for it the next day when Daddy woke up sober. He never mentioned the incident, and we didn't either. We had given Mama over thirty dollars taken from the table. The Lord works in mysterious ways, now that's a fact!

Food was always in short supply. We would make sandwiches out of mustard. Other times some of us would make a sandwich out of butter and sugar if we had any. A lot of nights we had to go to bed hungry.

Daddy started talking real ugly to Mama in the bed at night. Most nights he would be drunk. He would tell her how ugly she was and how other women pleased him better than she did. We had to lie in bed and listen to him, since we had no place else to go. I cried and my brothers and sisters did too. We snuggled up in the beds. I believe that during this time I began to realize that we had only each other and we needed to get along better if we were going to make it until he died.

When daylight came, Daddy never seemed to remember his nasty talks the night before, but I never forgot them. I never forgot either the fact that he would make the girls clean out the slop bucket every day but never the boys. He also made Mama light his cigarettes for him sometimes even though it made her sick at her stomach. I felt sick watching her do it. I never forgot that either.

Across the road from the Clinton's lived a lady named Mrs. Whatley. She was the head cook at the school. She was as nice as Mrs. Clinton. I began to go to visit her. She told me about one of her sons who had been killed by a hit and run driver. She also stated that she believed a lady in Lindale had seen the accident but had been paid off by the family and would not tell the police who the driver of the car had been. She was really pained by this. He was close to home when he was hit, and he got up and walked home with only half his head still attached to his body. Her son had died in her arms.

Mrs. Whatley started bringing food home that was left over from the school. Between her and Ruby Lee I began to eat really well. I began to feel round as a town dog. The house in front of Mrs. Whatley, across a different road from the Clinton's, was where her mother, Mrs. Smith, lived. I started visiting her too. Also, I began to spend the nights at their houses. I had a bed to myself at both places and didn't have to listen to Daddy's nightly ramblings. Sometimes Dollie would stay with them too. We were becoming closer.

When school started back in January, one of the teachers at school decided she would form a choir. She invited the students to try out for it. Not learning my lesson from my singing at the blackberry festival, I decided I needed to be in it. All my good friends were trying out too. The teacher had us sing the first stanza of America the Beautiful. By the time I had finished, everyone was laughing. I didn't make it. The teacher told me that I probably should use the recess time to study my lessons. "I don't need to study my lessons, I need to be in the choir," I told her. She said, "No, you can't be in it."

I was extremely sad. This was one of the times that the sixth grade was a bad time for me. I had always felt that a person could bear anything except a rock in their shoe. But, this was unbearable. Ernestine Phelps by now was my best friend and she didn't agree with the teacher. She felt like I should have been picked. Ernestine told me she had decided not to join the choir. That was something I could not allow. This was my pain and not hers. At my insistence, she was in the choir. I did go to listen to them though and tried my best not to be envious. I was glad for my best friend.

Daddy had made a lot of friends at Mineola during the Christmas holidays. One day he went back over there to visit. He came home telling us that he had bought a house in Mineola, and we were going to move there. We were all torn up about this. Mama decided she must stand up to him. She was shaking when she told him we were not moving; he could if he wanted to, but her kids were staying in school in Lindale. She also reminded him that she would not have a way to get to work if she lived in Mineola and that she would have to quit her job.

Mad as a hornet, the next day Daddy returned to Mineola and sold the house he had just bought. He sold it to a man who owned a grocery store. The man lacked ten dollars having enough money to pay Daddy cash for it. He gave Daddy ten dollars worth of Post Toasties. This cereal is still eaten today. The cereal sold for about twenty cents a box. Five boxes for a dollar times ten equaled fifty boxes of cereal, probably every box the man had in his store. We ate Post Toasties every meal for a long time, but at least we didn't have to move to Mineola.

Robert Lee had to have another project at school. This time he decided that he would raise a couple of pigs. We all helped him build a pigpen behind the outdoor toilet. That way we figured we would not be able to smell them. The Clinton's saved their slop for the pigs, and we fed them twice a day. Robert Lee did not work near as hard as the rest of us raising those pigs. However, when he sold them, guess who kept most of the money again. He did! We decided we were through with Robert and his projects. Robert Lee, who had failed at least one grade in school, mostly because he had not been allowed to go as often as other kids, decided that he would quit. He went to work with Mama at the rose nursery.

January turned into February. It was getting close to Valentine's Day. The kids at school exchanged valentines. We did not have any to give anyone. Miss Forrest had us all decorate a paper sack with our name on it. We hung them on the wall. We could put our valentines in our friends' sacks. Valentines were being put into mine and I felt bad about not having any to give.

The night before Valentine's Day one of Daddy's friends came to visit us. A miracle took place that night. Daddy's buddy had brought us a lot of valentines. We were very excited. Daddy, seeing our excitement, said to the man, "I don't know how to repay you." The man replied, "You can take me to see your sister, Bessie, this weekend." I saw Mama frown, but Daddy laughed, "Hell yes, I'll take you." Mama knew what they were up to. Daddy would come back drunk, and the friend would come back broke. A man had to pay Aunt Bessie for him to show her his respect.

We equaled out the valentines. Not having enough to give to everyone in my class, I decided to give them to my best friends. I was happy about being able to put valentines into some of the sacks the next day. One boy told me that he had gotten a valentine from everyone in the class but me, and that he was never going to give me another one. I was too embarrassed to explain to him that I had had only a limited amount to give out.

My best friend's boyfriend gave her a valentine that read, "They say that time changes things, but that is not always true; time could never ever change the way I feel about you." He was good looking so I just pretended he had given the valentine to me instead of her. It got so that I convinced myself that it was true.

We had ladies called "room mothers" who always came on holidays. They brought us cookies and something to drink, usually a fruit juice. I always looked forward to those days. They were coming today. Miss Forrest told us if we didn't want to drink the grapefruit juice the room mothers were bringing that we could leave a nickel on the tops of our desks and she would get us a cold drink from the store. *Well, who had a nickel?* I sure would like to have a cold drink.

At the beginning of our first recess, I went back into the room and stole a nickel from a boy's desk, and put it on my desk. After we came back in, this boy didn't have a drink on his desk. He asked the teacher why this was so. She told him that he did not have a nickel on his desk. He started to cry and told her that someone must to have stolen it. She chastised him for having such thoughts. Maybe he had lost it? I began to feel bad about what I had done, but I was not about to confess my crime. I told Miss Forrest that he could have my drink and that I would drink grapefruit juice. This pleased the teacher, and she told the room mothers about my generosity.

The room mothers rewarded me by telling me that I could have all the grapefruit juice I wanted to drink. I took them up on their offer. The boy I had befriended became a really good friend. He never forgot my kindness to him. *Who said crime doesn't pay?* The bad thing that happened to me over this incident was this: I drank so much grapefruit juice that I got really sick at my stomach and threw up. *Maybe crime doesn't pay.* To this day, I will not drink grapefruit juice.

Bo and Ruby Lee had gone to a café in town to eat supper one afternoon, taking Ronald Wayne with them. They pulled up in the yard about the same time as Daddy was returning from one of his visits to Aunt Bessie's. As Daddy got out of the truck, I could tell he was drunk.

I ran out to Bo's car to get the baby. He wasn't in there! About that time Ruby Lee remembered that she had forgotten him and had left the baby at the café. Daddy had gotten completely out of the truck. When he realized what she had done, he started cussing Ruby Lee telling her he was going to call the law on her. "What kind of mother was she, leaving her baby for someone to steal?"

Ruby Lee and Mama were both crying. Bo finally said, "Mr. Coomer, you had better go in the house now. We are going back to the café to pick him up." Daddy respected Bo and went in the house and passed out on his bed. I was half way back to the café by now, running every step. I would save my nephew. When Daddy woke up the next morning, he didn't even ask about the baby.

At the end of February, Bo and Ruby Lee moved back to Hobbs, New Mexico. Bo was going back to work in the oil fields. Ruby Lee had a secret. She told no one, not even Mama, that she was going to have another baby.

Daddy had bought us a radio that was battery operated. We would listen to it at night, especially on Fridays and Saturdays. It was really fun for us to sit on the weekends and hear such programs as the Cisco Kid, the Lone Ranger, Mr. & Mrs. North, Amos and Andy, the Screeching Door and others. My favorite programs were the ones that came into our home from Nashville, Tennessee. I learned to love country and western music. I might not be able to sing, but no one could stop me from listening to singing. It was my God-given right.

In March my right breast got real sore and swelled up. I didn't know what to do. *Was I going to die? Maybe God was now punishing me for my crimes.* I decided I had to tell Daddy about it, even though I was ashamed. *Maybe he would take me to see Dr. Kinzie.* I cornered Mama and Daddy, telling them that I had something pretty bad to show them. Promptly, I pulled up my dress and showed my sore breast to the world. Daddy started laughing. *What was so funny? Why was he laughing at my pain?*

Daddy told me that I was just growing up and that my titties would get a lot bigger and quit hurting. I was relieved. Later that night I heard him tell Mama in bed that I was going to be stacked like his sisters. Unhappiness washed over my body like a tidal wave. I didn't want to have big bosoms like them and have men coming around showing me respect. My decision was made. I would pray to God to make the sore breast go away. Another thing, as most people know, is that carrots are good for your eyes and beans will make your titties grow, so I quit eating beans. Now these things didn't completely work, but I never have had big bosoms like my aunts.

In early May, one of my classmates had a party at her house. She invited all the kids in the sixth grade. At first Daddy said that I could not go, but I kept on at him until he said it was okay. I was sweet on Whan Boaz and felt like that he might like me also. At the party we were having a great time. I told them how to play the game "Pleased or Displeased." When it came my time, I was displeased. What would it take to please me? A walk with Whan, of course! He held my hand and my heart was beating fast. *Would he kiss me? Would I like it as much as I did when Charles Roy kissed me?*

Down the road we went. Mac Gimble and a girl were coming up the road. When he saw us he said, "Whan and Annie Bell. I know something now." This must have embarrassed Whan because he dropped my hand and ran back to the party. I wanted to kill Mac Gimble. The next Monday at school Whan hardly looked at me. He never acted as if he might want to be my boyfriend again, but he would let me copy from off his schoolwork.

To console myself for not being able to get a kiss from Whan, I decided that I would start dipping snuff. I was old enough now. *Snuff must taste really good*, I thought, as Mama sure did like it. When a person is dipping snuff and the snuff runs down both sides of their mouth at the same time, then that person is considered to be level headed. Mama was as level headed a person as I had ever known. After finding her snuff can, I poured out a whole teaspoon of it. I put the snuff in my jaw and shut my mouth to keep it there. Good Lord! The snuff tasted awful. I spit it out into my hands and all over my clothes. I began to sneeze, as some of it hit my nose. Quickly, I covered my nose with my hands to stop a sneeze.

My eyes began to water, so I rubbed them with my hands. It was a bad mistake. My eyes began to burn. I was in an awful fix. To make matters worse, Mama caught me dipping her snuff. *I'll get a whipping for this.* To my surprise, Mama felt sorry for me and helped me get cleaned up before Daddy saw me. I promised her that I would never dip snuff again. It was a lie, of course, but after that my snuff dipping consisted of a mixture of Hershey Coca and sugar.

Robert Lee and a couple of his buddies done two crazy things that involved animals. They took a cow and put in inside a local church one Saturday afternoon and shut the doors. Imagine the smell the next morning when the preacher opened the building up for Sunday services. The agricultural teacher had a fat goat. These bad boys stole him and tied him by his neck to the goal post at the football field. The next morning they went to the field to turn him loose. Anybody knows that a smart goat can find his way home just like a smart dog. When these modern day Tom Sawyers got to the field, the boy goat had had turned into a girl goat. Holy cow! That girl goat had had a kid. The trauma of being tied up was just too much for her. She had tried to chew the rope up while giving birth to her baby.

These buddies took an old car, took the tires off it, placed it on the railroad tracks and drove it down the tracks. I have no idea what they done when they came to the first curve or met the first train.

At various times during the year Daddy had taken us to see Uncle Jack and Aunt Bessie in Gilmer and to visit Uncle Earnest and his family who were now back in Daingerfield. Other times our Sikes cousins would come to see us with their Mama and Daddy. My folks thought that we all needed to keep in touch. The bad thing, as you know by now, is that when we got home from visiting Daddy's side of the family, he would always be drunk.

Fourteen

Just as sure as chickens go barefooted, the Coomer kids left school the first week of May to go to Winnsboro to pick strawberries. At Winnsboro it was the same as the years in the past. We went to the fields early each morning, worked hard until right after lunchtime and rested up in the afternoons. Ever so often I would put my nose to the white gas can, but I never stayed long enough to get sick. Charles Frank Ragsdale was glad to see us and we all had fun playing with him. In about three weeks the strawberries played out, and we moved back to Lindale.

We moved back into the Clinton house. I went over to see Norvell Alvey. He was still as handsome as ever. I visited Mrs. Clinton, Mrs. Whatley and Mrs. Smith. They all seemed really glad to have us back in the neighborhood.

It was the last week of school. I re-enrolled myself. Good thing I did too. The six graders were graduating from grade school, as they would be in junior high the next September. We were having a party in the school gym after we walked across the stage to receive our certificates.

At the party Whan and I made eyes at each other half the night, but we didn't talk. He was still embarrassed about Mac Gimble catching us holding hands. When the party ended, I walked home alone. I was still mad at Mac Gimble.

One afternoon Nuse went to Daddy with a swollen nose. His nose looked like it was as big as the rest of his face. Daddy took a look inside and immediately decided he needed to operate. He took a small knife and started probing around in there. Mama started begging Daddy to take Nuse to see Dr. Kinzie. Daddy didn't listen.

Nuse was crying, and the rest of us were scared to death. *What was causing that nose of his to swell up like that?*

Daddy's probing brought results. Slimly stuff started running out his nostrils. When it was over, it was evident that Nuse had put a bean or a pea of some kind up his nose, and the thing had sprouted. Within a day his nose was good as new, and Daddy had saved a doctor bill, one that he probably would not have paid anyway. I thought that beans not only made your titties grow; they could make your nose swell up also.

A bench sat on the sidewalk by the drug store. There were usually a lot of old men sitting there. On a Saturday afternoon, Nuse and I were in town. We had been to the show. We stopped by the bench to talk to these fellows. One of them noticed that Nuse's blue jeans were unzipped. He told Nuse, "You had better shut your barn door. Your horse might get out." Nuse answered, "Oh, it's all right, it is just a little pony, and he can't hurt anybody." Well, those old men started laughing. I just shook my head and walked off. I sure didn't see anything funny about his remark.

The very next weekend, Nuse, Dollie, Joe, and I went strolling by the bench. I had intended for us not to say anything to those old fellows. One of them stopped us and asked, "What have you kids been up to?" Nuse, who couldn't just keep walking like the rest of us said, "I've been listening to three old mama cats talking." The men punched each other. One said, "Listening to cats, huh; what are the cats discussing these days?" "Let's go home, Nuse," I ordered. "Let the boy talk, girl, it's not everyday that someone gets to listen to cats talking," another one of the fellows said as he winked to the old geezers.

"Well," Nuse started, "These three old mama cats were talking about what they wanted for Christmas. The white cat said, "I want three white kittens for Christmas." The black cat said, "Well, I want three black kittens for Christmas." The last cat, a stripped one, said, "I want three black and white kittens for Christmas." Nuse paused a second, then continued, "Just then an old tom cat came around the corner singing, "Here comes Santa Claus, here comes Santa Claus!"

Those old men started laughing. I didn't know why. There was nothing funny about what he said. Maybe they were laughing about his bad singing. *Where had Nuse heard such a thing like that?*

They were all so stupid, including Nuse; it was not even Christmas time. With the sound of their laughter in the background, we went on home.

The Tucker kids had a bicycle so I decided I would learn to ride it. I felt sure I could ride it by just getting on it. I was wrong. It took me several afternoons to master the thing. Not only was balancing it impossible, steering was difficult, and I could not work the brakes. I ran into fences and ditch lines and fell over several times, but then I finally made the bicycle understand that I was the boss. From then on, riding a bicycle was easy, but I never made fun of anyone when they were first learning how to ride one.

The Clinton's had a pasture at the back of their house. Guys started coming over on Sunday afternoons to play baseball. I wanted to play too. There were not many gloves, and the boys had to pass them around. The boys did not want me to play, but I insisted. I felt I could play with the best of them. They would not let me use a glove to catch balls with, and I found out pretty quick that catching baseballs was not the same as catching softballs.

On the third Saturday, Nuse intentionally hit me in the head with a hard ball. I ran home, screaming. Mama went to the field and gave those boys a lecture. I had not told her which one had hit me. I had more sense than that. I had a headache all the rest of the day, but I never bothered those brothers of mine about playing ball again. Nuse had given me a reason not to.

A game that they would let me play was "Annie Over." The game consisted of throwing the softball over the house. Two kids would get on each side of the house to catch the ball and another person was the scorekeeper. One person would holler "Annie Over," and a kid from the other side would throw the ball over the house. If the ball made it over the house, someone on the other side tried to catch it. If the ball were caught, then that team made a point. If the ball hit the ground, no point was scored. Also, if the throwing team didn't get the ball over the house on the first try, a point was subtracted from their score. If you think this was a game where a lot of cheating could go on, you are right. However, keep in mind that we were the Coomer kids, and cheating just wasn't one of our things. Ha! Ha! and Ha again.

At night we would catch lightning bugs, pull their flashing tails off and make bracelets on our arms. We would lie in the grass at night, look up at the stars, and try to find the big and little dipper as well as the Milky Way. We would listen to the Katydids talking in the trees. I always wondered what they were saying to each other. Daddy taught us how to make seesaws and cups & saucers from a string.

One day we dressed Joe up like a girl, and had him pose for the camera. We put syrup bucket lids on our chests and pretended they were cars and drove them around and around. This was hard on my developing chest, but I never let it show. During the afternoons we talked to doodle bugs telling them to come out before their houses caught on fire. If they didn't mind us, we would cave their house in with our feet. We had always made our own entertainment and built our own toys. We were so tough, or so we thought, because we could run barefooted through the grass burs. We would walk on empty barrels with a stick in each hand so that we could turn the barrels. Sometimes we would fall off. It was a miracle that the sticks never went though our bodies and killed us. We did have some close calls with this.

Daddy got a bad hurting in his side. He finally gave up and went to Dr. Kinzie's office. After an examination, Dr. Kinzie told Daddy his appendix needed to come out. He was affiliated with a small hospital in Tyler where the operation could take place. "Hell, man," Daddy said, "I don't have any money to pay for an operation. Besides I have to work, keep the family in the berry patch, you know that." Dr. Kinzie told him not to worry about the money; if he didn't have the operation, his appendix would burst and he would die. His dying didn't fit too well with Daddy, so he reluctantly had the operation. I was kind of hoping that he wouldn't make it, but I was also hoping that he would. In a week or so Ruth Evelyn had to have the same operation. I don't know this for sure, but I heard that Ashley Clinton, the oldest Clinton son, paid Dr. Kinzie for the operations. One thing I do know for sure: Daddy didn't pay for them.

The rest of the summer was going pretty good, except for the blackberry picking in the mornings and early afternoons. I knew it would not be too many days before we would go back to South Texas and to the cotton fields. I was looking forward to that with mixed blessings. I sure wanted to see Charles Roy, but I was dreading the work. Blackberry picking was a much easier than pulling cotton.

Two bad things happened to me before we left for South Texas. Nuse was smoking cigarettes every time he could find or steal one. I decided I would smoke too. I would steal them from Daddy when he was passed out. That turned out to be a piece of cake. Now, a girl can't smoke alone, and I wanted someone I could trust to smoke with me, someone who wouldn't tell on me. Dollie came to mind.

We swiped a whole pack of Camels and went to the outdoor toilet where we smoked every one of them. We were so sick we didn't even fuss when we had to go to bed before dark.

The next day Dollie got caught smoking by some of the kids who were visiting in the neighborhood. They told Daddy on her. She was not about to take a whipping all by herself, so she told on me, and I joined her in the spanking session. We also had to listen to Daddy carry on about his sorry girls. *Well, what about his sorry boys*? Daddy said that I always acted like I was just one step in front of a fit.

I learned something from all of this. I learned you couldn't trust your sister anymore than you can trust anyone else. The whipping from Daddy ended my smoking career.

The other bad thing that happened is something that I am ashamed of to this very day. An old, old house that belonged to the Clintons sat next to the school bus. No one lived there. I got to thinking one Saturday afternoon that the old house needed to burn down, and we would have more yard to play in. With a little help from me, it could do just that. Mama and Daddy had gone to the store. I took matches and newspaper out there and started the fire.

I was the hero that day since I was the first one to see the flames and report the blaze to Mrs. Clinton. It was an exciting time. The fire department came, and Mrs. Clinton gave me some ice cream for being the first on the scene. My excitement soon turned to agony, and I confessed to the Clinton's what I had done. Even though they forgave me and decided not to tell the city marshal, they had to tell my daddy. I probably would have fared better with the law.

My explanation to Daddy was that I felt the fire department volunteers needed the practice. That didn't sit well, and neither did I after Daddy had gotten through with me. It took that incident to make me realize that I should quit being so bad about things. Maybe stealing, dancing in the streets, smoking cigarettes and burning down houses wasn't the way to go. It was the beginning of a new me. The new me would last until later on into the fall.

Daddy didn't have any poker games while we were living at the Clinton house. He knew Mrs. Clinton was a good Christian lady, and she would have made us move if he started that business. Mr. Clinton proved to be a really great friend. I hoped that we would be able to live in this neighborhood forever.

Things never work out the way you hope, of course, and it was time for us to head back to South Texas. Bo, Ruby Lee and Ronald Wayne moved their trailer house back to Lindale. They were going to pick cotton with us. When they drove up in our yard, I ran to get Ronald Wayne out of it. Ruby Lee had something in her lap, wrapped up. When I opened the door, I saw the baby. Now she might have written Mama about her having another boy, but I do not remember Mama telling me anything about it.

The baby boy was little. Ruby Lee told us that when he was born, he was so small that he looked like a rat. She cried and told the doctor that he was not her baby. He may have been short, but he had a beautiful face, and I knew instantly that I would be just as crazy about him as I was about Ronald Wayne. His name was Larry Edward Paul. I didn't want to give him all my attention and tried to share my spare time equally between the two boys.

We made our usual trip to the Valley and then back to Sinton where Charles Roy would be waiting for me. I wanted to tell him about my sore breasts, but I didn't dare do that, I was too embarrassed about it. The kids started playing our games, and the kissing began again. I loved it. In the field, Charles Roy and I would pretend we were married like Bo and Ruby Lee. This helped make the backbreaking work a little easier.

One weekend Aunt Leona and my cousin Orville came over. We all went to the Sinton Park to spend the night. It was exciting being around Orville. We got into the back of the truck and lay down on the bed, just talking you see. Before I knew what was happening, he was kissing me. *This wasn't right!* I knew it wasn't, but I didn't care. His lips felt good on mine. He put his tongue in my mouth. We kept smooching until we realized someone was getting up in the truck. If whoever was getting into the truck sensed what we were doing, they didn't let on. We got out of the truck and went back to playing. But he was no longer just a cousin; he was a kissing cousin. There were a few more weekends at the park that summer, and they were all the same. It was kissing Charles Roy during the week and Orville on the weekends. Life wasn't so bad. Kissing was something I knew I would miss when we went back to Lindale to go to school.

We were picking cotton in Wallis, Texas, when the rains began. It rained really hard for three straight days. We could not work in the fields. When the rain stopped, everyone was broke and everybody's trailer house was stuck in the mud. All the men were in a bad mood, and the women were worried. The kids were just happy that we had had a few days to rest and to play our games.

Everyone, including women and kids, had to help get the trailer houses unstuck as soon as the rain stopped. This was very dangerous as the trailers had a tendency to turn over. Daddy was afraid they would turn over on somebody. He told us all to be careful, and if one of them starting turning over, we were to run as fast as we could. I worked right beside everyone else. We hooked up trucks to the trailers, and we all pushed and shoved. Boards were placed under the tires on the trailer houses. It was unbelievable, but all the trailer houses made it out of the mud. I was proud that I had worked so hard, and in my mind, I felt we would never have accomplished this feat if it had not been for me. I was full of my own self worth.

We left that town, going north to where there had not been any sign of rain. In a few days, the men had money in their pockets again, so the kids got to go to the carnival and spend some of it. We spent our money at the Saturday picture shows too.

We should have been spending it on shoes. I didn't have any to wear, so I made me a pair to work in out of pasteboard. One Saturday while in town I decided to buy me a pair of shoes instead of going to the show with Charles Roy. He didn't like it much, but it was a decision that I had to make. I went to a second hand store and found a good pair at a price I could afford. I put my dirty feet in them and walked out of the place. That night Charles Roy kissed me even though he was still mad at me for standing him up at the movie.

One afternoon Daddy bought us a whole stalk of bananas at the grocery store. They had a sale on them. He put the bananas in the back of the truck along with us kids. We started right in eating them. Nuse started throwing the peelings out of the back of the truck trying his best to hit cars coming by. He hit one car's windshield, almost causing the driver to have a wreck. The man was furious and came around the truck honking for Daddy to stop. Daddy pulled over to the shoulder of the road and got out. "What in the hell do you want?" Daddy asked. He was mad too, not knowing what had gone on in the back of the truck.

"One of your damn kids is throwing banana peelings out of the back of your truck. My windshield was hit and I nearly wrecked my car. I could have killed my family. That kid needs his ass whipped," the man said. He was shaking. To my surprise Daddy apologized to the man and agreed he would whip whoever had thrown out the peelings just as soon as he got us to the house. This satisfied the driver and we all got back on the road.

I was scared now. We were too afraid to tell Daddy that Nuse had thrown out the banana peelings, a fact not lost on Nuse. He was going to get away with it. What he didn't realize was that I had decided I was going to tell on him. I was not going to take another whipping from Daddy because of his bad behavior. However, I didn't have to tell, because as soon as we got out of the truck, Nuse confessed.

Daddy was as surprised as the rest of us to hear his confession. He said that since he was taking responsibility for his actions that he would not get a whipping this time. Daddy also told him that if he did it again he would beat the hell out of him. I've said before that grown-ups are unpredictable. If that had been me making the confession, Daddy would not have waited until next time to beat the hell out of me. I was a simple-minded girl and would have deserved the whipping.

We were living in a house provided by a farmer that was located across the road from a Baptist church. The preacher came over and invited us to Sunday school. I was happy to go. Nuse and Dollie were in the same class as I was in. The Sunday school teacher passed the Bible around for each of us to read a couple of verses. I read first, then Nuse and next was Dollie's turn. When she had finished reading, one of the boys in the class exclaimed in a loud voice, "Cotton pickers that can read; I have seen everything now!"

That statement made me see red, and I jumped up in his face, fists clenched by my side. I told him, "You may have never seen a cotton picker whip your ass either, but that is exactly what is going to happen to you when you get outside this building." Now the Sunday school teacher was seeing red. He promptly got the preacher and took us across the road, back to the house. The preacher explained to Daddy what had happened and wanted me to apologize for what I had said.

Daddy asked the Sunday school teacher if he had heard the boy say what he had said. He said that he had. Daddy, now mad himself, got right into the face of that Sunday school teacher and said, "If that damn boy accused my kids of not being able to read, he should apologize. If he doesn't apologize, I am going to let these kids whip his ass. If they don't want to, then I am going to do it for them." The two men went back across the street.

We were proud of our Daddy for taking up for us like that. He was proud of us for taking up for ourselves. We waited, watching the church building, but we never did see that boy come out. Only God could have gotten him get out without our seeing him, and I guess that is exactly what happened. Lying on my cot that night I thought about the events of the day. We were a family and we would stick together. We did not get invited to that church again.

A few days later in the cotton field Joe was picking on a row next to Mama. She would get ahead of him and then pick on his row until he could catch up. All of a sudden he screamed. It is a scream I will never forget. All the workers in the field looked up, and some of us ran over to see what the matter was. Joe had stepped on a rattlesnake. He was working in his bare feet. It was the biggest snake I had ever seen. Joe seemed to be frozen and couldn't move. Mama grabbed him just as the snake took a strike at him. By now everyone was acting crazy, all the females were screaming.

A man who had started to work in the fields that morning and who was a stranger to us went to his car and returned with a gun in his hands. He came over and shot the rattlesnake in the head, killing him instantly. I thought the man sure looked familiar. He was bare-chested and had big arms and was very tanned. Now I assumed the rattler was a male snake because he was so big, so I walked very softly looking for his wife. I sure didn't want to disturb her sleep.

That night Daddy was thanking the man for saving Joe's life. I had never before been around anyone who had a real gun. During their talk he revealed to Daddy that he was an ex-Marine having served in Okinawa during the war. Now here is the amazing thing: the reason he looked so familiar to me was that his picture was in the book that the Veterans Administration had sent to Mama and Daddy. He was bare-chested in the picture and was giving an old woman a puff off his cigarette. His dog tags were hanging around his neck. This man had actually been in the same Marine Division as my brother, Franklin Eugene. Daddy was disappointed that he had not actually met Franklin and did not have any information as to the way he had been killed. As they say, "It is a small world." Even in 1954.

We were really enjoying the two nephews of ours. I spent as much time with them as I could. I was eating supper with Ruby Lee and Bo again as much as I could. Their trailer house had blinds in the windows. On top of one of the blinds Ruby Lee had placed a little glass slipper. The shoe could walk all by itself! At least that is what she and Bo made us believe. She would move the strings that were connected to the blinds, thus making the shoe move. We didn't understand that the shoe was sitting on top of the strings and was forced to move when the blinds were opened or shut. I was a grown girl before I ever figured out that mystery.

One Monday morning, I decided that I was going to pull cotton along side Bo, work real hard, and keep up with him. I was really sacking the cotton in. Each time I looked up Bo was right there beside me. This was unbelievable. I was very proud of myself. About halfway to the end of the row I realized that Bo was taking two rows to my one, and that was the reason I was keeping up. I just gave up. No one could pull cotton as fast as he could.

School started back in Lindale, but Daddy would not let us go home. I was buying little paper back books with my spare change, trying to keep up with my reading. I was so afraid that Daddy might think I had learned enough and make me quit going to school. I know for a fact that he would have liked to have kept us all out and follow the cotton crops on out to West Texas and Arkansas. Some of the families did that very thing. They even went to Washington State and picked apples.

We were lucky that Mama had the job in the rose nursery in Owentown. And too, I think Daddy was a little bit afraid of the laws, since they were now enforcing the law about children having to be in school a little better now. He would never ever admit to that though. He was tough, and he, not the law, was the boss of his kids!

We went back to Lindale. It was time for Mama to go back to work in the rose nursery. Daddy had decided that he would open up another fruit stand at another location in town. I was glad about that; at least he would be making a little money.

Starting to school in October of 1954 I was in the seventh grade. My teacher was named Mr. Land. I had never had a male teacher before, and this seemed strange to me. He was the most handsome man I had ever seen. I fell in love with him on my first day at school. The thoughts of Charles Roy were not with me all the time now. I suspected that all the girls in seventh grade were a little in love with him. I was going to have a wonderful year, or so I thought.

What messed it up for me was this: right after lunch each day, we had to go to choir. I could not believe it. Last year the teacher would not let me be in choir, but this year it was mandatory. I had accepted the fact that I could not sing, but each day all of us had to do it. The students laughed every time I opened my mouth. Well, I would laugh at them too. I tried to act like it didn't bother me, but of course it did. I did have feelings you know. I dreaded going to that class every day.

After a few weeks the teacher decided she would let some of us try out for band. This was my way out of the choir. I joined up. The school furnished all the instruments. Another student and I were assigned the same instrument to play. There was only one of them. I don't remember what it was, but it was big. I got to take it home one night and she would take it home the next night.

I sat outside in a chair and practiced, blowing as hard as I could. Before long I decided I didn't want to be in the band and turned the instrument back in. The Clinton's were glad that I did. My family hadn't given me any encouragement either. Right back into that choir class I went. The other girl who played my instrument stayed with the band for the rest of her school years and learned to play several more things.

My last class of the day was an English class. Mrs. Boulter, the high school English teacher, would come to the seventh grade to instruct us. She was pretty and was a very smart, wonderful teacher. One afternoon she was letting us play a game kind of like "I Spy." I was it. Standing in front of the class I said, "I see something you don't see, it's on a girl and it begins with a B."

A boy in the class named Daniel Duncan raised his hand. I called on him for the answer. "It's a brasserie," he said. Everyone started laughing. "It is not," I said. "It is boots." Mrs. Boulter got mad at Daniel. She told him that there were certain things that a boy might be able to talk about at home between his mother and his sisters, but they were not to be discussed at school. She told Daniel if he ever said that word again at school, he would be sent to the principal's office. We were not laughing when she was finished. We knew she meant business. She and Daniel had taken all the fun out of that game.

A few days later in English class Mrs. Boulter wanted each of us to make a wish. She went around the room. One by one each student wished for something like clothes, guns, toys, etc. When it came my time I said, "I wish that everyone would go to church and Sunday school every week." That bunch of hoodlums began laughing. Mrs. Boulter asked one of the boys why he was laughing. "If anybody needs to go to church and Sunday school, it is Annie Bell," was the reply. She was not impressed with his answer. Mrs. Boulter told the class that my wish was the best one that she had heard all day. If that boy had not been so cute, I probably would have jumped on him after school.

I talked Mr. Land into letting us have an Arithmetic race. I explained all the rules to him. When it came my time to go to the blackboard my opponent was Mac Gimble. Mac had started school a year after us, but he was so smart that he had been double promoted into our class when we were in the third grade. He had not been in my class in the sixth grade and had never participated in an Arithmetic race. He beat me. I was devastated, as I had hardly even been beaten last year. I never suggested that we have an Arithmetic race again.

At night we listened to the radio some and Mama helped us with our lessons. She would have us study our spelling words and then she would give them out to us. I always tried to make a 100 for her. One night she gave the word "fort" out for Nuse to spell. He spelled the word "fart" instead. He did it on purpose. Mama was mad; we all were laughing. I felt like she should have whipped him.

Since Daddy was working in the fruit stand during the day, we had to go home at lunch and cook our own food. I usually fried up some hamburger meat and an egg. Mama always cooked enough bread in the morning so that we could have biscuits to go with our meal. We had water to drink. It was not such a bad arrangement. The kids were always talking about how bad the cafeteria food was. I never really believed them though, because I knew who the head cook of the school was. She could do no harm.

We found a hickory nut tree down in the woods. When we cracked the hickory nuts open, we found the goody in the middle was hard to get out. Rusty bobby pins that were used to roll people's hair came in real handy in our being able to get the nut out of the hickory nut itself.

During the first week in December Mama got temporarily laid off her job. Daddy decided that we would run the firecracker stand in Mineola again this year. He went over there and got everything ready. We were ready too. I didn't like Mineola much, but I didn't mind helping Mama in the stand.

There was a house located next to the highway on the way to Mineola. They had a tree in their yard that was decorated for the holidays. The decorations were lights, ornaments, and a lot of homemade items. Daddy got it in his head that the people living in the house were Communists, and that they were sending secret messages to the Russians by way of that tree. Going past the house to the firecracker stand one afternoon Daddy said, "Those people don't have me fooled, I know what they are doing. I am thinking about going to the law about them. They want to take over our country." I thought he was sure dumb.

Naturally, I had to express my disagreement with him. "They are not Communists. Why would you think such a thing? You have never seen one before. All that is, is a tree, decorated by Americans for Christmas." He stopped the car. I knew I was in for it. "I know what I am talking about, you don't know everything. You ain't nothing but my damn old black Dutch daughter." He was fighting mad, and I thought that he was going to give me a whipping. About that time a car stopped. A man got out and asked Daddy if we were having car trouble. "No, just having daughter trouble," was Daddy's answer.

He didn't whip me, thanks to the car stopping. Daddy became more convinced of the people in that house being Russians when, after Christmas, they did not take the decorations down. He figured that they were at least trying to control our weather. Daddy went to the local laws about the Communists. They never did convince him that Lindale was not about to be invaded by another country. He kept his eyes on that house for years to come.

Two wonderful things happened to me that December. First the Hueys paid us a visit. They stayed for a few days. Nuse took Charles Roy to the show on Saturday, telling him he wanted to show him what really pretty girls looked like. They could not get away from me though. I followed them everywhere they went, even to the Lindale City Restrooms. Charles Roy didn't need to see any pretty girls. He only had to look at me. Because of Nuse not leaving him alone with me, we never got to smooch. It was nice to get to see him though.

Right after Christmas Aunt Leona and Orville came to see us. Uncle Earnest and his family came over too. There were kids everywhere. I told Nuse to leave Orville alone; I would show him around town. Nuse, not knowing my real reason for wanting to be alone with my cousin, said okay. He took Richard Earnest, our other cousin to the show. I found out that Orville was as anxious as I was to continue our kissing sessions. After they left to go back home, we never had the opportunity to kiss again. I vowed never to kiss another cousin, since I felt in my heart that God didn't like it. He was testing me, and I had failed the test.

For Christmas, Daddy bought Ruth Evelyn and Nuse a bicycle to be shared between them. He also bought a small one for Joe. He didn't buy Dollie and me one. He never would tell us why, but I asked him, of course. We were both hurt by his actions. Ruby Lee, who was now living back in Hobbs, New Mexico, sent all of us presents.

During the Christmas holidays some man Daddy and Mama knew died. They volunteered to sit up at the funeral home with his corpse. I asked Daddy why they did such a thing as the dead person was not going to get up and run off. He told me that someone had to sit up with the dead people or else cats would smell them and come in and get on top of the person. Now that was a good piece of information to know-that a cat could smell death. Later in life I would find out that it is dogs and not cats that can smell a dead body. Well, what do I really know? Cats may be able to smell it too.

Also during the holidays, before school started back, but after Christmas, Daddy pulled one of his drunks. Mama was sitting in a chair drinking coffee when he came into the room and started telling her how sorry and no good she was. If I had been at his back I would have hit him with something, like a chair. I wasn't though, and therefore, could do nothing but listen. Mama finally got enough of it and threw the cup at him. It landed in his face, and she had thrown it hard. He fell over backwards. We all got out of there, including Mama. In a little while he came outside, but because Mrs. Clinton was in the yard with us, he never said a word. The next day he was sober, but he did have a knot on his head. A well-deserved knot it was too.

Daddy had discovered a way to get sober pretty quick; he would break six eggs into a glass, stir them up and drank the eggs raw. He said that the raw eggs would either cure you or kill you. Unfortunately for us, they always cured him.

Fifteen

School started again in January. We no longer were required to attend choir. The students in band could stay there if they wanted to. The rest of us could take P. E. Of course, I said good-bye to the choir teacher, who was also the band director, and got into the P. E. class.

Now I was in great form here. We played dodge ball, kick ball, volleyball, and basketball. Just as much as I hated choir, I loved P. E. twice as much. The kids who had laughed about my singing wanted me to be on their side in the games that we played.

Daddy had never let us wear shorts. He thought it was sinful, but we had to have a pair for P. E. One of the students asked her mom to make me some. She did. No one had ever seen my legs in shorts, and most of the boys made comments that I liked. One guy said, "You are so skinny that I thought your legs would look like bird legs, but man was I wrong." My legs were the biggest things about me. I had never thought much about them until he made that remark. I never did tell Daddy that I was wearing the homemade shorts in P. E. class.

Robert Lee, now almost nineteen, had gone to work at Tyler Pipe, a factory that manufactured plumbing supplies. He had had it with the work in the cotton fields. However, he discovered that work in the factory was pretty rough also. So, after a month, he had decided that he would join the U. S. Army. He and a friend had gone to Dallas to talk to an Army recruiter. Both of them had backed out.

They had come back to Lindale. In January 1955, he and another friend went back to Dallas to talk to a Navy recruiter. They wanted to join up under the "Buddy Plan." The recruiter promised the two young men that they would not be separated. Lies, lies, all lies! After they completed boot camp, they were sent separate ways, almost immediately. Robert is still mad about it.

Later in the month Bo and Ruby Lee came to visit us with the two boys. Ruby Lee announced that they were in town to purchase a house and that they were probably going to move to Lindale in the near future. She was tired of being away from her family. They looked around and bought one from a good friend of theirs, Claude and Imogene Jordan. It was a cute, small two-bedroom house on the highway going toward Tyler. Bo was making good money in the oil fields. They had a new 1954 Chevrolet car. It was just about the prettiest thing I had ever seen. The car was orange. Ruby Lee was mad at Bo mad for buying it. She wanted them to save every penny they could.

Bo told Daddy that he and Ruby Lee wanted us to rent the house from them and live in it until they could move to Lindale. Daddy agreed. I said good-bye to all the kids in the neighborhood. I was crying when we took the last bit of our old furniture from the Clinton house and loaded it into our truck. Mrs. Clinton and Mrs. Whatley stood in the Clinton's yard and waved at us. I knew that I would not get to see them too often anymore, since we were moving to the other side of town. I would miss them terribly and hoped that they would never forget me.

We moved into the new place. I was thrilled to see that the house had a bathroom in it. We would no longer have to take our baths in a #3 washtub. Our new home consisted of three rooms and a kitchen. Beds were put up in all three of the rooms. Mama and Daddy would sleep in the front room, the girls in the middle room and the boys in the back one. The kitchen was neat. It had a sink and nice cabinets. I might miss my buddies across town, but this was really something.

Our first night there, I filled the tub with nice warm water. I started to get undressed when it dawned on me that one of those brothers of mine might come into the bathroom unannounced. There was not a lock on the door. I got into the tub, but I left my slip on. After that, as long as we lived there, I took a bath in my underclothes.

Behind the house across the road is where an old couple lived. I went right over to their house and introduced myself. They were the Browns. Two sons had been born to them, but both had died; one had drowned and the other was killed in a car wreck. They were happy that kids were going to be living in the neighborhood. I knew immediately that I was going to like this couple and they were going to like me. I would eat a lot of meals with them prepared by Mrs. Brown. She turned out to be as good as Mrs. Clinton and Mrs. Whatley had been.

Walking home from school to our new place for the first time, I realized a girl who was in my class at school was walking in the same direction. I let her catch up with us. Her name was Treva Loving. She lived in a two-story house in the same neighborhood that I would be living in. Treva and I became instant friends. I told her about Daddy running the fruit stand. So each day, on our way home from school, we would usually stop by, and Daddy would give all of us a piece of fruit. We would eat it on our walk to our homes.

There was a clothesline behind the house. We would no longer have to dry our clothes on fences and weeds. Daddy decided that he would let Mama go to the washateria to get our clothes washed instead of having to use a rub board in the washtub. He also told her she could buy washing powder and quit making lye soap. The building where we had at one time had our café was now the washateria. We went on Saturday mornings to wash the clothes.

The washing machines consisted of a tub that we washed the clothes in and three tubs that had rinse water in them. In the first rinse tub we put some blue liquid in it and wrung the clothes from the washer into this it. The bluing in water was supposed to help the clothes. From the bluing washtub the clothes were wrung into the next two tubs. We went to the washateria early on Saturday, and it took us until lunch to get all the week's clothes washed. We then took them home to be hung on the line to dry. The first time I went to the washateria I got my arm caught in the wringer. I was a lot more careful from that day forward doing the wash.

Ruth Evelyn, boy crazy now, had a special boyfriend. His name was Bud Praytor. Daddy would not let her date. She was seventeen years old, and he probably thought she would turn out to be like his sisters. Ruth Evelyn was pretty and in love. Robert had helped her sneak out to see Bud before he had gone into the Navy.

In fact, before Robert Lee had gone to the Navy, Ruth Evelyn had already had a fight with another girl over Bud. One day, during their lunch hour, they had gotten tangled up on the lawn of the

Central Baptist Church. Both girls were expelled. When Ruth Evelyn went home, scared to death, she told daddy that she had been expelled from school for fighting with another girl. Daddy asked. "Did you beat the hell out of the other gal?" Ruth Evelyn told him that she did. Well, that satisfied him.

It didn't satisfy Mama. She had to take a day off work, which Daddy didn't like, but she marched Ruth Evelyn back to school the next day, right into the principal's office. She told the principal that Ruth Evelyn did not fight on the school yard but on the church yard. Mama told him that God would punish Ruth Evelyn so the school didn't need to. The principal let Ruth Evelyn stay in school. He must to have been a Baptist too. The other girl's mother did not bring her to see the principal, and, in fact, the girl never came back to school again. Too beat up, I guess.

Daddy finally told her she could go out on a date with Bud. The night Bud came to pick her up, we were there to see the big event take place. Daddy was not at home. I think he was off someplace getting drunk. Ruth Evelyn only had one pair of shoes. Nuse hid one of them from her. Bud came and she was still looking for the shoe. Mama finally told Nuse she was going to beat the day lights out of him if he didn't give Ruth Evelyn the shoe. He did. Ruth Evelyn went on the date with stars in her eyes. She was so in love. By the end of summer she would be married to someone else.

We got a letter from Robert Lee. He was in Quincy Point, Rhode Island. Everything there was deep in snow. He was really homesick. He hated the Navy and wanted to come home. Enclosed was a picture of him hanging out clothes in the snow. I felt the picture was staged, since Robert Lee had never had to do that at home. But, as I read his letter, tears started running down my face. I missed him too. *Would I ever see him again?* The letter instructed Mama to give all of us hugs and kisses.

A letter from Robert Lee came almost every week. They were always filled with the same stuff, dislike for the Navy, and homesickness for his family. One letter stated that he would be on a ship for six months, and that he would trade it for a chance to go back to the cotton patch. I figured things must be really bad for him.

In a store downtown there was a television set in the window. The owner of the store left it on at night. About two nights a week Daddy would take the family to town to watch it. We would sit on the concrete sidewalk or on the bumper of the truck and enjoy the show through the glass. Never mind that we could not hear what they were saying. Daddy would get mad if a baseball game was on, and he would take us home. The set was only capable of getting one channel. This was in the early days of television, and the picture always looked like it was snowing.

In April, Daddy took us on our first Easter egg hunt. Mama dyed a lot of eggs with rags boiled in the water with the eggs. She also cooked a bunch of food. One of the farmers that we picked blackberries for was named Lee Hicks. He owned a lot of land. Mr. Hicks gave Daddy permission to hide the eggs in one of his pastures. It was a wonderful time for us.

While we were hunting the eggs, we found a tree full of bees. Daddy promptly stole their honey. He put his hands in the hole real slow, and he did not get stung one time. He was a very brave man. When the time came for us to go home, Daddy made a decision. We would always get the family together on Easter and have the egg hunt. That was 1955, and we have not missed a year since.

Nuse, now fourteen had learned to drive a car. One Saturday afternoon Daddy let him drive Dollie, Joe, and me to Gilmer to spend the night with Aunt Bessie and Uncle Jack. Mama had fixed a lunch for us. When we got into the car, Dollie and Joe got into the back. They were the youngest and it was their place to get back there. I climbed into the front. On our way to Gilmer we pretended that I was married to Nuse and that Joe and Dollie were married.

At a roadside park we stopped and ate the lunch Mama had made us. We had a really good time. Aunt Bessie and Uncle Jack did not know that we were coming as we did not have a telephone, but they were real glad, as always, to see us. They took us into Longview to see a movie. We reluctantly went back home the next day.

The next Saturday Daddy and Mama went to Gilmer to see them without us. They felt we were old enough now to stay home with Ruth Evelyn taking care of us. She was not our boss. And she didn't want to be. Bud Praytor was coming over. She did not care what we did. We didn't have any money, but Dollie and I decided to go to the Saturday movie. Not having any money had not ever stopped us before.

I had recruited Dollie into this venture sometime back. We would stand around out front waiting for several people to go into the show all at once. We just went in behind them. It had always worked. I rationalized that it was okay because they would show the movie whether or not we were in there. No one was hurt, so no crime was actually committed. Well, as our luck went, the owner of the show caught us. He had gotten suspicious of us and had been watching us. On this day not too many people were in the show. He counted heads and then counted the number of tickets that he had sold. He was two tickets short.

The owner's name was Earl Reece Wood. His son, Richard, was in my grade at school. Mr. Wood came and sat down by Dollie and me and told us he would like to talk to us when the show was over. I shook my head okay. I didn't have anything to hide. When the show was over we were nowhere to be found. You talk about Elvis leaving the building. We had snuck out.

I knew that Mr. Wood was going to tell Daddy. I waited on the front porch until Daddy and Mama came home the next day. I didn't even go to Sunday school. I was responsible for the mess we were in, so I felt that I was the one to tell Daddy. Dollie said it was okay with her. She went to Treva's to play, so she would not be at home when they came in.

Daddy and Mama had not gotten out of the car good when I ran up to it saying that I had something to tell them. It shook them up, as they could not imagine what terrible thing had happened to us in their absence. My explanation came out of me slowly. I was shaking and stuttering. Daddy seemed to understand, saying that he should have given us the money to go to the show. I was surprised. He stated that he would go and talk to Mr. Wood. He did, and offered to pay for the times we had sneaked in.

Mr. Wood did not take any money from Daddy. He knew us well and knew there were a lot of mouths to feed. He told Daddy he was glad that I had confessed and that all was forgiven. We didn't get away scot-free however.

By the time he got back from town, Dollie had come home. He took his belt off and gave us a good whipping. *Richard would make fun of me at school the next day just as sure as the sun was going to come up.* However, to my surprise, he didn't say a word about it. It was several weeks before I got the courage to go back to the show. When we finally went back on a Saturday afternoon, Mr. Wood smiled at us as we were purchasing our ticket. He apparently had not told his son about our sneaking into the show because Richard never mentioned it at school.

Daddy started playing poker at our house. We started selling coffee to the players, but I didn't like for them to be there. One day I told Daddy that I didn't want to come home again and find that bunch of men in Ruby Lee's house. "I'm renting this house," he told me. "You try one more time to tell me what to do, and I will wear your little butt out." I knew he meant it, but I meant it too, and he knew that I did. He also knew he was the boss. The other kids thought I had a lot of nerve talking to him like that. They would never have done it, not even Ruth Evelyn.

One Saturday night Ruth Evelyn was going to a church party with a friend of hers named Ruby Foshee. I wanted to go too. The girls of course did not want me to tag along. Ruth Evelyn was going to meet Bud Praytor, and I knew it. Mama told her she had to take me if she wanted to go. Ruth Evelyn was mad. On the way, walking to the church, Ruth Evelyn was telling me off, saying I was too young to be with them and that she wished that I would go home. I knew she was right, but I was too stubborn to go back. She hit me across the face. She must have been desperate.

I began to cry, telling her I was going to tell Mama on her. She told me that I had better not. I told her that I had a headache. By that time we were in front a filling station in town. Ruth Evelyn went inside and bought a box of aspirins. She made me take all twelve of them. Ruby Foshee got scared. She felt I would die.

I realized that Ruth Evelyn meant business. I told her I had decided to go home. When I got back to the house, Mama asked me why I had come back. I told her that I had just changed my mind. With my headache cured, I went to bed and went to sleep almost instantly. When Ruth Evelyn got home, she felt my heart to determine if I were still alive. Ruby Foshee came to the house early the next morning to check on me too.

A man who lived close to us had a garage. He also sold used cars. He kept them backed into the yard beside of the garage. Ruth Evelyn and Ruby decided that they would run away. Ruth Evelyn had had enough, cooking, cleaning and babysitting. They were boy crazy girls. One night they each packed a small suitcase and hid them in the tall grass close to the house. On the appointed time, around ten o'clock that night, the two of them stole one of the cars by the garage. They had also stolen some money out of their daddies' billfolds. Ruth Evelyn could not drive yet so Ruby had to do it.

The two thieves drove to Tyler. They went to the bus station. The plans were to catch a bus to anywhere USA and to leave the car at the station so the owner could pick it up. The ticket agent at the bus station told them there were no more buses leaving out until the next morning. Several policemen were having their coffee break at the bus station. They began to study the two girls. Ruth Evelyn and Ruby decided it would be in their best interest to go back to Lindale. The car was driven back into its place in the parking lot. Ruby did not know how to back up a car, so she just drove it in facing the different direction than it was in when they took it out. Did they return the stolen money? You try to guess.

It was mostly Ruth Evelyn's job to do the cooking. I didn't much like to, but sometimes I would help her out. One Saturday afternoon around 4 o'clock I was the only one at home. I decided that I would cook supper. I peeled and fried potatoes and cooked hamburger meat. I opened a big can of ranch style beans and corn. I liked to work in this kitchen with the sink. The dishes were kept washed up as I cooked. The table was set.

I wanted to see the surprised, happy faces when they came home. All I had to do was wait. No one came. I do not remember where everyone was, but not a one of my family came home until after 9:00. The supper I had so lovingly prepared was cold. All of them had already eaten. I was sad and mad. Into the kitchen I went. All the food was thrown into the trash. From that day forward I have hated to cook. I do not like being in the kitchen, not even to get a drink of water.

Mama was not happy about my throwing good food away. She had to work hard to make money to buy it. Usually she didn't say much about the high jinks I pulled, but this ate at her. She was mad at me all week, hardly speaking to me, but she didn't whip me. The next Saturday we went to the washateria as usual to wash our clothes. I worked really hard, hoping she would forgive me. It really hurt me for her to be so unhappy with me.

It was a custom at the time for girls to wear a headscarf on her hair if she were having a bad hair day. Well, most days were a bad hair day for me. This day was no exception. The headscarf was held on by bobby pins. Mama, Dollie, and I were hanging the clothes on the clothesline. Dollie and I got into a fuss. Mama came over and slapped my face and pulled the headscarf off my head. I was astonished. And I was hurt. I knew what was wrong with her. She was still thinking about the wasted food.

I would not cry; she could not make me. I braced myself for another slap. My precious Mama had never slapped one of her kids that I could recall. All of a sudden Mama put her arms around me and began to cry, "What have I done? Oh, Lord, forgive me." I thought forget the Lord, you need to ask for my forgiveness. Dollie came over and joined in on the hugging; she held my hand as I walked back into the house.

The incident was never mention again. The headscarf was not picked up. Wind, rain and sun destroyed it. I never put another one on my head. I did forgive Mama. After all, I had thrown good food away. I've always wondered if maybe Mama wasn't really as mad at me as she was at life in general. Daddy was drinking a lot and probably seeing other women, and, of course, he was throwing our money away. Mama and I never had a cross word about anything again.

By the time we were going to move to Winnsboro, two families had moved to Lindale; Bo and Ruby Lee, their boys, and of all people, the Huey family. The Hueys were going with us to Winnsboro to pick strawberries. I was thrilled to see Charles Roy. Ruth Evelyn was also excited about seeing Billy Ray. I had never realized that Ruth Evelyn liked him, since I usually just had thoughts of my own feelings.

The Paul family moved into their home. Daddy bought a house for us close by. It was not nearly as nice as the one Ruby Lee and Bo owned that we had to move out of, but at least it had a bathroom. In the bathroom was an old, old bathtub, the kind that people pay a lot of money for now. I hated that thing, but it kept me clean. The house had four rooms. One of the rooms was pretty big, so Daddy decided he would put two beds up in it for the kids. Three girls slept in one and the two boys slept in the other one. Daddy and

Mama slept in the second bedroom. The front room was used as a living room. We got a couch and a chair or two to go in it.

Our first week there Ruth Evelyn decided she was going to learn how to drive. We all knew how to pull the cotton truck up the rows, but driving on the highway was a different thing all together. Daddy had never taught any of his boys or Ruby Lee to drive. They had learned on their own. Nuse decided to teach Ruth Evelyn how it was done.

Our house had a small front porch on it. Dollie, Joe and I knew that Nuse had taken Ruth Evelyn down the road in the car. She was going to drive it back home. Mama was at work, and Daddy was asleep in the house. The three of us stood on the porch. Here came the car with Ruth Evelyn behind the wheel. She was doing pretty well, or so we thought. It was evident that she could not steer the car very well. The closer she got to the porch the more we could tell she was headed right to it. We jumped off just about the time the car came crashing into the porch.

The porch was torn off the house. Ruth Evelyn, Nuse, or the car however did not have a scratch on them. Daddy, hearing the crash, came running out of the house in his drawers. Man, I can't tell you how mad he was. Worried about that car! *What about all his kids that had nearly gotten killed?* Daddy didn't get the porch fixed for a long time after that. Ruth Evelyn was unstoppable now. Nuse finished the driver's education course, doing a good job of teaching Ruth Evelyn how to keep the car between the ditch lines.

Nuse also took it upon himself to teach a pretty girl how to drive, and she had a wreck in daddy's truck. She drove it into a ditch. In the back of the truck was a lot of trash; Nuse decided this would be a good time to get rid of it. He threw all of it into the ditch. He told Daddy that he was driving when the truck ditched. He did not tell him about the ditching the trash. The next day the constable came to our house. He had found Daddy's name on something in the trash heap. We had to go pick all the trash up. I was so mad I wanted to trash Nuse. He didn't even get a whipping for letting that girl drive or throwing the trash in the ditch. He was a boy, you know.

We left our furniture at the house and took our camping stuff and went to Winnsboro. There were not any locks on the door, but

Daddy felt our stuff would be okay. He was right; no one came in and took a thing.

When we returned a few weeks later, Bo had bought a filling station. Daddy went to work for Bo at the station in the evenings after we had finished picking blackberries in the morning. Our family now was actually making a little money and Daddy did not pull a drunk. He worked there about a month and a half before he quit so we could go back to South Texas. He would return to work there when we returned in the fall.

Ruth Evelyn came back from Winnsboro in love again, this time with Billy Ray Huey. Around the middle of June, Billy Ray and Ruth Evelyn paid Daddy a visit at the filling station. Daddy was pretty suspicious about what they were there for. Billy Ray was nervous when he asked Daddy if Ruth Evelyn could marry him. Ruby Lee did not have his permission to marry when she was fifteen, but her marriage was okay. Ruth Evelyn was seventeen, and Daddy knew Mama would just sign for her anyway. He gave them his okay.

When I heard the news, I thought it was a joke. I just knew that Ruth Evelyn was in love with Bud Praytor. Both of the boys were good looking, but I could not understand why a girl could be hugging and kissing one boy one day and the next day be getting married to another one. Sadness fell across my soul for Bud Praytor. I had no way of knowing that he had about as many girlfriends in town as there were blackberry patches.

Mr. Huey bought Billy Ray and Ruth Evelyn an old trailer house. It was eighteen feet long. The only things it had inside it were a bed and a sink. Ruth Evelyn got her a box to put her Coleman stove on. On June 25, 1955, they were married at our new place. I had mixed feelings about her getting married. On one hand there would now be just two girls in the bed, but on the other hand, more of the cooking chores would be passed on to me. One good thing always messes up something else.

Ruth Evelyn and Dollie had always made me sleep in the middle. A lot of nights they would pull the covers back and forth. An argument usually followed until Daddy would get up and whip them. He always whipped me too, even though I was innocent of any wrongdoing.

I knew I was going to miss having Ruth Evelyn around. She was a good person and had been basically good to us younger kids, just as Robert Lee had been. She and Billy Ray ate their meals sitting on the bed, as there was not a table in the trailer house. They were as happy as if they had good sense.

In July when we pulled out of our yard to go to South Texas to the cotton fields, the newlyweds were behind us with their trailer house. They were on their own now and had a living to make. Billy Ray's daddy and mother were traveling with us too. They had a new car in which to pull their trailer house. Charles Roy was riding in the back of the truck with us. I was happy. I was thinking about another marriage that would take place in about four more years.

Uncle Earnest decided that his family would also go with us to pull cotton. It took all of us nearly a week to get to the Valley. Our kinfolks seemed glad to see us. We picked cotton for three weeks there.

One afternoon Billy Ray and Ruth Evelyn stopped at a large field where cabbage was growing. It was the largest patch of vegetables that they had ever seen. They decided that the owner of the property would not mind if they got out and gathered some of it. They worked as fast as they could. An old pick-up pulled up, and an old man got out. "How is the cabbage?" The man asked. "It is a good crop," Bill Ray answered. "When we finish up, we will help you get some." "Well, no need to do that, the man said, "This field belongs to me. Now you can keep the cabbage that you have gathered, but I do not want to catch you in my fields again." Both of them thanked the man and promised not to come back. They didn't either. They just told some more cotton pickers where the patch of cabbage was located, but they kept their word not to return. Most cotton pickers were good about keeping their word.

As in the years before, after we left the Valley, we went north to Sinton, seeing our aunts and uncles. For some reason I was no longer interested in kissing my cousin and I could tell he felt the same way. No one else but me knew I was going to get married in about four years. I felt that maybe he had a secret marriage date too.

We rented a small cabin at Victoria to live in while we were pulling cotton there. The cabin was in a place called "Hilltop Cabins." The cabins could be rented by the day, week, month or whatever. I saw several people just stay in one an hour or so and never be seen again. I guess they just needed to take a quick nap.

One Saturday Daddy took us to town and let us out at the picture show. He told us we could walk back to the cabin, since it wasn't that far. We liked to walk anyway, so we said okay. I knew how to get home.

After the movie, Nuse wanted us to take a shortcut back to the house; we agreed. Instead of following the main highway back, we turned right and waded through a small creek, and crossed a barbwire fence. We were just taking our time when I turned and saw a bull coming pretty fast in our direction. I started to run; we all did.

Dollie and I were screaming. The bull seemed to sense our fear as he got closer and closer to us. To this day I do not know how we managed to outrun the bull, but we did. Nuse got across the fence first and held it up until each one of us was safe on the other side. The bull, now defeated, turned around and went in the other direction.

We all four had faced death. Nuse did not cry, but the other three of us did. We sat down a few minutes to catch our breaths. There was never another mention of our taking a shortcut home from anywhere.

While we were living here, Nuse and Joe went skinny-dipping in an old pond. When they got out of the water, they discovered someone had taken their clothes. They had to walk back to our cabin naked as the day they were born. Now, I am not going to confess who had gotten their clothes, but for some strange reason the clothes were waiting for them when they came walking up. I guess maybe the clothes took legs and walked home. What do you think?

Daddy was mad about their going swimming and told them not to do it again. Well, Nuse, half crazy and half mad about being told he couldn't do something, decided they would go swimming again. He was a little cautious though and asked permission from another grown up. She gave it to them. Daddy, coming from town in his truck, spotted the two swimming under a bridge.

Daddy stopped the truck, got out and cursed the boys, telling them to get their asses back home that he was going to beat the living hell out of them. They were really scared. Big, brave Nuse and his little brother got to Ruby Lee and Bo's trailer house and hid under their bed. They had to stay there for two hours before Bo could talk Daddy out of beating them to death.

Nuse, not learning anything from this episode, decided that if Robert Lee was old enough to be in the Navy and Ruth Evelyn was old enough to get married that he was old enough to smoke. He told daddy that he thought he was old enough to smoke and that Daddy should buy his cigarettes for him. Daddy took his belt off, tried to strike Nuse with it, telling him to get his sorry butt back to the cotton patch and go to work. Nuse dodged the belt, but he got this message. He still had to sneak around and smoke and steal cigarettes.

A farmer in Edna, Texas let us live in an old house of his while we were pulling his cotton. At night as we lay on our cots thinking about the hard day ahead, we began to hear a noise in the ceiling. It sounded like someone was walking around up there. We were scared to death. During the day the sound seemed to disappear. One afternoon as we eating our supper on a makeshift table, a raccoon fell out of the ceiling right into the middle of the food. We scattered. The raccoon was as scared as we were. Mama ran him out of the house with a broom. I thought that maybe the animal had smelled the food and could not wait for the groceries to go out the backdoor. That night we thought all would be quiet, but we began to hear a cat crying under the house. During the day we all looked for that cat, but we never found one. I was glad when we left that haunted place.

One day Mama boiled her famous red beans. We ate about half of them. I cleaned up the dishes, putting a lid on the uneaten beans. For some unknown reason, no one thought about those beans for several days. I finally took the pan and opened it up to throw away the beans. The smell was awful. There was something else to make a person with a weak stomach sick. Maggots! They looked like a bunch of white worms, hundreds of them. I never showed them to any one, as I knew I would get a whipping for leaving the beans in the pan. I went a short distance from the house, dug a hole and put the maggots in it. Water was drawn from the well, and the pan was cleaned up good as new. Mama boiled some more beans in it that very day. Everyone said they were the best she had ever cooked. I was the only one who knew where they had gotten their flavor.

We traveled north to Hearne, Texas. Daddy went to town to find a farmer to ask if we could pick his cotton. This time he let me go with him. On the street he met a man that we had worked for before. The man was very friendly, and he told Daddy that he would buy him a cup of coffee at the café while they talked over business. I was glad, as I knew he or Daddy one would buy me a cold drink.

On our way to the café another man appeared. He spoke to the farmer and shook hands with him. The farmer introduced Daddy to his banker. Daddy held out his hand for the banker to shake it. The banker did not shake his hand, thinking he was too good to even acknowledge a cotton picker.

The farmer was embarrassed, and Daddy was sad. I was mad. I drew back my foot and kicked that banker's shinbone on his right leg just as hard as I could. He screamed with pain. I didn't care if I got a whipping for it. I wasn't all that crazy about Daddy, but I didn't like anyone thinking they were better than him.

We went on into the café. The farmer was actually laughing about what I had done. I felt I wasn't going to get into trouble for it since the farmer thought it was all right. He told Daddy that he didn't like that banker very much, but he couldn't let him know, as he was the man who loaned him money to plant his crops. Thoughts of the stuck up banker bothered me for a long time, but Daddy never mentioned him again.

I spent the summer playing games at night. I probably kissed Charles Roy a thousand times that summer. *After all we would get married someday, wouldn't we?* Ruth Evelyn had married his brother, so it would just be natural for us to marry. These were just thoughts in my head because Charles Roy sure never mentioned anything about marriage.

School started in September, but we passed up Lindale and went on north to Princeton, Texas. We moved into a camp that had cabins in it. The rumor was that this place had served as a POW camp during the war. At night I would lie awake and think about the Germans, and I could see their ghosts in the room. I didn't sleep much in that place.

One Saturday we went into town. I had a little money in my pocket. When we had been in the fifth grade back at Lindale School, we were shown a movie about our teeth. In it a little man with a pickaxe got into the little boy's teeth and picked away at his teeth, causing them to decay. The only way he could stop this decay was to brush his teeth with toothpaste, thus killing the man with the pickaxe and saving his teeth. I had thought about that movie a lot, but I never had money that I thought I could waste on a toothbrush. I did, however, pretty regularly, put some salt or baking soda on my teeth and wash them with a rag. I also chewed gum a lot.

This day I decided I would buy a toothbrush for myself. I didn't spend any money on toothpaste. That would have to come later. I went outside of our cabin several times a day with the saltbox in my hand and brushed my teeth. There was running water outside. I would brush a little bit and then I would look up to see how many kids had gathered around. I made a big production of rinsing my mouth out. I sure wanted Charles Roy to see me.

One other thing worth mentioning that happened to me that summer was this: several of us kept picking a fight with a certain little boy who was living in the camp. One afternoon I was giving him a bad time. He picked up a board and hit me on the side of my head. Never again did any of us torture him. In fact, he became one of the gang after that show of bravery.

Also that summer the Coomer kids started saving, finding and stealing empty Coke and Dr Pepper bottles. About once a week we would take them to a filling station and sell them. The owners of the stations would then sell them back to the bottling companies, probably for double what they had paid us for them. That didn't bother us any, since we had probably stolen about half of the ones we sold them from them. We had a plan that always worked: one of us would go in and get into a conversation with the owner or worker at the filling station while one or two of us would sneak the empty bottles from the boxes that were always sitting outside the place. We were a team. Now you might say that we were a team of thieves, but we felt that the owners should have paid us as much for the bottles as they got from the bottling companies. We were just thieves stealing from other thieves. That was our reasoning anyway.

In October we went back to Lindale to our house that had our nice furniture in it. I was going to be in the eighth grade. I wondered on the way home if Mr. Land would still be there and if he would be one of my teachers. I sure hoped so.

I read the Burma-Shave signs on the side of the road:
"SPEED WAS HIGH...WEATHER WAS NOT-TIRES WERE THIN...X MARKS THE SPOT."
    "AROUND THE CURVE...LICKETY--SPLIT-IT'S A BEAUTIFUL CAR...WASN'T IT?"

Sixteen

The first day of school did not produce a sighting of Mr. Land. I wondered what kind of year it was going to be, since it was evident that he was not going to be a teacher of mine this year. *Would I be able to survive?* Life was hard on a teenage girl who had a crush on one of her teachers. I thought surely he must have a crush on me too. Later I would realize that a girl should not believe everything she thinks. *Life just wasn't very kind to me sometimes.* Now there is a thought that most teenagers have, even the boys.

Nuse had failed another year, so now here we were, both in the eighth grade. He didn't seem to mind, and I didn't either. I didn't think that we would both show up in the same class though. This would be our first year to "change classes." We would have to go to different teachers' rooms for different subjects for the first time.

I was enrolled in a "Citizenship" class. Up to that time I don't believe I had ever heard that word before. If I had heard it, I sure didn't know what it meant. One of the high school football coaches was the teacher. He was also going to be my Math teacher. It seemed funny to me that Arithmetic had turned into Math during the summer. Arithmetic had been my best friend, but I didn't know how I was going to fare with this Math business. It sounded kind of hard. Well, I didn't have a choice, so I was about to find out.

The principal also enrolled Nuse in these classes with me. It didn't make me feel any better about it when he told me that he thought I could help Nuse with his lessons. Nuse and I both knew that wasn't going to happen. He could get his own lessons. This same teacher had coached Nuse in junior high football last year.

Nuse had made one touchdown. The trouble was he had run the football in the wrong direction. The coach had run him through the belt line for that. I'm pretty sure he knew what he was doing all the time. He just didn't think about the belt line. Another thing this coach done was to make Nuse swallow a whole cigar when he caught Nuse with it in his mouth of the bus one night going to a football game. It may not have been so bad, but the cigar was lit at the time.

In English class my teacher was named Mrs. Wood. She was older than my Mama, and mean looking. Her daughter was the high school counselor. I had no idea what a high school counselor was, but I didn't dwell on that much, as I was not in high school yet. I could deal with that next year, if I made it through this one.

That first day at school, I got one good piece of news. We would have P. E. everyday. It was mandatory that we attend this class unless we had a doctor's excuse not to attend. I could not imagine anybody not being able to do P. E. No doctor was going to stop me from going to it. If they had tried to put me a choir class though, I probably would have paid Dr.Kinzie a visit for one of those excuses. He could have always written me an excuse for "broken vocal cords."

I didn't sleep much that night wondering about the eighth grade. I also thought of Charles Roy. *Was he in school? Did he have a crush on one of his teachers?* He'd better not. It was okay for me to have a crush on one of mine, I just couldn't help it. I hoped that he could help it.

Billy Ray and Ruth Evelyn came back to Lindale too. He went to work at one of the local plants, and after only one week, he quit. They moved to Alice, Texas, so he could go to work in the oil fields like Bo had done. We all cried the day they left. My stomach hurt. Her moving so far away was a sure indication that I might never see her again. I was really stuck with Dollie now, and I made a silent promise to try to get along with her.

Daddy went back to work for Bo at the filling station. Mama got her job back in the rose nursery. I was glad about Daddy and the job. As long as he was working, he would not have those dirty old men at our house playing poker. His job and my luck wouldn't last for long. That was the way it had always been, why was this year going to be any different?

The grass at our house had died, but Daddy bought a second hand push lawn mower for Nuse and Joe to use. This was only right because Dollie and I had to do all the inside work. But, as it turned out, I liked to push that thing, so I got another unpaid job. I also started going to the filling station on Saturday and Sunday after church helping Daddy and Bo. I didn't get paid for that either. Sometimes a customer would not let me fill their car up with gas, as they either thought I was too young to be doing this kind of work or they didn't want a girl doing it. I thought they sure were stupid. A baby could fill a car up with gas, boy or girl.

We all began to walk to and from school with Treva and her brother Bobby. He was in the same grade as Dollie. Treva and her family turned out to be a wonderful thing for me. I firmly believed the Lovings had to be rich, living in a house as big as theirs was, having an upstairs and all. Why, they even had a phone. And only two kids were still at home. Well, let me tell you, I practically moved in with them.

Treva and I spent countless days seining for crawfish, gathering chinquapins, swinging in the pecan trees and playing in the yard with Bobby, Nuse, Joe, and Dollie. Mr. Loving built us a pair of stilts so tall that we had to get on top of the garage just to be able to begin our stroll on them. Treva had a pair of skates. It took us several weeks to learn how to use them. She would skate a few minutes, take them off; I would put them on and do the same thing.

I spent as many nights as I could at their house. Mrs. Loving would let us get a snack when we got home, usually a bologna sandwich. Living in a family where food was scarce, bologna was as good as steak. She also had fresh cow milk, butter she had churned, and sometimes a cake.

The Lovings had a record player so we would learn songs and put on plays for them. What a talent we thought we had! Mr. Loving had been a schoolteacher, so at night he would help us with our lessons. Because of his helping me, my grades begin to really improve, and the eighth grade was becoming one of my favorites.

The Lovings raised chickens. Together they grew a really big garden. They had a lot of vegetables. Until I knew them, potato, corn, and beans were the only vegetables I had ever eaten. Mr. Loving made his own fish nets, fished a lot, and Mrs. Loving did too.

She had her own personal worm bed. I learned to eat fish in their home.

That fall the Lovings had their annual reunion. I was invited. Cousins came from Oklahoma, girls and boys. One of the boys was named Pete. Well, you know me by now. I became sweet on him. Another secret I would hide from the rest of my school friends. I knew I wouldn't let Charles Roy know about him either. The Oklahoma cousins stayed at the Loving's house for several days. By the end of the week, I had gone from being sweet on Pete to being really in love. However, we did not kiss. I guess he felt we were too young for that. His not kissing me didn't worry me though, since I knew he would be back the next year, and sooner or later it would happen.

Daddy purchased the vacant lot next door and put up a basketball net. All of the kids in the neighborhood came over as often as they could. The Coomer kids were short, but we could play ball pretty well. All of us could do gymnastic stuff. I would go to Treva's house and do the back bend from one tree limb to the next on a huge pecan tree in the front yard. One afternoon I fell out of the tree and landed flat on my back. I was hurt just long enough for Mrs. Loving to give me some sort of snack; then I got well. That ended my gymnastics performances in the tree.

I decided I was old enough now to drive. Daddy had purchased an old car, so he told me to get in it and give it a try. Mama said that she would teach me. I had the same problem that Ruth Evelyn had. I could not steer the car too well. The car had a standard shift in it, but that was not a problem. After a while, I went on my solo drive to church. For several Sundays after that, Daddy let me drive Dollie and Joe to church. We had to go on the back roads.

One Sunday after church, Joe talked me into letting him drive home. Well, wouldn't you know it? Joe went right through town. We had a four way stop on the square. He stopped, and then started off slowly, making the right turn toward the house. The city marshal recognized him and knew he was too young to drive. He pulled us over. After a good lecture from him, I promised I would not let Joe drive again. The city marshal did not realize that I was also too young to drive. Dollie and Joe both promised that they

171/Baldwin/Meager Beginnings

would not tell Daddy about my letting Joe drive, his going through town, or the city marshal's stopping us.

We were hardly inside the front door at home when Joe spilled the beans. Daddy got mad, not so much about my letting Joe behind the wheel, as his driving through town. It was several weeks later before he would let me drive to church again. You can bet a dollar, the next time Joe begged me to drive, I didn't let him. Well, he didn't deserve to, now did he? He would just go back through town and get stopped again. No, I wanted the city marshal to trust me.

Joe thought he was really tough and formed a gang at school. He charged twenty-five cents to be in the gang. If you didn't want to be in the gang, or didn't have the twenty-five cents, he would try to beat you up. Perry Mac Hutchens, one of his classmates, told his mother one day that he had to have twenty-five cents so that he could be in Joe's gang. Well, when his mother refused to give him the money. I guess more mothers refused to give their sons the money too because Joe's gang fell apart before he got into big trouble, like stealing something.

We got into sort of a routine around the house. Mama got up early with Daddy. She cooked a good breakfast, fried potatoes for me, fixed gravy for Joe, fixed pancakes for Dollie and Nuse, and prepared bacon, eggs and biscuits for all of us. We also had butter and ribbon cane syrup for anyone who would eat it. I was one of the ones that didn't eat the syrup. Daddy liked to eat cow brains with his eggs. Daddy had bought Mama a gas stove to cook on, and our food tasted good. We had a bench on both sides of the table where we sat. Breakfast was the one meal we shared every day.

Dollie and I would wash the dishes, make the beds, and sweep the floor before we left to walk to school. When we got home from school, Dollie and I would cook supper. I didn't like to do this, but I didn't have a choice. Ruth Evelyn was married. After supper Dollie and I washed the dishes. The two boys did not have any chores to do. That was because they were boys. Daddy always said that it just fell a woman's lot to have to do all the household chores.

In the evenings, I would get my lessons. At times I would go to Treva's house for her dad to help me. The other kids did not always get their lessons. I just could not be responsible for them.

One afternoon when I got home from school, a strange car, and two strange men were in our yard. The men were talking to Daddy. I knew they were not poker players; they were too clean and too dressed up. They were also driving a nice car. It scared me. Daddy had a strange look on his face.

Daddy told me the men wanted to talk to me. "I don't want to talk to them, and I am not going to," I told him. "Yes, you are, now come over here girl." I can tell you, I wasn't going to tell them any family secrets. *Maybe they had come to arrest me for something, like driving a car without a license. Had the city marshal figured out that I was just thirteen?*

Well, I would face them like a man. "What do you want?" I asked them, just as hateful as I could sound. "Young lady, we are from the VA office, and we just need some information from you," one of the men said. "What is a VA office, and what has that got to do with me?" I asked. Sensing that I didn't trust him, he smiled. It didn't make me feel any better though.

"We are from the Veterans' Administration office in Waco. We are here to check on your parents to make a determination if they can continue to receive their VA checks." *What checks? My parents didn't get any checks.* I didn't let on though. He continued, "Is this man your Daddy?" I really didn't want to admit to a stranger that he actually was my Daddy. I looked at Daddy; he shook his head yes. "Wait until my brother gets home from school," I answered, "He looks just like him."

Daddy, now red faced, said, "Damn it, gal, tell this man who I am." "Now just hold on Mr. Coomer," one of the men said, "It appears she is a little afraid of us." "I am not afraid of you or anybody else from the veterans' office," was my reply. He had no way of knowing that my insides were shaking.

"Yes, he is my Daddy," I finally said. "What is his name?" he asked. "Good Lord," I answered, "You just called him Mr. Coomer, didn't you?" The other man smiled, almost to a point of laughing. Seeing that Daddy was really getting mad at me, I finally said, "His name is Buford Franklin Coomer, now what are you going to do with that piece of information?"

The two VA guys asked me a lot of questions, like what was my Mama's name, where did she work, and how much money did she make. I told them her name was Mrs. Coomer. *What else did they expect it to be?* How much money did we spend a week on food; how much did it cost to wash our clothes each week; how many kids were left at home; and what were their names and ages.

One of the men wanted to know how much we spent on personal items and entertainment. I told them we didn't spend a dime on entertainment. There was no entertainment to be had in Lindale except for the show, and we didn't have any money left over at the end of the week for that. This was a lie; we always got to go to the show on Saturday. I had my fingers crossed behind me when I said that; so it really wasn't a lie.

The men finally left, shaking hands with Daddy on their way to getting into their fancy looking car. They actually thanked me, and told me I had done a good job, giving them all the information they needed to make a decision. I had no idea what they were talking about. After they left, Daddy was going to have to answer some questions himself.

"What were those men talking about, what kind of checks have you been getting, and for how long?" I was mad at his answer, but also happy. Daddy confessed that he and Mama had been getting three checks a month from the government every since Franklin had been killed in 1945. They had been Franklin's dependents, and this was the reason for the checks. Franklin had also taken out an insurance policy, and Mama was named on it to receive the money. That is why she got two checks and he only got one.

For ten years, we had been getting these checks. I was stunned. Why had we nearly gone hungry? The answer, of course, was that Daddy had been drinking, playing poker, and spending it on women, instead of his family.

The cat was out of the bag. Daddy was now afraid that they might stop the checks. He had never been checked on before. Later on, we realized that they could not stop their checks. They were entitled to them until they died. The reason for the visit was to find out if Mama and Daddy were still living. We were never checked on again. In a few days, a letter arrived from the VA informing my parents that their monthly allotments were being increased. It must have been because of my good answers; that was my thinking anyway. When the checks arrived the next month, Daddy showed them to us. They were not all that much, but they could help some, if spent in the right manner.

Ronald Wayne and Larry Edward begin to stay at our house almost every night. We didn't have a bed for them, so we made pallets on the floor. Most of the time Dollie or I would sleep in the floor with them, so they wouldn't be scared. We loved to take care of them. Sometimes I would go to their house and baby-sit with them when Ruby Lee and Bo went out. They liked to go dancing and go to the show. She didn't pay me, but she always left milk and Oreo cookies to eat.

On Saturday night a person could go to what was referred to as the "midnight show" in Lindale. It started at ten o'clock; this was a time where guys usually took their dates. I decided one Saturday day that I was old enough to go. I had some money stashed back to buy a ticket, no more sneaking in for me. When I asked Daddy if I could go he said, "Hell no, you know you are not old enough to go to that." The disappointment was awful. He didn't know how bad I wanted to go. I needed to find out what went on there.

After everyone was asleep, I got up, dressed and walked to the show. Almost everyone there were grown-ups. I bought a ticket and went in. The show was good, but I didn't enjoy it much, as I was afraid Daddy was going to come in and get me. When the show was over, I walked home. It was real dark and after midnight. I had to go the back way, since I didn't want anyone driving down the main highway to see me.

On the way home, I was scared. I began to run. Down the back road I saw a figure walking toward me. I could see that it was a man. He had already seen me. *Be brave,* I thought, *he is not going to say a thing to me.* I picked up a rock that was next to the road. The closer I got to him, the harder my heartbeat. Almost instantly he was upon me. The voice said, "Hello Annie Bell, what are you doing out this late?" I recognized the voice as being Tommy Shacklett, and I was relieved. He asked me if I wanted him to walk me on home, but I declined. We both went on our way.

When I got to the house, I realized that I was in a lot of trouble if anyone in the house had awakened while I was gone. As I turned into our street, I could tell there were no lights on, a good sign. However, I wasn't all that assured, as Daddy could be playing a trick on me. No one was awake. I slid into bed with my clothes on. Sleep eluded me the rest of the night. I knew I would never pull that stunt again. The next morning Daddy asked, "Did you enjoy the show last night?" Before I thought, I answered, "Yes sir." *How did he know?* "I went there to check on you, and after seeing that you were okay, I came on back home. I will whip your ass if you do that again." I didn't say a word to him, since I was not about to tell him I was sorry, and I would never even think about doing it a second time.

At school things were going well for me. They were not going all that well for Nuse though. He kept getting into fights with people, usually boys about his age. He could whip anybody and he knew it. One afternoon after school a man came to the house to confront Daddy about Nuse's scuffle with his son. Daddy got really mad, not at Nuse, but at the man and his son. Daddy asked the man how did he know that Nuse caused the fight and not his son. After an argument, the man left. Nuse and Daddy had a talk, and of course, Nuse convinced Daddy that it was the other's boy fault. Maybe it was, I didn't know, but I doubted it. I wasn't going to put my two cents in it, telling Daddy what I had heard about the fight at school.

Nuse hitched a ride to Hawkins, Texas, for one of our high school football games one Friday night. As usual, he got into it with some guys there. They were older than he was. Our football team was the Lindale Eagles. They were called the Hawkins Hawks. Nuse told them that an eagle could do anything better than an old hawk. These fellows brought him back to Lindale and tied him to a tree after they had removed his clothes. He managed to untie himself and walked to the house, going the back roads so not to be seen. He had a knack for shooting off his mouth and losing his clothes in the process.

I had thought I would not like my English teacher, Mrs. Woods. But as it turned out, I liked her just fine. We were doing our lesson for the day in class. One guy had to fill in the blanks of this sentence: *Sam went to the carnival and got sick, riding all the rides, and he didn't (never or ever) go there again.* The student stated the correct answer was, "ever." Mrs. Woods, pleased that he had answered it correctly, asked him why he had used ever. His answer was, "Because you don't never use a double negative." Mrs. Woods rolled her eyes around in her head. I began to laugh. Mrs. Woods and I were the only ones to realize that in his answer to her question, he had used a double negative. Who says English can't be fun?

Robert Lee was still writing us the most pitiful letters, telling us how unhappy he was. He wanted out of the Navy so that he could come home to his family. Even though the letters were sad, I still was glad when they arrived. I read them over and over. We all missed him, especially Mama. Daddy even wanted him to come home. Mama and Daddy were afraid he might get killed while in the service.

Daddy got up about 4 o'clock each morning to listen to the radio station for news and weather information. His favorite station was KTBB. At six o'clock a program called "Wake Up and Live" came on. Robert Lee wrote to us and told us to be sure to listen in on a certain Friday morning, as there might be a surprise for us. At the appointed time we were all up, circled around the radio. The surprise was that he was having a song dedicated to his family in Lindale.

The song was sung by Jimmie Davis; he was the governor of Louisiana. The name of it was "Come on Home Son, It's Supper Time." There was not a dry eye in the room when the song ended. Daddy got up and walked outside to smoke. I suspected he went out there to have a good cry. Every few weeks Robert Lee would have a song dedicated to us. It was his way of our not forgetting him. Fat chance of that happening!

In December, Daddy opened the firecracker stand in Mineola. We helped out on the weekends and some nights. I enjoyed working there and meeting all types of people. Daddy installed a stove for us inside the firecracker stand that was powered by butane. It was a wonder that we didn't get blown to kingdom come.

It was the first week in December. A couple at Garden Valley, a small community to the west of Lindale, had a huge Christmas tree. Rich people donated presents to them. The schools in the surrounding communities could pick a boy and girl from each grade to take there on the school bus to get a present. It was usually the poorest kid in each class.

Dollie was in the sixth grade. This year they picked her. I was embarrassed to death for her. I was glad that I was in different building from her, so the kids in my class could not see her board the school bus. She was glad to be getting a present, but I was mad at her principal. To think that we were the poorest people in town! I just felt awful about it.

One of the kids in Dollie's six-grade class had a Christmas party at his house. His mother let him invite all the kids in his class except Dollie. His mother was supposed to be very religious, and she just didn't want a drunk's daughter to be at the party. The night of the party, I made it a point to stay with her. We popped popcorn, rolled each other's hair, and went down to visit Treva. I slept real close to her in the bed that night, with my arms around her. I could fuss with her, but I sure didn't want anyone else to hurt her in any way. She was hurting now.

The next Monday at school, some of the kids told her that their mothers had said that if they had known about her not being invited, their kids would not have gone to the party either. Some of the mothers actually called the boy's mother and let her know what they thought of her actions. One of them told her that she needed to get down on her knees and pray for forgiveness.

I knew if Daddy found out about it, he would not call her, her would go see her. There would be hell to pay. He never found out about the party. She must have asked God to forgive her, since she sent a note to school in which she asked for Dollie's forgiveness too. Now Dollie was not God, and she did not answer the woman's note. The hurt stayed with her a long time.

The week after the party, we came home as usual from school. Daddy had a really big surprise for us. He wouldn't let us go into the house until Mama got home. He wanted us to guess what he had inside for us. I knew it would be a dog or a cat. Mama finally got there. We all had to shut our eyes as we went through the door. The biggest shock of my life was in our living room. A television set was sitting in the corner!

We all started jumping around, clapping our hands. Mama was really in shock. "Where did you buy that?" she said, and "Where did you get the money, from a poker game?" "No," Daddy said. He explained that Robert Lee had sent the money to the owner of the local furniture store, and he had delivered it to us. It was a Christmas present from his son. Daddy was really proud. We didn't have any shoes to wear, but we had a television set.

Daddy sat us down, explaining to us that we could not go to the show on Saturday morning any more, or any place else for that matter. The television set would use a lot of electricity, and he would have to use our show money to pay for it. I saw right away the television was going to be a mixed blessing. That very night Daddy let us go to a ball game, he said, for the last time.

The next day at school when I reported the good news about the television, no one believed me. One boy said to me, "Annie Bell, you are the biggest liar in school. You know you do not have a television at home." Several of the kids went home with me after school so that they could see if I were lying or not. I really had something to brag about now, as there were very few families in Lindale at that time that had a television set. Well, very few families had a good son in the U. S. Navy either, something else I bragged about often.

Robert Lee still sent us individual presents. Dollie's and my present was a record player and some records. That present was better to me than the television. When school started back in January, I reported this to the kids. No one doubted me now. If we had all of this before Christmas, Dollie would not have been picked to get a Christmas present from that couple in Garden Valley. I made a promise to myself to see that she was never picked again. It bothered me as much as it did her. No one in my class ever found out that she had been picked, and I was glad about that.

Daddy had bought a washing machine and all the tubs that went with it. He put it in the back yard. We no longer went to the washateria. Mama cooked starch on the stove. On Saturday mornings we had to do the wash outside in the cold weather and starch our school clothes. We would then hang them on the clothesline. After the clothes dried, we would sprinkle them with water and rolled them into a ball. We had fixed up a coke bottle that had a cork with holes in it screwed into the top of it. That is what we used to sprinkle the water on the clothes.

In the afternoon, Dollie and I had to do the ironing. We now had an electric iron instead of one that was run on gasoline. That gasoline iron had to be pumped with air just like the Coleman stove and lantern. I was glad to get rid of it. As we ironed, we watched the television set. That made ironing a lot easier, but I sure did miss going to the show on Saturday afternoon. Daddy soon realized that the television set was not going to use as much electricity as he had anticipated, and he announced one day that we could start going to the show on Saturday again if we got our ironing done in time. Dollie and I got up earlier on Saturday, and, with Mama's help, we got our work done in time for the movie. Life was pretty good!

Uncle Earnest had moved his family to Lindale. They were living in a house with a man who had never married. It was in the country, on a hill, and was a pretty nice place. That guy also had a television. We could only get one channel on our television, which came in from Tyler, but the television at Uncle Earnest's house could pick up a station from Ft. Worth. On Tuesday nights, we would ride out to his house and watch "Tuesday Night Wrestling."

Everyone except me believed that the wrestling was real, but I enjoyed it anyway. We also got to see our cousins. We went there early enough so we could play outside until the wrestling came on. Sometimes I would get sleepy and would lie down on the pallet Aunt Kate made for us. The cover always smelled of pee.

Daddy was still drinking and playing poker and spending our VA money. One day he announced that we were broke, and he didn't have enough money to buy us any food to eat. We all went to bed hungry. Daddy went to see the man who owned Neeley's Grocery Store in Lindale. He made a deal with him to buy groceries on the credit until we could pick blackberries in the summer and pay him back. After that, any of us could just go in and get food, and they would just put it on our bill.

One afternoon I went by there on my way home from school. There was no one in the store. I got the groceries I needed; including hamburger meat, already weighed and wrapped up. When I got home, I made a list of what I had gotten and the cost of each item. The next afternoon I stopped by the store and told Mr. Neeley what I had done. He simply wrote the total amount down on our bill. We were never really hungry after that. Daddy got the same deal for Uncle Earnest and his family.

That winter we visited our Sikes cousins a few times, and they came to Lindale to see us. We were always glad to see each other.

I was the captain of our basketball team, and I loved the game. The P. E. teacher decided that we would play the seventh grade girls one afternoon after school. I was really excited about this. My excitement turned to disappointment. We lost! Since I was the leader of the team, I felt like it was my fault. I went home and cried all afternoon. When Mama got home, she hugged me and told me that everything would be okay. She explained to me that I could not have won the game by myself. The reason I felt so bad about it was the fact that they were younger than we were. The next week this same seventh grade team beat the high school girls. I felt better after that.

In April, all of the eighth grade students were going to State Park for a party. I began to save my lunch money instead of eating lunch. I wanted to be able to go like everyone else. I kept my money hidden in a sack in my desk at school.

One morning when I got to school, my money was missing. I was sick and mad. The teacher had everyone look for it. Mrs. Woods gave everyone a lecture about stealing. The principal came in and stated that if the money were not found by the next morning, no one was going to State Park. I didn't want that to happen, as everyone would blame me for our not getting to go. I did not sleep at all that night. The next day, the sack with my money intact was back in my desk. The party was back on. No one ever confessed to taking the money, but I didn't care. I was happy it had made its way back into my possession.

On the Friday we were to go to the party, several girls came to my house after school to get ready. Mama was at home, but Daddy wasn't. We were walking back toward the schoolhouse to catch the bus to go to State Park when I saw Daddy driving toward us in his truck. He pulled over and handed me fifty cents to spend at the party. He told me not to leave the schoolhouse, as it looked like a bad cloud was coming, and he might have to come after me if a storm came up. I told him that we were going to State Park and were not going to stay at school.

Right there, with all those girls listening, he told me that I was not going to State Park. He stated that the park was too dangerous for kids my age and something bad would happen to me out there. I told him I would be okay; that several teachers were going, and all the kids in my class were too, including Nuse. "No," he said, get in the truck, you are going back home with me." I could not believe it! All the work I had done and plans I had made to go to the party. He told me that it was okay for Nuse to go because he was a boy. Nothing would happen to him.

When we drove up in the yard, I was crying silently. Mama came out to console me. Daddy gave her a good cussing for giving me permission to go to that damn party. He told her, "You know that nobody but wild girls go out there, to dance and fool around with the boys. Well, no girl of mine will go out there."

I went into the house, and cried until I could cry no more. Daddy sat down outside on an old couch we had beside the house. I had a sack of candy that I had bought to take with me to the party to give to the other kids. I went outside and sat down beside him, and offered him some of it. I gave the fifty cents back to him. He tried to explain to me why he just couldn't let me go. I told him it was okay, that I was all right. I lied. I felt like he had my best interest at heart and I would forgive him. It would take me a long time to forget though.

I didn't rest all the weekend; I cried most of it. I felt as if I were the only person in the entire eighth grade that didn't go to the park. I knew my girl friends were embarrassed for me, and no one ever mentioned about my not getting to go to the park. For some reason, I will always believe that Daddy realized he had done the wrong thing, but just couldn't back out of his decision.

Ruby Lee and Bo had already built them a new house, bigger than the one they had rented us. It was rented to someone else now. Bo had sold his filling station and had gone to work learning to lay brick. It would prove to be a very wise job move for him.

When it was time for us to pick strawberries in Winnsboro, Daddy made a decision that we would drive the thirty-six miles each morning, pick strawberries until about eleven o'clock, and then drive back home. That way we could go to school in the afternoon. I liked this idea. We would come straight from the strawberry patch, and Daddy would put us out at the schoolhouse. We didn't have a chance to go home and clean up.

One morning Richard Earnest, my cousin who was my age, rode in the back of the truck with us. He was a strong, healthy boy, a lot bigger than I was. We all were lying on pallets, trying to catch a few minutes of sleep before we got to the strawberry patch. Richard was beside me, at my backside. All of sudden, for some reason, he pulled me up against him, reaching around me and putting his hands on my breasts. I almost stopped breathing. *What was he doing?* I pulled away from him, and didn't say a word. I didn't want to

182/Baldwin/Meager Beginnings

disturb the rest of the kids. They would tell on him, and his Daddy would give him a beating, and I might get one also.

I was embarrassed to look at Richard when we got to the field and got out of the truck. He didn't say a word, never apologized. I guess he just did that deed on the spur of the moment; maybe he couldn't help himself. I never told anybody about the incident. Later, I thought about what I would have done if Richard had been my other cousin, Orville. *Would I have pulled away from him?* I probably would not have.

The last week of school, we all took our final tests. As it turned out, the Citizenship class turned out to be a class that I really liked. My average was 100 for the year. A boy named George sat in front of me. The Monday of the last week, George reached back and grabbed my legs with his hands. I jumped up and hit him in the back of the head, almost knocking him out of his chair.

The teacher looked up and said, "Annie Bell, don't pick on poor little old George. Everybody is always picking on poor little old George." I sat down and didn't answer. *I'd do more than pick on him if he touched me again!* Poor little old George never again looked like he even wanted to be around me, much less touch me.

In Math, the teacher let me grade the final papers. I thought this was only right for him to do, since I had finished a problem he was working on the board one day when he had gotten called out of the room. I had walked right up to that board, took the chalk in my hand and found the right solution. He was giving the papers back to us on the last day of school, when he realized that Nuse, Helen Carter, a good friend of mine, and I had all made ninety-nine. The teacher was about to question me about it when the bell rang. "Saved by the bell I said," and ran out the door taking my paper from his hands on the way out.

Blackberry season was in full swing. Each day Daddy stopped at the icehouse in town to get the amount of ice he thought we would need for the day. Later in the morning, he would go back to town and pay for it. The owner had given him a key to the place. One morning about 4:30 a.m., on our way to the berry patch, Daddy approached the four way stop sign in the middle of town. As usual he didn't stop, even though he saw the highway patrol car parked there.

When we pulled up to the icehouse, the highway patrolman pulled up too. Daddy just ignored him and started into the icehouse to get the morning ice. The highway patrolman asked him what he was doing. "Hell man, what does it look like I am doing, I'm getting ice to take to the berry patch." "How do you plan to pay for it?" The lawman asked. Daddy explained the plan, and it seemed to satisfy the fellow.

"We need to discuss your running the stop sign back there," The highway patrolman said. "I run it every morning, been doing it for twenty years, and I'll be running it for the next twenty. What's the problem?" Daddy asked. "What if another car is coming close to the sign?" The man replied. "There ain't no cars coming through this town this time of the morning but mine." Daddy was getting mad now. And so was the highway patrolman.

"Besides," Daddy said, "It sure as hell ain't no business of yours. You don't have any business being up here, this is Lindale; you are supposed to be patrolling outside the city limits." "Now look here sir, I patrol all the highways," he told Daddy. "This ain't no highway, it's a town street," Daddy reminded him. "Don't you know the difference?"

By now we were all out of the truck. Mad as Daddy was, we all knew to keep our mouths shut. I sure didn't want to. *Daddy did have a point; this man did not have any business here.* "I could arrest you," the highway patrolman told Daddy. "If you think you need to, let me take these kids to the field, and get my crew started. Then I will come to town, and we will discuss it," Daddy assured him. I knew he was not coming back to town, just to get arrested. If this man wanted to arrest him, he had better do it now.

About that time the city marshal drove up. He was a good friend of Daddy's. He asked the highway patrolman if there were a problem. The man explained to the Lindale law about Daddy running the stop sign. He also said that he thought he was going to steal something from the icehouse. After the city marshal explained the situation, the highway patrolman, reluctantly, let us go on to the field. The next morning Daddy didn't slow down when he got to the stop sign. We never saw another highway patrolman there at that time of the day again. I guess Daddy had straightened him out about the difference between a highway and a town street.

184/Baldwin/Meager Beginnings

That week, a wife of one of Daddy's berry pickers had a baby in the hospital at Mineola. When the husband went to bring his wife and baby home, the hospital administrator told him that he could not have the baby unless he paid for it. He said to them, "That's okay, you can keep him, I know how to get another one." They let him take the baby home. Listening to Daddy telling this, and hearing the folks laugh, I really could not quite figure it out. I didn't know a person had to pay for babies. I knew that there was something about this having babies that I was not aware of. *Maybe I would figure it out when I got married.*

When we started picking blackberries, Daddy began to pay off our grocery bill at Neeley's store. By the end of the season, we had a zero balance. Uncle Earnest had moved his family back to Daingerfield, and he had not paid off his debt. We paid it for him. Daddy was a man of his word, even if it were his brother's word.

One day while I was in the grocery store, I noticed an old black man looking at the labels on the canned goods. It was obvious he was trying to figure out the printing on the cans. I asked him if I could help him. He seemed embarrassed but said, "Yes, young lady, if you don't mind. You see, I can't read, and I am trying to find a can of hominy." "Why can't you read?" I asked him. "Well, I am an old colored man, and the white folks would not let me go to school when I was young. It is hard not knowing how to read, but I do the best that I can." Tears came to my eyes. I understood about not being able to go to school. I told him that I would help him find anything he needed. He and I became sort of pals, and I helped him with his grocery shopping several times after that.

One evening we were all at home listening to country music on the radio, straight from Nashville, Tennessee. I was clapping my hands and moving my feet. I was afraid to move them too much. Daddy would surely not like it. To my surprise, he got up, grabbed Mama around the waist, and they started dancing. I could not believe my eyes. My parents doing something as sinful as that! It was embarrassing. It was wonderful!

The dance they were doing could not have had a name to it. They took mostly in one spot, their bodies hardly moving, but their feet were flying, up and down. Their feet landed on the floor so hard, they made a lot of noise. Mama was laughing, not embarrassed a bit. I felt warm and happy for her. That night I slept like a baby.

Seventeen

Before the blackberry season ended, a medicine show came to town. I decided to forego the evening television shows, and I walked to town to find out what this was all about. They were selling the latest medicine that could cure anything for just $1.00 a bottle. I felt it would work too, since they had a lot of folks whom I didn't know testifying what that stuff had done for them. One lady said that it had cured her addiction to Dr. Pepper, after drinking just one bottle of it. I didn't have a dollar, and since I was pretty healthy, I felt I really didn't need any of it. I just didn't want to drink anything that would make me no longer want to drink Dr. Pepper. That was the best drink in the whole world.

The show was going to be in town for a week. The first night of the show, the owner announced that a queen would be crowned at the end of the week. The girl who turned in the most empty snow cone cups would be the winner. Now, I didn't realize that this was just a scheme to sell snow cones, and I didn't care. I wanted to be that queen. Daddy would be so proud of me.

I enlisted the help of my brothers and sister. We begged, borrowed and stole more empty snow cone cups than anyone else, and I was crowned "Queen of the Medicine Show." My prize was a beautiful necklace, bracelet and earbob set. I would only have to wait about ten more years to be old enough to wear it.

After I won it, I got to thinking that maybe Daddy would not let me keep something that was for a grown-up girl. I decided to hide it in a dresser drawer. Twice a day I would look at it, just to make sure no one, especially Dollie, had stolen it. About two weeks after the medicine show left town, that expensive jewelry turned green in its box. I didn't really care. It had become a liability, having to keep it from Daddy and checking on it so often. I threw it away.

The good thing about my winning the jewelry was the realization that, if we worked together, we could do a lot of things that we couldn't do by ourselves. We had worked so hard for me to win. Now I had a better attitude toward Dollie, Nuse, and Joe. They had made me "Queen for the Day." What a group!

Flies were plentiful that year. So were cockroaches. Daddy explained that the cockroaches flew in from West Texas. They could eat a loaf of bread in a day's time. We learned to put food away from them. The flies were a different problem. Mama bought flypaper from the grocery store. We put the paper on the table. When the flies walked on it, they would get stuck. We had them then. Another way to handle the fly problem was to run them out of the house with towels. We had to open up the doors and all the windows that did not have any screens to do any good at this.

We also used a spray gun with fly spray in it (usually DDT) to rid the house of these pests. Oftentimes, while we were eating, a fly would buzz over the table. Daddy would get up; get the spray gun and spray. Sometimes he actually killed the fly, but more than likely he just sprayed all his kids.

Time came for us to go to South Texas. Daddy decided to leave all our furniture, including the television set, in the house until we got back in the fall. We loaded all our camping stuff into the truck. Daddy put up a full size bed close to the cab so that we could sleep on it on our way south.

We got into a big poker game in the back of the truck. Not having any money was not a problem. There were several boxes of matches packed away in one of the apple crates. We used them as a substitute for money. Sometimes I would have a big pile of pretend money in front of me, and at other times, I would be almost broke. It was the same with the other three kids.

This was the only time that I could remember actually having fun while riding in the back of the truck with just my siblings. After the game ended, we carefully put all the matches back in the boxes. We re-hid Daddy's cards in the same place that he had hidden them from us. He didn't have to know anything about our gambling. After that day, poker playing became a normal thing for us to do while traveling.

I was anxious to see Charles Roy. We stopped in Sinton for one day. We didn't get a chance to kiss at all. The next morning we went on to the Valley. We picked cotton there for about two weeks while waiting for the cotton to open up back at Sinton. Every day I was anxious to get back to Sinton.

Aunt Ellen fixed lunch for us each day, just as she had done in the past. We slept in their yard at night on our cots. I lay awake at night wondering what it would be like to be inside the house on a nice bed. Uncle Harley was nice to us, and sometimes his wife would cook supper for us. I was always ill at ease around the Valley cousins. It just seemed to me that they might be a little better than we were. They didn't have to work in the field. I didn't realize it at the time, but Aunt Ellen's girls worked in the dairy. A lot of my thinking that they didn't like us was just that, in my mind. They may have been just as ill at ease around us.

When we got back to Sinton, Daddy and Mr. Huey decided to be partners. Both of them hired hands and delivered the cotton to the gin in the afternoon. That summer Daddy hired a couple of "hobos" to work with us. One of them, we called Happy Henson, and the other one was known as Turkey. Both of these guys formed a bond with us. Daddy trusted them and would let us go any place with them. We walked a lot of miles together, since I don't think either one of them could drive. Happy came from somewhere in Louisiana, but we never did find out where Turkey came from.

One day Turkey and I went into a café to eat dinner. We were looking at the price of the Chicken Fried Steak on the menu. Turkey asked the waitress how much the gravy cost. "The gravy is free," she answered. "How much is the bread?" was his next question. "The bread is free too," she answered. "Give me some gravy and bread and a glass of water," Turkey said to her. I wanted to laugh, but I was scared to. I didn't know if the waitress would think that was so funny. She did. Several patrons, who were listening, laughed also. I began to laugh too. We only had enough money for a hamburger and a coke. Eating Chicken Fried Steaks was just a dream that all cotton pickers had, never a reality.

Happy was also funny. He, like Turkey, told us a lot of stuff about his past. We had no idea if any of it were true. We didn't care. It was funny stuff. Two of his tales concerned his days when he was attending grade school. Below are the stories.

If a student needed to go use the outdoor toilet, he/she raised their hand and the teacher would shake her head yes. One afternoon after lunch, one of the girls raised her hand, but the teacher shook her head no. After raising her hand a few more times and getting the same no, this girl got us, pulled up her dress and panties down and used the bathroom in the floor. What she did was not known as #1 either.

One of his male teachers, who was poor, could only bring biscuits and syrup for lunch each day. There was a girl in the class who was from a well-to-do family and brought a good lunch each day. One day when the students were at recess, the teacher ate the girl's lunch and hid her lunch sack. When the students came back to class, everyone looked for the girl's lunch. The teacher even helped look. Her lunch sack was found before the day was over, but it was empty. The teacher gave a good lecture to the class about eating a lunch that didn't belong to you.

Happy and Turkey helped Daddy a lot too, taking care of things. As soon as we started loading up our stuff to move to another town to find new cotton, they would help us. When we got to the next town, they would help us unload. These two guys helped carry our cotton sacks to the trailer and helped empty them. They knew Daddy worked us too hard, but they liked him anyway. Just like me, they didn't like him, but yet they did.

In one of the towns, one Sunday morning, Daddy, Happy and I went to a farmer's house to ask him about his cotton. I was barefooted, hair a mess, and, of course, my blue jeans and shirt were wrinkled. I probably had slept in them the night before. Daddy knocked on the door. A beautiful, blue eyed, blonde haired girl opened it. I could tell that she was about my age. She was dressed in a really pretty dress with ruffles on it. Her hair was cleaned and combed. She apparently was ready to go to church.

I stood back behind Daddy and Happy. The farmer came to the door and asked us to come in. Daddy told him no, that we couldn't do that; he wanted to talk to him about pulling his cotton. As they talked, the girl stood next to her dad, looking at me. I was staring at her. I was ashamed of the way I looked and tried to rearrange my feet so that she could not see that I was barefooted. She was fair skinned, almost sickly looking. I felt sick to my stomach. Oh to look like her!

She finally came over to me and asked, "Why is your skin so dark?" I wanted to start crying, but I would never do that. I wanted to ask why her skin was so white. "From the sun," I finally answered. Jealousy was building up inside me. "Kids make fun of me because of my white skin," She said. "I wish I had yours." I couldn't believe what she had just said. *Why would anyone want to have anything I had?* I didn't know what to do or say to her. I didn't say another word.

After what seemed like a week, Daddy shook hands with the farmer, telling him we would be in his fields by daylight the next morning. Still looking at the farmer's daughter, I climbed into the truck in the middle, between Daddy and Happy. As we were driving off, I saw her wave. I hoped that I would see her someday while we were pulling her Daddy's cotton, but I never did see her again.

At night I would think about her and how she had looked, beautiful, but sad. I wondered what she had thought about me. One thing for sure, she could not have thought that I was beautiful. She probably thought about how dirty and unkempt looking I was. It was weeks before I got her off my mind. Whenever I had a few minutes to myself to think, it was her face that I saw. For some reason, a part of me felt sorry for her with that skin so white, the way I pictured angels.

We had seen Ruth Evelyn and Billy Ray for a day or so when we were at Sinton. They had come down on a weekend. We also played at the park in Sinton and got to see Daddy's sisters and my favorite boy cousin. He never attempted to kiss me again. It didn't bother me much; I still had Charles Roy, and Orville was still my cousin, you know.

While pulling cotton at Sinton one morning, I was in the cotton trailer emptying my cotton sack. Mr. Huey got into the trailer with me. I didn't think anything about it, as he often got in it to throw green boles and leaves out of the trailer. However, today he came over close to me. In an instant he grabbed me, knocking me down into the cotton. The burrs hurt, cutting at my legs, arms, and hands. He put his hand down the front of me, between my legs and said, "I want to feel right there." I almost screamed, but decided not to. Mr. Huey was a small man, and I kicked him hard, knocking him over backwards. Let him see how the burrs felt!

We heard someone coming up the ladder to empty his cotton sack. It was Turkey. Mr. Huey was already exiting out the other side by the time Turkey got to the top of the ladder. "What happened to you?" Turkey asked. "Nothing, I just fell down," was my reply. "Well, let me help you up," Said the voice from the top of the ladder. "Thanks, but I am all right," I answered back.

When I climbed out of the trailer, Mr. Huey was talking to Daddy. *What was he saying to him? Was he telling him a lie about what happened in the trailer, trying to pin the assault on me?* My arms were bleeding. Mama came up and asked, "What happened to make your arms bleed?" I told her the same lie as Turkey, "Nothing, I just fell down in the trailer." I could tell Mr. Huey was relieved. He had saved my life once, remember.

I got a drink of water and went back in the field to go back to work. I never told anyone what he had done. It would have been the end of Daddy's friendship with him, and they would have taken Charles Roy and moved on. It would be for the best if no one knew but me. For the rest of his life, I hardly looked at Mr. Huey, and he never mentioned the incident to me.

The kids at night were playing our games. One night a boy that we called "Bootlegger" was playing Spin the Bottle with us. He spun the bottle, and it landed on me. "I want to kiss you," he said. "No, you can't," I answered. "Oh, yes I can," he said, as he grabbed me and laid the kiss on my lips. Charles Roy was watching, and I pretended that I had not enjoyed the kiss. But, to tell the truth, I did. Charles Roy, unhappy about the matter, kissed another girl when it came his turn.

I went to bed and cried. I didn't understand my body. *Why did I enjoy Bootlegger's kiss when I was in love with Charles Roy? Why was I mad because Charles Roy had kissed another girl?* The next day in the field neither one of us spoke to each other. The girl that he kissed was now telling everyone that she was Charles Roy's girlfriend. I never played the games with the kids again that summer. I didn't want to take a chance of kissing Bootlegger again, as I knew that I might like it more than I had the last time.

Later in the summer, Charles Roy and I did begin our kissing again. This time things were different. He began to put his hands inside my blouse, touching my slowly developing breasts. At first I was hesitant to let him, but began to enjoy the way it made me feel.

I knew too that if I didn't let him, the other girl might. *I didn't want to lose him, now did I?*

I had begun to have doubts about the stork story, although I had not figured out who brought the baby to the house. Maybe the local doctor or the local grocer brought it. Any guess was as good as mine. I sure was not going to ask anyone about it. One Sunday, we were parked under an overpass near a river. Joe found something in the pocket of Daddy's old truck. He showed them to Dollie and me. We did not have any idea what they could be.

Joe said he knew what they were. He was ten years old. He explained about the birds and the bees, saying that these rubber things kept new birds from being born. The explanation of how this took place took my breath away. Nuse was the one who had told him all about it. I didn't believe it. *How could the two of them come up with such a thing?* I told Joe that he had better not mention this again to anyone. We threw the rubber things away. *What did Daddy need with them?* He hadn't had a new bird born in ten years.

As it turned out, the rubber things didn't belong to Daddy. He was secretly keeping them for another younger man who didn't want his wife to know he had them. We did not confess to know anything about what had been in that truck pocket. I thought some on what Joe had told us, but I just didn't want it to be true. A baby needed to come in through the window or the front door, just like I had always believed.

Daddy and Mr. Huey had amassed a big crew, fifteen families. The crew could pull fifteen bales of cotton a day. When they hit the fields and started to work, it looked like a herd of sheep had gone through the fields, eating up the crops. In one town that summer Daddy rented a big old house. It had fifteen rooms in it. He did not tell the man that fifteen families were going to move into it. Daddy assigned each family a room. We had to camp out in the yard, as there was not a room for us.

When the man who owned the home found out about all the people, he went to the local sheriff to have us evicted. The sheriff told him that he could do nothing about it. The house was in town, and we became the talk of the county. People would drive their cars around the place just to gawk at us. They yelled at us, telling us to get out of town, that we were not welcome here. To Daddy's credit, he saw to it that the folks kept their rooms clean, and no damage was done to the house. After two weeks, we all pulled out, moving to another town to work. The owner of the house had aged ten years.

It was in this town that a Mexican girl about fifteen years old was walking down the street when a big storm came up. She was running, trying to get inside a building when lightning struck the earrings that she had on and killed her. I remember thinking that would not ever happen to me, as no self-respecting white girl would wear earrings in the first place. Who was I kidding? I didn't wear them because I didn't have any.

Another hobo came into our lives. His name was Slim Robinson. He had been in prison and was on parole. Slim was smart and talented. He had learned a lot in the penitentiary. He could make paper flowers that he let us sell from house to house. He let us keep all the money. I became good at this. He could draw and paint and make lamps and tables out of matchsticks. It was unbelievable all the things he could do. Slim was a good addition to our little group. He was kind to us; just as the two other hobos were. They all became good friends.

That year when we got back to Hearne, Texas, Bo, Ruby Lee and the boys came to visit us. The joy of seeing those four people was indescribable. They were going to stay for a week and pull a few boles. On the weekend we all went into town. Bo took Ruby Lee, the boys and me into a drug store. He bought me my first banana split. That thing was as good as a Coke float. I knew I was going to be buying me these splits from now on.

Daddy was drinking as usual, but he was in a buying mood. He bought two bedspreads for our beds back in Lindale. They had big peacocks on them. He bought us some clothes and a lot of groceries. He was going to feed the Paul family good while they were visiting. The stuff was put into Bo's car, in the back seat.

All the kids, including Ronald Wayne and Larry Edward, went to the show. There was a carnival in town, and we all got to go to it. If it had not been for Daddy being drunk the day would have been wonderful. I tried not to dwell on it though, since I was so happy that my sister was visiting with her husband and her kids.

About eight o'clock that night, we began to get into the cars to go home. The stuff that Daddy had bought was gone from Bo's car. He had not locked it up, never had locked up a car. Bo went and got the law to investigate.

When the investigation was over, it was proven that Daddy had not put any of the stuff in Bo's car but into a car that was similar to his. All the money we had made that week was thrown away. I was very sad, since I really wanted to put the bedspreads on our beds back home. Bo went to the grocery store and bought us a bunch of groceries. In a day or two, they went back to Lindale. Bo went back to work laying brick.

One morning I woke up feeling really bad. I told Daddy that I couldn't go to the field that day because I was sick. He promptly gave me a dose of Black Draught. Daddy thought this could cure anything. It was a laxative and tasted awful. It came in liquid and powder forms. Both of them made me throw up when I tried to swallow the medicine, but the powder form was the worse. Daddy always kept it handy. His kids didn't get sick too often. We had better sense than that, since we didn't want to take the Black Draught.

Today I felt so bad that I didn't care if he made me take the bad stuff. I didn't feel well enough to go to the field and pull cotton. Daddy was not happy about my being sick. He got the box of Black Draught, and stuck a spoonful of it down my throat. I threw it right back up. He shoved another spoonful down me. "You ready to go to work now?" He asked. "Yes sir," was my reply. "Okay, that's better, now go get in the truck and stop that damn bitching. Getting just like your Mama!"

The laxative began to work its magic. I had to go to the woods several times that day. When anyone in the field had to go, they would take a big handful of picked cotton and go to the woods and do their job. Everyone knew whenever anyone went. I was really embarrassed that day. However, by the time we were through working, I felt a lot better. Good enough to smooch that night. Maybe Daddy wasn't so bad of a doctor after all.

Working in the fields was still hard on me. I would sleep on our cotton sacks in the back of the truck on our way to the field each morning. I dreaded going to work each day. As always, the cotton patch was my enemy. Some fields were really big. It seemed you could see cotton for miles and miles.

Daddy always went to town by ten o'clock to buy the pressed ham for lunch. We drank water from the same dipper as all the other hands. I took to holding the dipper away from me, letting the water fall into my mouth, but not touching the sides of the dipper. Several of the workers dipped snuff, smoked, and most of them never bathed. I didn't want to come down with some kind of disease and die young.

Several families from Lindale were now traveling with us. The Warrens, Browns and Wards, to name a few. All of them had children for us to play with in the afternoons, after we all had eaten our supper. These three families were pretty clean, finding ways to take baths, even though we might be in a place that didn't have running water. Some of the places we stayed at had wells. Make shift baths were put up with #3 washtubs, and water would be pulled from the wells to put in the tubs.

Most of the time the water would be cold unless it was warmed on the Coleman stove. I had gotten used to bathing every night back in Lindale, and I sure missed that old tub at home. I hated taking baths out in the open, so to speak. I was always afraid some boy would be looking at me, and I am sure they did.

About two weeks before school was to start in September, Daddy made an unexpected announcement. He had decided we were going to go home so that his kids could start to school. I was so happy I started to cry. "Well gal, ain't you glad? You have bugged me enough about it," Daddy asked. I did something unexpected too. I ran over to him and hugged his neck. He sort of hugged me back, but I could tell he was embarrassed.

When we left the hobos, Daddy told them to come to Lindale during the blackberry-picking season. They would make some money and could ride back to South Texas with us for the cotton picking. I told them good-bye and hugged them too. I sure hoped that they would come to Lindale. I figured we would never see them again.

I wondered if our television would still be in our house when we got home. I was happy. We were going home. I had to tell Charles Roy good-bye; with my happiness always came some of the opposite. When we got back to Lindale, our television was still in the house, as was all the rest of our old furniture. I jumped out of the car and ran to Treva's house. She was happy to see me.

We got home in time for me to join the pep squad. I don't know how Mama got the money to buy me the uniform I had to wear. The kids at school were in shock that the Coomer kids were starting to school on the first day. Nuse didn't start however. He was sixteen, and Daddy felt as if he had gone to school long enough. He went to work with Bo learning to be a bricklayer. By now Nuse was smoking and buying his own cigarettes. Mama went back to the rose nursery to work. She had been promoted to a line foreman, and she loved going to work.

My friend, Mary Shacklett, was not going to be in school either. She had gotten married. This was a fact that hit me like a ton of bricks. *Why would she do something like that? Would I ever see her again?* One thing for sure, I was really going to miss her in school.

Being in the ninth grade brought changes for the students. We would have to take at least four subjects besides band. We could take five courses if we wanted to. Each course was worth one credit. We would have to have sixteen credits to graduate. I decided right quick that four courses each year was all I needed. If a student took four courses, he/she would have two study halls each day to get his lessons. If he/she took five subjects, he/she would have only one study hall. If a student was enrolled in band, then he/she could only take four regular courses, leaving him/her one study hall each day.

I decided to take the required subjects: General Math, English 1, and General Science. Homemaking was my elective. Taking Homemaking really didn't appeal to me, but it fit into my schedule for the other classes. Something wonderful was going to be going on too. Mr. Land was my Math teacher. I had not seen much of him last year, but I would see him every day this year. What a reason to go school! I was elected as an alternate to the Student Council.

One sad thing about going to school that year was the fact they had dropped high school P. E. for girls. My favorite subject would be lost to me forever. P. E. for boys was still in though. It was unfair, but I could do nothing about it. I didn't make the rules, and I was so glad to get to come back and to start school that I wasn't about to make any trouble.

Ruby Lee had gotten a job in a factory in Tyler working on an assembly line. She was so fast with her hands that they had to put two people on each side of her to keep the line flowing properly. She and Bo were doing quite well with their lives, saving up a lot of money, just like they had been doing since the very first day they had gotten married. I was very proud of these two people.

Ronald Wayne was now in first grade. He had seen a lot of country in his young life. His being old enough to go to school was a shock to me. I guess I wanted to keep him a baby. He would spend the night at our house, and walk to school with us a lot of times.

Life was great. Daddy was still drinking and being mean to us, but it seemed it wasn't as often as it used to be. He would go to the post office each day to get the mail. He started our account back at Neeley's Grocery Store, and he bought groceries for us to cook each night. Daddy also decided to sell fruit again and rented a place in town. When we walked home in the afternoons, he would give us fruit, just as he had done in the past.

The pep squad was a yell group for the football team. We had four cheerleaders, one from each grade. In addition we had a head cheerleader who was a senior. They were the leaders of the pep squad. We practiced in the afternoons after school. On Friday nights, we would march out onto the field, going to the bleachers on the other side. I really looked forward to Friday night football games. For some reason, I felt that most of the people had their eyes on me when we marched across the field. I was still full of my own self worth.

One day, one of the cheerleaders got the brainy idea that we should march with the band at half time. Now the band members took their marching seriously, and they didn't want us to march with them. A big fuss was started. The pep squad won. We practiced all week with them, with most of the band members not speaking to us. When the big night came, the pep squad members messed up, thus making the band members mess up too. People in the audience were really laughing. I messed up as much as anybody did. Marching wasn't as easy as it looked. We never got to march with them again. It took several weeks before the riff between the two factions healed.

The Lovings had their annual reunion. The Oklahoma cousins came. I was there too. When Pete's family drove up in the yard, I was there to meet them. I had plans for him this year. We started kissing that first night. He didn't put his hands inside my blouse like Charles Roy had. For some reason I wanted him to, but I never said a word about it. That could come next year.

Back at school, in our General Science class, one of the guys secretly made some hydrogen sulfide gas. Now H2S gas smells exactly like rotten eggs. He took some of it, and let it out on the bus on the way home. Several of the kids on the bus got sick. The principal got several complaints from parents that night.

The next day at school, the principal and the teacher tried, unsuccessfully, to get someone to confess to having made the gas. We all knew who had done it, but we were not about to tell. There was a code of ethics among kids back then; even good kids didn't tell things on the bad ones. The teacher decided to punish us by making everyone in the class copy the complete glossary in the back of the Science book.

I got busy and completed mine within a few days. I sat at the kitchen table at night after the others had gone to bed and wrote all the words and the definitions. I was the first one to turn my work into the teacher. One of the guys in the class offered me five dollars to copy the glossary for him. Five dollars was a lot of money. I went back to work at the kitchen table.

When I finished his work, I turned it in with his name on it. I had not thought about the possibility that the teacher would know it was not the boy's handwriting. I worried about that for a few days. I knew the boy and I both would get into a lot of trouble if the teacher figured out what we had done. Apparently the teacher never even looked at all the glossaries that were turned it, since we never heard another word about it. About a month later, I finally got enough nerve to spend the illegal money.

Some of the boys in the Science class, still mad about having to write the glossary, decided they would take all our Science books and throw them out the window. They waited until the teacher had left for home before they pitched them onto the grass outside. Someone alerted the principal, and the books were brought back inside. It was a good thing too, since it rained that night. Since the teacher found out pretty quickly who the guilty parties were, he did not punish all of us.

Homemaking became a class that I liked. I didn't hate it as much as I thought I would. One day in class we were studying the shape of people's faces. The teacher said the ideal face was one that was oval shaped. We were sitting in a circle at a table. She asked the class what shape face they thought I had. No one said a word. *What did we know about shapes of faces?* I was afraid of what one of them was going to say. *Why did she pick me first?* Finally she said,

"Her face is oval shaped. That is why Annie Bell is pretty." I was embarrassed, but pleased. No one had every told me that I was pretty. I had always wanted to be, but I didn't have the clothes to be pretty. One of the reasons I had always acted kind of tough was that I thought I was ugly. That one statement from her gave me a lot of self-confidence.

After that day I began to do better by my hair and took an interest in the clothes that I did have, most of them given to us by our cousins. I had this secret summer life and the boy friend that I had never mentioned to my Lindale friends. I knew none of them had been experiencing kissing in the summer times. I began to look at the Lindale boys to see if maybe I could have a good boy friend in Lindale. My old buddy, Norvell Alvey, had moved from Lindale after seventh grade. Try as I might, I just could not like any of them. They were just not Charles Roy! I don't think any of them liked me either.

When we made a mistake on a paper in homemaking class, our teacher would put a big, and, I mean, a big red X on the part we had wrong. One day she asked us to write a paper on what religion we were and why we had chosen that particular religion. That made some of the girls really mad. One of the girls wrote on her paper. "My religion is none of your business, and when I get to hell you will be right down there with me giving everyone big old red X's." Now, listen, that girl was not me. I am telling the truth here. I made good grades in homemaking and hardly ever got a red X on any of my papers. Really!

Right before Christmas, in homemaking class, we made divinity candy that we were to take home for the holidays. The teacher had supplied all of us with coffee cans. I wrapped the candy in wax paper and put it in the can. I wanted to take it home so Mama and Daddy could taste it. I was proud of that stuff. When I got home, I realized I had left it at school. I ran back, but the schoolhouse was all locked up. I would not be able to get in again until after Christmas. I knew by then the candy would be ruined. I hung my head down and walked back home.

Just as the Christmas before, Daddy opened the firecracker stand in Mineola for us to run. Mama was off from her job for the holidays. We made a lot of money in the firecracker business, but Daddy gambled it all away.

At Christmas time Mama made all the pies and cakes that by now was a tradition. She had bought a rotary beater, so whipping up the egg whites were not so hard. She always made a couple of butterscotch pies for me, browning the sugar herself. We never had any of these sweets except at Christmas. My family was not much on desserts anyway.

When I went back to school after Christmas, I went into the homemaking class and opened up the coffee can expecting to see green candy. To my surprise, the candy was in perfect condition. When I discussed this with the teacher, she told me that I had put a good seal on the can, thus not letting air in to destroy the divinity. As soon as school was out, I took the candy home for my family members to enjoy. I didn't like candy much, so I let them have all of it. I guess it tasted good, since they didn't complain.

When the second semester started in homemaking, we began to learn to sew. I was not interested in that at all. We had several electric machines in the class, but several them were older machines run by foot power. The teacher asked for volunteers to use the old machines. I felt that since I was not interested in learning to sew anyway. I volunteered for one of them. It was a mistake that I would regret for the rest of my life.

We made a skirt and a blouse that year. It was hard work, and my stuff looked awful, even though the teacher helped me as much as she could. When I got my skirt sewed up, I realized I had the back of it turned right side out. I had to rip out the seams and redo it. Since I had not bought enough material to make the blouse, I went back to the store. They did not have any more material the exact shade of blue, so I had to buy a lighter shade of material. On the day we were to have assembly so that all the students in all the homemaking classes could model the clothes they had made, I was conveniently absent. My new outfit ended up in our trash.

Sometime during the year the homemaking teacher paid Mama a home visit. This was a requirement to complete the class. Mama had to take an afternoon off work to accommodate her. Thank goodness Daddy said that he would stay away. I had the house all cleaned up, but I was anxious about the visit. Mama was too. *What would the teacher say about me?* I wanted to impress her, but I was kind of afraid that Mama might embarrass me.

To my surprise everything went well, without a hitch. Mama told the teacher that I was the best kid she had, and that I helped in the cooking and the cleaning. The teacher in turn told Mama that I was a good student, never giving her any problems. I slept really great that night, thinking about the wonder of it all. These two women thinking so much of me! However, I decided that I was not interested in taking Homemaking again.

After that visit I began to take pride in keeping the house clean. I cooked supper every night for us. We always had hamburger meat, chicken or sometimes steak, but we never had dessert. Sometimes Dollie would help me clean up the kitchen after supper, but it seemed to me it was like pulling teeth getting her to do her part.

Our English teacher informed us one day that we were going to have to read at least one book each six weeks and make a book report on it. We had to follow a certain procedure in this. First we listed the name of the book, the author, the list of characters, the setting, a summary of the story and then the conclusion. Man, a lot of people were hot about this, especially the boys, who we all know didn't read much back then. One boy, who I am sure didn't even read the book, turned in his first report. He wrote the first four things down, and then, in the summary he wrote "If you want to know what this book is about, read it yourself." Well, I will write the conclusion for him here. Seeing the teacher's red face as she was reading his report, he said to her, "I am probably not going to make a good grade on this am I?" He not only made a bad grade, he made a trip to the principal's office. You want to know his punishment? He had to read two books and write two book reports each six weeks for the rest of the school year. In Lindale High School in the 1950's reading two books was just about the worst punishment you could deal out to someone whose life long ambition was not to become a librarian.

A local dry goods store held a contest. To win it, a person had to turn in the most buttons. The prize was a beautiful blonde, Hollywood, bedroom suit. Ruby Lee decided that she was going to win it. She would do this by enlisting the help of all her family members. We all went to peoples' houses asking them to give us all the extra buttons that they had. She even took us into Tyler. We asked a lot of folks there too.

Ruby Lee was like a crazy person. She had to have that bedroom suit. She just about worked all of us to death. We were busier than termites in a sawmill. But, it was worth it. She won! I don't recall if anyone was even close to her. I don't see how they could have been. She always had good luck. We were all standing close to her when she was awarded the first prize. We could not have been any prouder of her. To her credit, she did buy each of her brothers and sisters an ice cream cone.

Billy Ray and Ruth Evelyn surprised us with a baby boy, Rickey Glen, born in March. Their old house trailer had fallen apart. They moved back to Lindale. It was wonderful to have another nephew to help care for. Daddy fixed up a building behind our house for them to live in. Later on Mr. Huey helped them buy a better trailer house. Then they moved to McKinney so Billy Ray could work, but he assured Daddy they would come back in time to go to South Texas with us to pick cotton.

My freshman class turned out to be my best year ever. I made excellent grades. When the time came to pick strawberries in Winnsboro, Daddy decided that we were not going to go there anymore. We were going to get to stay in school all day until it let out for the summer. I did worry about who was picking the Ragsdale's strawberries, since they had always depended upon us to do that. I sort of missed seeing Charles Ray too, and I wondered if he were missing me. I am pretty sure that he did.

Right before the blackberries got ripe, Happy and Turkey came to our door. We were all happy to see them. Daddy let them stay in the building that Billy Ray and Ruth Evelyn had stayed in. They rode to the field with us every morning in the back of the truck. I had no idea where they had spent the winter. *Had they stayed together?* I never did ask them.

That year while picking blackberries, Daddy let us keep half of what we made on Saturday. I saved my money to buy Kelpen's Ice Cream at Bo's old station. It cost twenty cents a pint. My favorite kind was banana nut. Each day, after the mornings in the blackberry patch, I would go home, wash my hands with Purex to get the purple stain off, and then go buy the ice cream.

Daddy left the field one morning to go into town to buy our lunch. When he came back, he had another hobo in the truck with him. This man had on all the clothes that he owned, several shirts and pants. He also had a coat on. It was very hot. Daddy told me to show him how to pick berries. I tried to get the guy to take off some of the hot clothes. He would not do it. I figured that he didn't trust us; that he thought we might steal some of them.

I asked the hobo what his name was. He told me that it was none of my business. He was right, of course. Since he would not tell us his name, we just started calling him "Hobo". Hobo kept to himself. He lived with the Happy and Turkey, but he didn't talk much to them. He did tell them that he did not drink beer or whiskey and for them not to offer him any. Because he didn't drink, I liked him and tried to be his friend. He saved all the money he made in the field except for money he had to spend on food. I began to think that someday I would get him in a poker game and relieve him of some of it. It didn't happen; he didn't play poker either.

It was very hot that summer. We all began to sleep outside on our pallets to stay cool. We did it most of the time in South Texas, so why not do it right here in Lindale? We would study the moon and stars, trying to make out all the shapes in the sky. We would go to sleep with the beautiful heaven above us. Each star represented a person who had died and had gone to live with God. Sometimes, I would think about when I died, how nice it was going to be to live up there. Usually before daylight came, it would get cool enough for us to go back inside to our beds to finish the night.

Something awful happened to me that summer in Lindale. Several of us were stealing watermelons in a man's field. Lindale was knee deep in sand. After we loaded the pick-up, we discovered it was stuck. We had to unload half of the watermelons in order to get the pick-up out of the sand. All of us were getting nervous, as the farmer could drive up any second. As soon as the pick-up could be moved, we all climbed back inside the cab. One thing we had forgotten to do was to shut the tailgate of the pick-up. When we got back to town, we didn't have one watermelon; they had all rolled out.

As soon as the pick-up slowed down, I opened the door and jumped out. When I hit the ground, blood began to pour out of me. I was scared to death, having no idea what had just happened to me. I ran all the way home. Mama wasn't there. I got in the bed, under the covers with my clothes on. *What was I going to do? Was God punishing me for having stolen the watermelons? Was I dying? Would this blood stop running before I did?*

When Mama got home, I told her I had something awful to tell her. I told her I had started bleeding, for no reason at all, after I had jumped out of the pick-up. I was not about to confess to stealing watermelons. She told me she would go to the store and get me something to wear. *What was she talking about? Something for me to wear, it didn't make sense.* When she returned from the town, she told me to go into the bathroom, and I would find what I needed.

I slowly got up and did what she told me. There in the bathroom was a box of Kotex. I still didn't know what to do. I picked up the box and read the instructions. I finally put one on and some clean panties. I wanted to throw the bloody panties away, but I washed them out instead. I didn't have very many pairs of them.

Still not understanding what had happened to me, I decided to go to Ruby Lee's to discuss the matter with her. I was embarrassed when I went into her living room and began to cry. After listening to my story, Ruby Lee realized that Mama had never told me anything about the birds and the bees. She had never told her anything either. She had learned all she knew after she had married.

Ruby Lee sat me down and told me all about having babies and why women had to go through this kind of stuff. I asked her, "Now that I have done this, will I ever do it again?" She was crying, as she shook her head, "yes."

What a day this had been for me. I not only had started my monthly periods, I had also found out where babies came from. I just couldn't figure out exactly how they could get out of a woman's stomach, but I felt I would learn this later in life, maybe when I got married. Right now I had all this new information to study. In her explanation to me, Ruby Lee never said the word sex, not once. It would be later in life before I would hear that word.

On my way to South Texas that year I wondered about this body of mine. *Did my South Texas cousins do this every month? Would I tell Charles Roy about it? Would I even let him kiss me now? Was kissing what led to all this baby business in the first place?* Mama never mentioned my predicament again, but there was always Kotex around for me to use. She put the box in a secret hiding place for me; a place the boys wouldn't find out about.

Before the summer was over, Dollie had to start using them too. She and I never discussed it though. Things like that were not to be discussed among sisters back in the fifties.

Letters from Robert Lee kept coming. We looked forward to them. Someday he would be home just like Billy Ray, Ruth Evelyn, Bo and Ruby Lee were. My family would be complete again. That was a dream I held on to every day and every night.

There was a certain town on our way to South Texas where daddy believed that Hitler was now hiding out. Daddy knew that he had not died in Europe, wherever in the hell that was, but had pulled the wool over everyone's eyes but his. Somehow he had been smuggled out and was living in this German community. Daddy said if he had the time he would find him and kick his ass for getting his son killed in the war. Well, I would have kicked his ass too. I hated Hitler worse than I did my daddy, but I didn't fear him half as much.

When my brother had been killed, his death was on the front page of our Lindale newspaper. On back in the paper it told how Hitler and Mussolini had died. Mussolini had died like the coward he was- shot in the back. In Lindale their deaths had not even been front-page news. At that time in East Texas not all that many people knew who they were anyway, so there had been no need to talk about people who no one had ever met, on the front page, anyway.

When my daddy got something in his mind, he wouldn't let up. He argued that the earth was not round, but flat. In the Bible, according to him, it reads, "God put an angel on all four corners of the earth." Now, how could it be round if it has corners? He did have a point.

On the way to South Texas I read the Burma-Shave signs: "PASSING CARS...WHEN YOU CAN'T SEE-MAY GET YOU A GLIMPSE...OF ETERNITY."

"NO MATTER THE PRICE...NO MATTER HOW NEW-THE BEST SAFETY DEVICE...IN THE CAR IS YOU."

Eighteen

We did not go all the way to the Valley that summer; therefore, we were not able to visit with our cousins. I felt they were probably glad that we had not shown up on their doorsteps.

We had Ronald Wayne and Larry Edward with us. Ruby Lee had agreed that we could take them cotton picking while she stayed in Lindale. The boys were happy until Daddy made them pick cotton just like the rest of us. I felt sorry for them, and they missed their parents. Within three weeks the parents came to get them. I missed them, but was glad they had gotten out of the fields.

Charles Roy and I would have the best summer two people could ever imagine. He now had a car of his own. I didn't have enough nerve to ask Daddy to actually go out on a date, but I could sneak out with him, couldn't I? That is exactly what I did. We would go to a drive in picture show and never put the speaker on the car window. The petting between us was heavy now. My body was responding in a way I couldn't figure out, but I liked the response. We would lie side by side usually in the back seat and smooch and smooch and smooch. His hands were all over me now, especially down my blouse. I kind of figured he wanted to carry the petting one step farther, but I was not about to let him, even if he asked me too. I was no fool; I knew a little something about where babies came from. I wondered if he did.

After I would sneak back into my bed at night, I would lie awake thinking about our kissing and our wanting to do more. I was resolved not to let it happen. He never did ask me to. He probably was as scared as I was about not letting anything happen that would cause pain to our families.

Slim Robinson met up with us at Sinton. I was glad to see him. He made more paper flowers for us to peddle. The hobo that we had named Hobo came into our lives again. On the weekends the hobos would escort all of us to the Saturday movies or take us to a carnival. The hard work during the week would just be a memory during those times. When Monday morning came, the drudgery would begin again. I did have the weekends to look forward too, however, and always the nights with Charles Roy. Life wasn't always bad.

As usual, in Sinton we went to the park on the weekends to see our aunts who lived close by. Uncle Earnest and his family would go to the park too. One weekend all four of them went to the Valley to see their other siblings. They did not ask Mama or Aunt Kate to go with them. Well, they had to stay back and keep the kids. I don't think either one of them minded, as they knew that the entire bunch would be drunk before they got to the Valley.

In Wallis, Texas, one Saturday morning, Slim did a bad thing. A stupid thing! He stole a farmer's pick-up and drove it around the block and then parked it. *Why did he do it? Just to see if he could get away with it?* He didn't! By the time he had the pick-up parked, the sheriff handcuffed him. I saw it happen. He was taken to jail.

Daddy went down to talk to the sheriff, and the farmer told him that he would not press charges because he had actually driven off in the pick-up. The sheriff had no choice; Slim was on parole. He was sent back to prison. All the cotton pickers were sad. Daddy was mad. "Why in the hell did he do such a stupid thing?" Daddy asked to no one in particular. "He only had one more year on his parole." At night I would think about him, see his smile and his handsome face. I also wondered why he had done it. It was as if he had done it on purpose, as if he wanted to get away from us. *But why, I wondered.* I would be seventeen years old before I would know the truth about the pick-up theft. It would involve me.

We were all unhappy about Slim going back to prison. Happy decided to pull a really big drunk. To the surprise of all of us, Hobo got drunk too. It was late afternoon. Happy had a big tub of water boiling. He had bought some live lobsters from someone who had come by selling them. Happy told us that the way to cook the lobsters was to throw the lobsters into the hot water while they were still alive.

Hobo, now really drunk, told Happy not to put the lobsters in the hot water alive; that it was not right. He said that they should knock them in the head first, killing them before trying to cook them. The two friends, now enemies, got into a fight. Happy took a lobster by the tail and threw him into the boiling water. Hobo, trying to rescue the lobster, reached into the tub to retrieve him.

When his hand hit the hot water, he screamed. Being drunk, he stumbled and fell face down into the tub before anyone could catch him. Daddy and some other men grabbed him and took him to a doctor's office. The doctor promptly sent him to a hospital in another town. We never did see Hobo again. I worried about him for a long time, wondering mostly about what happened to all the money he had hid in his clothes. If he lived, I knew he would be scared. Happy never said a word about the incident to us, but he never drank alcohol again. The lobsters never got cooked. I think they just walked away in all the commotion.

Dollie and I were not exactly bosom buddies, but we got along better now. However, I was so wrapped up in Charles Roy and myself that I didn't pay as much attention to her as I should have. We had spent most of our life fussing about one thing or another. She was bigger than I was, and could whip me. Mama said that I always started the fights, but Dollie always finished them. The fights were usually finished when Mama halted them, after I had gone to her crying.

Nuse was still smoking and I suspected drinking beer. Joe was sneaking around and smoking too. I sure wasn't going to smoke. I was having too much fun kissing. Smoking seemed to me to be trouble, especially if Daddy caught me. Joe was a fool. If daddy had caught me kissing, I would have been in trouble too.

One couple that was picking cotton for Daddy got into a fight every weekend because they would both get drunk. It was "honey this" and "honey that" during the week, but just let the weekend come around, and it was a totally different story. They didn't work on Saturday morning, as the drinking and the fighting had started on Friday night.

By Monday morning at least one of them had a black eye, and sometimes both of them did. I believe jealousy was the devil between them. Both of them were nice looking. Thank goodness they did not have any children to witness their craziness. We did though, and I hated it. Drinking alcohol brings out the worst in people. They were proof of this.

Sometimes, when the husband had drunk so much whiskey that he had passed out, Daddy would pick that exact time to visit them for about an hour. My Mama had to witness that. She never expressed her displeasure of his going to see them or his buying the man an extra fifth of whiskey.

Mama was still cooking on the Coleman stove, and in most places we just lived out in the open. Every now and then we would have an old house to stay in while we were picking a farmer's cotton. There was always coffee made in the little percolator that sat on the stove. Mama cooked beans every other day with dry salt meat in them for flavor. Daddy had started buying canned biscuits, and Mama now had a little oven on the stove in which to cook them. I loved to eat them; they were much better than homemade biscuits, to my way of thinking.

We got a letter from Robert Lee sent General Delivery. Mama read it to all of us. He still hated the U. S. Navy. I was glad that he didn't like it, for that meant he would not stay in it like Thurman was doing in the U. S. Army. Daddy began to cry as Mama was reading. When she was finished, Daddy started talking, telling us some things about his past. I listened with both ears. Mama just sat and looked at him. I really didn't know if what he was telling us were true or not. Mama would never contradict him.

He told us that before he was married to his first wife he had been a great baseball player in Kansas. He was playing in a state championship game. His team was made up of poor guys. They didn't have uniforms or good shoes. They won the championship. After the game was over, he was at a well, getting a drink of water, when one of the other team's players came up to him. The man was mad that they had been beaten. He had a girl on each arm. He started mouthing to Daddy, and a fight ensued. When the fight was over, Daddy was the winner. He left the man on the ground and walked off with the man's shoes and the two women. *What a lie, I thought.* Everyone but me laughed, and I just kind of shook my head. Daddy picked up on my reaction. He continued.

About a year after he and his first wife had split, he was sitting at a café drinking coffee. A man came into the café and asked, "Are you Buford Coomer?" "Depends on who is looking for me," was Daddy's answer. "Well there is a woman out there who wants to see you." Daddy looked out, and there his ex-wife sat in a car. He went out and approached her. She was smiling as she said, "Buford I have something here to show you." She poked a baby in his face. "Why are you showing that to me?" Daddy asked her. "It's yours," was the reply. I could not believe what I was hearing. We might have an older brother or sister somewhere!

Mama sat up straight too. She apparently had never heard this story before. We were silent for a moment. I broke the silence. "Was the baby a boy or a girl?" "I don't know, I left and I never saw her or the baby again." Daddy said. Mama looked relieved. *Could this be another lie?*

Daddy, sensing he was making us uncomfortable, began another tale. After he and Mama were married, but before any kids were born, they had gone to a dance. He and Mama sat at the door and charged couples twenty-five cents to get in. After a couple paid, Daddy pinned a yellow ribbon on them. That way they could come and go outside to smoke it they wanted to, and wouldn't have to pay to get back in. One man came in with his girl friend, paid the money but told Daddy that he was not going to pin a ribbon on him. No man should have to wear a ribbon.

Daddy explained the reason for it to him, but the man still refused. So, Daddy and him stepped outside and got into a fight. Of course, Daddy whipped him. When the man went back inside, he had a yellow ribbon pinned to his shirt. He and Daddy became good friends after that. *Daddy was so short, how could he have whipped anybody?* I didn't believe this one either, but at least it was humorous.

Nuse was enjoying the tales so he encouraged Daddy to tell us something else. The story went like this. When the older kids were small, he and Mama were sharecroppers in Oklahoma. The man they worked for was extremely mean. *Meaner than you?* I thought. One afternoon the owner was mad at one of the other sharecroppers. The sharecropper was taken to the lake and shot. He got up from the water and was shot again. The other sharecroppers watched, but were helpless to do anything; they may have met the same fate. Every time the man got up, he was shot and fell back into the lake. They watched him die, begging for his life.

210/Baldwin/Meager Beginnings

After he died, the owner ordered Daddy and some other men to dig a hole and to bury him. They obeyed. During the night, Daddy got Mama and the little ones up, and they got in the car and left. By the time they were missed the next day, they were safely across the state line in Texas. *Is this a reason to believe this was true because a Texan told it to me?* Mama shook her head in agreement. I knew then that this tale must have been true.

Daddy's hair had always been thin on the top. He asked, "Want to know why I have thin hair?" Without waiting for us to answer, he continued, "women pulled it out while helping me into their windows at night." I was uncomfortable with this tale, but he went right on, telling us another one. "You know, women always told me that I was uncouth, and I will tell you why. I would never help them put their clothes back on. I might help them take the clothes off, but they could get dressed by themselves." I really didn't want to, but I laughed. Mama rolled her eyes around in her head.

Since it appeared that everyone was enjoying this story telling, Mama decided to get in on it. She told us about the time they had a pet chicken. The chicken would ride with them in the truck. She would sit in the front on the floorboard. Every once in a while they had to stop and let her go outdoors (use the bathroom) just like a dog would. They were in the Valley living in a house with some people. Mama was working at a place that made ketchup. She trumped around in the tomatoes all day barefooted, crushing them to make the ketchup.

One day while Mama was working, the chicken laid several eggs on their mattress. They just let the chicken set on the eggs and hatch them. Mama and Daddy slept on the floor. The other people in the house hated that chicken. One afternoon, when Mama got home from work, the chicken's neck had been rung and the chicken herself had been cooked. Mama was hurt and Daddy was mad. He caught two rats and put them in the chicken killer's flour bin. The couple moved out of the house. Mama and Daddy never saw them again. I even enjoyed this one. Mama was telling it, so it had to be a true story.

When Mama and her brother, Jean, were little, they had a pet cat. One day they gave the cat some of their mama's snuff and put a pair of shoes on his feet. The shoes were made out of paper. The cat got sick or drunk from the snuff and he couldn't walk in the paper shoes. When the two got caught, Mama put the blame on her brother. His mama decided he needed a whipping. She got a hickory switch and he started running. Mama got at the end of one side of the house. Every time Jean came by, she hollered, "Run Jean, run." Well, this got her a whipping also. The cat got well, so they felt they had gotten a bad whipping for nothing.

Mama had one more tale. Our cousin, Edith, one of Uncle Jean's girls, had a friend over. They were teenagers, and the friend had a car borrowed from her parents. The girls, who lived in Dekalb, Texas, wanted to go to Texarkana, a bigger town not to far from Dekalb. Aunt Pearl, Edith's mother, told them they could not leave the city limits of Dekalb. No problem. These two enterprising teenagers went to the edge of town, dug up a Dekalb city limit sign and put it in the trunk of the car. Since they had not left the city limits, they set sail and went to Texarkana.

Daddy had one more story for us before we had to go to bed. He had not witnessed this first hand but had heard others telling it. Years before in Lindale a local businessman had a dog that followed him everywhere he went. All around town people would see the dog at the man's heels. One afternoon the KU KLUX KLAN was marching through the streets. On the street corner several old men sat watching the proceedings and wondering who was under the sheets. They felt like they probably knew most of them. Right behind one of the sheets was a dog, making every step the clan's member took. They may not of known who was under the sheet, but they sure knew who the dog belonged to.

With that story ending, we all washed our feet and went to bed. I had a lot to think about that night. *Did we really have a brother or sister, and if so, where did he/she live?* I wished that Daddy had not told that. I really didn't know if I should believe him or not, but the possibility was there. For a while after that, I studied faces of strangers, trying to decide if they favored my Daddy.

Summer came to an end. It was getting close to time to go back to Lindale to go to school. *Would Daddy let us go back when school started this year?* He had not mentioned it, so I asked him in late August. "No," he said. He explained that he had borrowed $150 at the bank for Billy Ray and Ruth Evelyn. They were supposed to pay it back but were unable to do it. The note was due in October, so

212/Baldwin/Meager Beginnings

we were going to have to pull cotton a little while longer to get the money to pay off the bank.

That night I cried myself to sleep. I tried to make sense of it. I was mad at Billy Ray and Ruth Evelyn, but I loved them so much, and I knew they would have paid it if they could have.

We traveled north to Greenville, Texas. Going into town, in any direction, you could see a big sign that read, "WELCOME TO GREENVILLE, THE BLACKIEST LAND, THE WHITEST PEOPLE." I didn't think it was funny. Daddy told me there was a town in Oklahoma where folks would let you live there only if you were black. "That is hard to believe," I challenged him. "Hell, girl," Daddy defended his statement. They had a sign going into town that said, "WHITE MAN, READ THIS AND RUN. IF YOU CAN'T READ, RUN ANYWAY." Okay, so maybe I believed what he said was true. He could not have made that sign up.

The Burma-Shave signs beckoned to us: "A GUY WHO DRIVES...A CAR WIDE OPEN-IS NOT THINKIN'...HE'S JUST HOPIN'."

"AT INTERSECTIONS...LOOK EACH WAY-A HARP SOUNDS NICE...BUT IT'S HARD TO PLAY."

School in Lindale was in its sixth week when we returned to begin classes. I signed up for Algebra 1, English II, Typing I and World History. I had never heard the word Algebra, didn't have a clue what kind of class I was getting myself into.

Algebra turned out to be a Math course. The teacher told me the first day that if I studied really hard that week and took the test on Friday, she would give me the grade that I made for a sixth week grade. I told her that I would do it. Every afternoon of that week I went to Treva's house. She grilled me on the subject, and I did all the exercises in the book, getting all the lessons up to date. When Friday came, I was ready. Not only did I turn in all the homework, I made a 100 on the Algebra six weeks test. When she graded my homework papers, I had missed only two problems. The teacher was pleased as punch. I enjoyed that class the rest of the year.

The typing class was another matter. I had never sat down in front of a typewriter before. In fact, I had never seen a typewriter before. The first day in class the teacher got on to me about my gum chewing. She made me throw it out the window. All the other students had been typing for six weeks, so she had to deal with them one-way and with me another way. At least once a week she made me spit my gum out. I always felt that if she would have let me continue to chew the gum that I would have been a much better typist. I did not catch up with the rest of the class, but I did manage to type enough words per minute to complete the course by the end of the year.

Robert Lee was home from the Navy. He went to work at a local foundry, working strange hours. He had to get up around two o'clock in the morning. Daddy, who had a clock hidden inside his body, always woke up in time to get Robert Lee off to work. Daddy always encouraged Robert Lee never to be late for work or miss a day. He said to him, "Take care of your job, and it will take care of you." *What did he know about a job, or what it could do for you?* He sure didn't have any first-hand knowledge of this.

Robert Lee told us some funny stories about the Yankees. He said that he had told them that people from Texas got an extra thirty days vacation each year because when they got to the Texas border, they had to go the rest of the way on a stagecoach. They had believed him.

He told us that one night while they were on leave, they were in one of the guy's car. The radio was playing. He reached over and turned it off. "Why did you do that," one of the guys asked. "Because," Robert Lee said, "radios use gas, and we don't have much gas or much money." Another one of the guys laughed and said, "That just can't be true." He turned the radio back on. Robert Lee told us, "Kiss my foot if we didn't run out of gas before we got back to base." After that he said that most of the guys believed anything that he told them.

The ship that Robert Lee had been on was really big. He told us that it had airplanes on it. We could hardly believe this piece of information. In our minds, we could not imagine that anything could be big enough to have planes on it. Well, he said that they could play football on the deck. I didn't believe that either. It just couldn't have been that long. He told us that once he was going out for a pass, wasn't watching where he was running, and fell off the side of the ship. He had to be rescued.

Robert Lee gave Dollie and me his bellbottom pants. We hemmed them up and wore them to school. We sure made a fashion statement in those breeches.

Not too long after Robert Lee came home, Aunt Bessie died. She had gone in for some tests and didn't survive. Daddy told us that one of the tests had dried up her blood. I was very unhappy about this. We all went to her house in the country so that we could attend her funeral.

All her neighbors were black folks. They brought food over for us to eat. We were going to spend the night. They brought quilts for us to use too. The black neighbors came over to set up with Aunt Bessie's body so the cats wouldn't come in and lay on top of her.

That night as I was going to sleep under an old black granny woman's quilt, I thought about how nice it was of her, and wondered why white people had bad thoughts about them. I also wondered why the quilt didn't have a bad smell. I had always heard that everything they owned smelled. *This was another lie that white people told.*

About nine o'clock the next morning some people from the funeral home in Longview came to get her body. We were in Robert Lee's car following the hearse into town. Uncle Jack, Daddy and Mama, Uncle Earnest and Aunt Kate were in the limousine. I think the sisters from Corpus Christi and Taft came to the funeral, but I am not sure about the kinfolks from the Valley.

We thought it was really neat, getting to run all the red lights. This was my first experience to be in a funeral procession. During the funeral, I kept turning around, looking for the good black folks. None of them came. They were Aunt Bessie's best friends, but they must have felt they would not have been welcomed to come to her funeral. They would have been wrong. I cried for them, for the injustice in the world, and for Aunt Bessie. I was surely going to miss her.

After the funeral, we went back through the country to Aunt Bessie's house, so we could pick up a lot of the leftover food. On our way home, when we got into Gilmer, Robert Lee ran the first red light. When the officer pulled him over, Robert Lee explained about the funeral and said that he thought he was still in it when he ran the red light. The officer let him go, didn't even give him a warning ticket. It was never said that Coomers were not good liars.

The next week, I decided I wanted to go to Tyler to get my drivers' license. I had been old enough for over a year to get them.

In Texas, in 1957, a person could get their license at age fourteen. Neither Mama nor Daddy would go with me to sign for me. Robert Lee took me. Dollie and Joe went too. A friend of Dollie's, Patsy decided she would go with us. Robert Lee said that he would state that he was married to Patsy and that I lived with them.

When we got to the driver's license office, I had my birth certificate ready. I did not look like I was fifteen. I looked more like a twelve-year-old. The man behind the desk looked at my birth certificate, and he looked at me. "This birth certificate belong to you?" he asked. "Yes sir," was my answer. "Where is your mother?" was his next question. At the very same instant, Joe and I gave different answers. I stated that she was in Colorado and Joe said that she was dead.

Robert Lee said to the man, "This is my wife, and Annie Bell lives with us. I will sign for her." "If you do not have legal custody of her, you cannot sign for her," the guy told Robert Lee. Getting frustrated, Robert Lee said, "I am a veteran, been in the U. S. Navy. And I really liked it too, I might add."

"Well sir, that is mighty noble of you. I was in the Army myself, but the law is the law. She will need to come here with one of her parents, if they are still living, to sign for her," the officer stated. He was beginning to get frustrated himself.

I was so anxious to get my license that we went home, resurrected that dead mama of mine, got her home, back from Colorado, and to the highway patrol office in little over hour. Dollie, Joe, and Patsy stayed in Lindale.

When Mama went up to the counter, the same man asked, "Are you this young lady's mother, ma'm?" "I sure am," Mama said. "How long have you been her mother?" The guy asked. "Since the day she was born. You can figure out how long its been; you are holding her birth certificate in your hand." My mama wasn't going to take any flap from that fellow. "I have come to sign for her so she can drive a car legally," Mama told him. "You mean she has been driving a car without a license?" The man asked. "Since she has been twelve years old," Mama answered. The man rolled his eyes around in his head, but he gave the tests to me. I made a 100 on all three of them. I had really been studying. The written parts were the ones that I had been dreading. The same person gave me the driving part of the test. I passed that too.

When we pulled up into the yard, everybody in the house came running out to see if I had succeeded. The smile on my face said it all. Robert Lee let me take his car for a spin, just around the block. I went straight to town. It was at least thirty minutes before I got back to the house. Robert Lee was sort of mad at me, but I didn't care; a girl doesn't get her first set of driver's license but once in her lifetime.

I was going to Sunday school all the time now. I enjoyed the classes and driving to church, and it was legal for me to do so. I would go through town, not having to skirt around it. I really was showing off. *Just let the city marshal stop me*! I would have a surprise for him--my driver's license. Not too many of my classmates had a license yet.

We did not have driver's education at school, and some kids could not find a way to get to Tyler to take the test. Most of them were driving though, but not within the law. I thought about turning some of them in, but it might not be the Christian thing to do. I would have tried to whip someone if they had turned me in before I was legal. I decided to leave them alone.

To our surprise, Daddy gave us some money and told me I could take Dollie and Joe to Tyler to a show to celebrate my getting my driver's license. After the show we decided to go shopping, never mind that we didn't have any money to shop with. It was Dollie's idea, of course, not mine, to steal us a bathing suit at one of the shops in Tyler. We took several dresses and bathing suits into a dressing room, and when we came out we each had a bathing suit on under our original dress. We looked so sweet and innocent, no salesperson suspected a thing. We went on home. Well, as one could guess, Joe told on us as soon as we got home.

Mama took us back to Tyler and made us go into the store and confess to the owner what we had done. He thought about calling the law but decided not to because we had brought the bathing suits back, and I kind of led him into thinking that it was our idea to bring them back. Our conscience was hurting us a little. Daddy let it be known that if we ever pulled another stunt like that and he found out about it, I would never drive a car again. Well, if we did pull another stunt, he didn't find out about it. The main reason is because we didn't let Joe go with us again.

All of a sudden I was everywhere. I would sit around the house thinking about what I could go to town to get. I volunteered to go to the grocery store. I would throw away perfectly good bobby pins, just to have an excuse to drive the car to the store to buy some more. Billy Ray and Ruth Evelyn would let me drive their car around the block, if I would wash it. So would Robert Lee. I was busier than a "one legged man at a butt-kicking contest."

Joe got a goat to raise. She was going to have a baby. I am not sure if Daddy knew about this or not when he bought her. We had all forgotten about the goat that Robert Lee had tied to the goal post at the football field a few years earlier. She was tied with a rope to our basketball pole on the vacant lot. Daddy planned to use her to mow the grass. The second day that she was a member of our family, I was playing with her, pulling on her rope. She started to go around and around the pole. Before I realized what was happening, I was pinned to the pole, and breathing was becoming a big problem.

What was I going to do? I was beginning to panic. Trying to get her to go in the opposite direction did not work. I was at home alone. A lone car came slowly down our street. I could not scream, as I didn't have enough breath. The car went on by. I was crying now. Feeling sure I was about to meet my maker, I began to pray, out loud in a very weak voice. "Please God let someone come home. I need it to happen right now."

In what seemed an eternity, I saw the car that had just passed coming back around. It stopped. A man got out of it. Seeing that I was in some kind of distress, he began to run over to me. This praying always worked for me. He grabbed the goat and started to walk her in the opposite direction. When I was completely free, I fell to the ground.

The man's other family members were out of the car by now. Together they picked me up. One of their kids ran into our house and brought me a drink of water. In a few minutes I was okay. A young boy in the back seat of the car had just happened to look back as they passed. He had convinced his dad that I was in some kind of panic. I hugged them until they were blue in the face. When my family members got home, I told them what had happened to me. I don't think any of them believed me. That ended my love affair with that nanny. I wasn't about to like her kid either.

218/Baldwin/Meager Beginnings

The goat had the yard to herself. She also could get into the house through the back door that wasn't too secure. She almost had her baby inside our house, getting out just in time for the delivery. I watched the birth, fully realizing now how babies got out of their mother's stomach. *It was something that I would never experience.* Later on, the new mother got on top of the hood of Bo's new car. Daddy knew then that she and the baby goat had to go. It was hard to believe, but I missed seeing her around. It also meant we would have to start mowing the grass again.

Joe was also raising pigeons and he had a cat. Dollie had a parrot. They both really cared about their animals. I didn't like any of them. One afternoon, as I was going into the house from school, I noticed Dollie was choking Joe's cat. Joe was trying to stop her. "What is going on here?" I asked. "Why are you fighting?" Joe answered, "Dollie is trying to choke my cat to death." Dollie screamed, "This stupid cat ate my parrot. I am not trying to kill him. I am just trying to make him spit my parrot back up."

"If he swallowed the parrot, she is dead," I told Dollie. How did the cat get her out of her cage?" Dollie, crying now, said, "Somebody left a chair under it. The cat got into the chair, slapped the bottom of the cage out and grabbed her. If I find out who left the chair under her cage, I am going to kill them." I was not going to confess that I was the one who left it there. Feeling really sorry for her, Joe and I both helped her clean up the mess on the floor. Together we took the cage down and put it away. Joe's cat took a good long nap and he didn't eat a bite of supper.

Daddy came home from town one afternoon, and he had another hobo with him. I do not recall his name. I took an instant dislike to him. Daddy let him live in the shack behind our house. He didn't have anything but the clothes on his back. Mama took him some supper and gave him one of our cots to sleep on and some cover. The next morning we left to go to school. We had just gotten out of the sight of the house when I realized I had left a book at home. I ran back into the house to retrieve it. The hobo was in the refrigerator eating our ranch style beans out of a bowl. I startled him, and he scared me.

Looking embarrassed, he said, "Are you going to tell your folks?" I could tell he must really be hungry, but I didn't want him in our house when we were not there. I was a little afraid of him, but

I was a Coomer, so I was not going to let him see that I was. "No," I assured him. "If you want to eat, just ask us for food, but do not come into our house again when we are not here, as Daddy will kill you. He's done it before," I lied. "I won't," he promised. I kept my word and never told a soul. Daddy found him some odd jobs.

We didn't know anything about him. We did find out that he had two sons who were in an orphan's home in Dallas. He was trying to get them back. They had been there for about two years. He told us his wife had died and that things had been rough on them. I didn't know whether to believe him or not. Daddy talked to the welfare workers, and they promised to see if the boys could come for a visit.

Sure enough, one day a car drove up in our yard, and the two boys got out. One was about my age and the other one was younger. Watching them hug their Daddy, we all cried, even our Daddy. The man from the orphan's home said that he would be back in a couple of weeks to pick them back up.

The two boys proved to be kind of mad at the world, and I didn't like them very much. I tried to understand them, since they had had a bad time after losing their mother. One afternoon Daddy was pretty drunk. I was getting on to him about it. He slapped me across the face. The two boys were in the yard, and they saw what he had done. They didn't like me much either. The younger boy came over to me and said, "My Daddy has never slapped me in the face." "Well, so what," I smarted back to him. "My Daddy never left me at an orphan's home." The young man began to cry, and I was instantly sorry for what I had said. I would not apologize though, as I was still mad at my Daddy for slapping me, and them seeing him doing it.

In a few days the boys were taken back to the orphan's home. It was a sad day when they had to leave their daddy. In a month, the hobo left Lindale to go to Dallas to try to get a job and to get his boys back. To this day I regret what I said to that young man. I can only hope that he realized that I was hurting too.

On a Sunday afternoon before Christmas, Daddy took me with him to see Uncle Jack. When we got there, he was entertaining a woman. She had recently lost her husband. Her son, who appeared to be about two years younger than I, was there with her. It

220/Baldwin/Meager Beginnings

was almost dark so Daddy decided we would spend the night. He would help Uncle Jack pay his respect to this woman.

Within a couple of hours all three of them were drunk. Daddy told the boy and me that we would have to sleep outside. He made us a pallet on the front porch of the house. It was cool, but he gave us enough cover to keep warm. We lay down on the pallet, side by side. I began to get the feeling that I always had when Charles Roy was this close to me. *Don't do this; he is a kid.* I could not help it. In a few minutes I turned to him and found his mouth. He was startled. We did not even know each other's name.

We lay on that pallet and kissed for a very long time. Finally sleep overcame us, and we both dozed off. Sometime during the night, our parents came outside and carried us into the house. Two "innocent children" were sleeping like babies. Before the rest of the household woke up the next morning, Daddy and I were on our way back to Lindale. I never saw the young boy again.

Treva and I were the best of friends. We went to the movies. On Friday nights we attended the football games. I spent countless nights at her house. We slept in the upstairs bedroom. We shared our hopes for the future. She wanted to become a beauty operator. I just wanted to be able to finish high school. I had no plans to go to college. There was not any way Mama and Daddy could afford to send me, even if Daddy would let me go. I could not see beyond high school.

The Lovings held their reunion, and I saw Pete and all the girl cousins. Pete and I continued our kissing sessions, but no hands down the blouse. I struggled with wanting to make him do it, and with my conscience; I knew it was not right.

Christmas vacation came. We were in the firecracker business gain. This year we also opened up a stand in Lindale. Business was very good at both places. My only wish was that I could keep the money I made or for Daddy to pay grocery bills with it. Neither one happened.

Thurman came to see us that Christmas. We had not seen him for some time. He brought his wife and two little boys, Stephen and Johnny. They were very handsome and really clean looking. I loved them just like I did the other nephews. The sun was shinning on Christmas day in Lindale. They lived in Colorado, and it was always snowing there. It was the first warm Christmas that they had ever seen.

Robert Lee bought all of us presents. So did Ruth Evelyn and Ruby Lee. We had a real Christmas tree that was decorated. Thoughts of a real Santa Claus were all gone now. I felt that I was almost grown-up; Dollie was too. She and I decided that we needed to open the Christmas presents. They were wrapped in brown paper brought home from the grocery store. We became experts at unwrapping them and then wrapping them back up undetected.

After Thurman and his family went back to Colorado, a strange thing happened. It snowed in Lindale, and then the temperatures dropped into the twenties. There was ice everywhere. The trees and the bushes were beautiful. Robert Lee took a hood from an old car, tied it to the back of his car, and rode us all over town. He also tied a ladder to the back of the car so that several people could ride all at once. It was the best Christmas season that I had ever had. Robert Lee's being home made all the difference in the world! The Paul boys, as well as Little Rickey, spent a lot of time at our house. Bo and Ruby Lee kept working and saving their money. If it had not been for Daddy's drinking and gambling, I would have been really happy.

On Saturday nights I hardly ever asked to go anywhere. I enjoyed staying home with Mama and Daddy and watching television. First we would watch Matt Dillon and next watch Perry Mason. It was a sport between all three of us to decide who was going to get murdered on Perry Mason, and then figure out who the person was that had done the killing.

In our World History class the teacher gave our tests, not from our notes, but from tests provided by the state. These tests were very hard. I noticed that the teacher kept the tests in an unlocked cabinet. A plan was devised so that I could borrow the tests over night.

Since Dollie and I got to school before anyone else, except the janitors, she would stand guard in the hall. I would take a test home that evening and look up all the answers. The next morning the test would be replaced in the cabinet. I was always careful never to make a 100 on a test. I didn't want to raise the suspicion of the teacher. No one could have made a 100 on those state tests. I usually made the best grades in that class though. The other students thought I spent a lot of time studying the history book.

Uncle Earnest and his family were living in a house in our neighborhood. His beautiful daughter, Betty Jo, had a handsome fellow. She was in love with him. Now, she had had a lot of proposals for her hand in marriage, and she had had several engagement rings. But, this was the real thing. The boyfriend decided that he was going to ask Uncle Earnest for her hand in marriage. I was afraid for him to do it. I felt like Uncle Earnest would run him off. I volunteered to ask Uncle Earnest for him. The boy had better sense than to listen to me. To the surprise of all of us, Uncle Earnest said yes. I would miss her; I loved her. She got married and moved.

Winter turned to spring. Before long the blackberry season would be upon us again. On a Saturday morning Mama went to the post office as she or Daddy did every day. When she pulled up into our yard, the city marshal pulled up behind her. He said, "Mrs. Coomer, whose car are you driving?" "Its my daughter's," she answered. The city marshal was smiling. "I believe you need to look again. That car belongs to someone else, and they want it back."

The car looked exactly like Ruby Lee's. No one took their keys out of their cars, so Mama had just gotten into it and driven off. She quickly took the car back to town where the anxious owner was waiting. No harm was done. Mama knew the owner. It was just a simple mistake, but it shook us all up. We surely didn't want our breadwinner to go to jail!

Uncle Earnest's kids came down to play with us all the time. We all played on our vacant lot. The families were just like one as far as the kids were concerned. One afternoon our cousins came down to play with us. In a few minutes Uncle Earnest called for them to come home. We could tell by his voice that he was mad. *What had they done?* I went home with them to find out what laws they had broken.

Uncle Earnest told them they had not asked him if they could go down to our house. He was going to give all of them a whipping. I begged him not to do it, explaining that he had always let them come to our yard to play. He wanted to whip me too. "I will let my brother take care of you young lady, after I whip my own kids," he said to me. "Now get your ass out of here." I saw him get his razor strap. His children were crying. How I wished that Aunt Kate were home, but she was at work with Mama.

By the time I got back into our yard, I could hear the screams of my cousins. I was crying as hard as they were. Daddy saw me come into the yard, crying. *Well, I was probably going to get a whipping too, as soon as Uncle Earnest told him about my fussing with him.* "What's wrong with you?" Daddy asked. He too could hear the kids crying. I told him. He appeared to become mad. I didn't know if he were mad at us kids or what.

To my surprise he said, "That sorry son-of-a-bitch. I will kick his ass for whipping those kids with a razor strap." He momentarily had forgotten about all the whippings he had given us with his belt. "You stay here," he instructed me. He need not have to worry. I was never going to go back around Uncle Earnest.

Daddy was gone for what seemed like an eternity. When he came back, I wanted to ask him what had happened, but I didn't. The next day was Saturday, so the kids didn't have to go to school. I told no one about the whippings. My heart ached for them.

After a week and a half, they came back to play with us. If he had left marks on their bodies, they had healed, but not the scars in their hearts. I never liked Uncle Earnest after that, and I never could figure out the real reason for his anger. Whatever the reason, he had taken it out on his innocent children. I was glad that at least Betty Jo was safely away from him. I hoped that she was happy with her handsome husband.

Robert Lee had been taking flying lessons ever since he had been home from the Navy. The Veterans Administration was paying for the lessons. I thought that the VA might have a tow sack full of money if they could pay for my brother to learn how to fly a plane. I bragged about his abilities to everyone. In the afternoons we would stand in our yard. He would fly by and swoop down like he was going to land on top of us. Sometimes he came real close to the top of the house. He was showing out.

I always worried that he was going to crash that plane, and I was glad when the lessons ended. Robert Lee became interested in other things- like girls.

One interesting thing about Robert Lee: for some reason he had a way of finding out when the soldier boys on summer camp would be coming through Lindale. He always relayed that information to Dollie and me. Some of my favorite memories are the times when we stood on the street corner waving at the soldiers when they went through town. The convoy did not have to stop at the stop sign but just drove right through them, thanks to our local city marshal. I guess it was a good thing they didn't have to stop as me and my sister might have climbed aboard one of the trucks and joined the U. S. Army.

Nineteen

Blackberry season was in full swing. Daddy was now contracting with farmers for their crops. He would pay them an agreed upon amount of money for the berries in the field. He would then have the responsibility of getting the berries picked. Prior to the harvest the farmer would have plowed and pruned the berry patch. We had a lot of people working for us.

Daddy paid each person when they brought a lug of berries to him. If Daddy was gone to town, the person would pay himself out of the money Daddy left there. As soon as we got a truckload of lugs of berries, Daddy would take them to a canning factory in Lindale. Several canneries were operating in town during the 1950's.

Each morning Dollie, Joe, and I would compete to see who could pick the first lug of berries. Daddy would give that person fifty cents. Since I was the oldest, it was naturally expected that I would pick the first lug that consisted of three gallons of berries.

That was not always the case. Joe had really become good at being the first to get his lug picked. I began to suspect him of cheating. Not that I hadn't done it myself at times. Sure enough, one morning I got on a row next to him. When he had his lug almost full, the hobo, who was picking on the same row with him, gave him enough berries to fill his lug. I was mad, but Dollie was so mad she threatened to destroy his lug of berries. Love of money was breaking up this family. She told Daddy on him. The competition ended.

One day in the field, a woman had picked several lugs of berries, and she had a lot of quarters in her pants pockets. Her husband, who hardly ever worked, came to the field with his brother. The husband tried to get his wife to give him her money so that he could go to a poker game. She would not do it. The two men picked her up and turned her upside down. The quarters fell out of her pockets onto the ground. The good-for-nothing men picked up the money and left. The poor wife went back to work. Her family had to eat.

When the blackberry season was over, we had one week to get prepared to go to South Texas to pick cotton. I was happy about our going. The reason, of course, was to see Charles Roy. I was sad about our going too. The reason of course was Bo and Ruby Lee and the boys were not going with us. They were doing too well on their jobs.

Daddy told us we would be pulling out on Sunday morning. The last day that we were going to be in town I went to Ruby Lee's to play with the boys. I was downhearted. When I got to her back yard, I noticed that she was talking to someone in her front yard. They were in a car, and she was standing next to it. I went into to her house by way of the back door.

Inside the house the beds were unmade and dishes needed to be washed. I got busy. I knew Ruby Lee would not want her company to see the mess. Ruby Lee was good about keeping her house clean. I did not know that she was telling them that she would invite them in but her house was a mess, and she didn't want them to see it. Her company convinced her that it was all right for them to see a dirty house. They really wanted to come in and visit.

About the same time I got everything straightened up, the door opened, and my sister with her company walked in. I had made beds, washed dishes, swept the floors and dusted really fast. I knew Ruby Lee would be proud of the clean house. Instead, her face was red. One of her company said, "Ruby Lee, if I had known that you didn't want us to come in for a visit, I would not have stopped by. You didn't have to lie to me." Ruby Lee tried to explain that she didn't tell them a lie. I told the company what I had done, but Ruby Lee felt they had not believed either one of us.

I felt just awful about trying to help out. I should have minded my own business. When the company left, I thought she was going to get on to me for coming in and doing what I done. Instead she was laughing about it. She said she didn't like that bunch much anyway and really didn't want them to come in, as she knew they would be a long time leaving. This way they had left a lot quicker than expected.

She knew I was unhappy about the situation, and also the fact that we were leaving the next day didn't help either one of our feelings. She wanted to cheer me up, so she got out the milk and the Oreo cookies. She began telling me tales about things that had happened to her when she was younger.

She remembered the day that she had tried to kill Daddy by grinding up spider webs and putting them in his beer. That particular day several kids had climbed Lover's Lookout tower in Jacksonville, Texas. She was eight years old. Daddy had given her a really hard whipping for being one of them. She was the only kid to have gotten a whipping. That was the reason she decided to end his life. Daddy never did find out what she had done. If he had, he may have ended her life.

When she and Thurman were young, they were riding in the back of a pick-up. The family was moving from one town to another one to pick cotton. They had a box of big matches. For some reason, they began to strike them and throw them out of the back of the pick-up. When the family arrived at the next town, the cotton was not quite ready to pull, so Daddy decided to return to the town they had just left. This way they could scrap the cotton and make a little money.

The next day on the trip back to the old town, she and Thurman realized that half the country was burned up. Land, barns and equipment looked like they had been torched. They knew they had set those fires. She and Thurman took a knife and made a blood oath never to tell a soul what they had done. Ruby Lee told me that this was the first time that she had ever told anyone about it. I promised her I would not tell. I could picture it all in my mind, and I didn't laugh.

Robert Lee had been a young boy, about seven or eight years old. They had been pulling cotton in Richmond, Texas. One of the couples that picked cotton had taken a bus to another town to spend the day. During the morning, the rest of the pickers decided to move to another town to work. There was no way to leave the couple a message.

Daddy decided that he would sit Robert Lee beside the road on a box. He could stop each Greyhound bus as it came by. When the one stopped with the cotton pickers in it, Robert Lee was to tell them about the move. Robert Lee sat there until after dark before the right bus came along. He stopped, and then boarded the bus, just as he had done all day. The couple didn't have a car. Daddy had taken their belongings with them. It just happened that the bus was headed to the new town. Daddy had not left Robert Lee with any money to ride the bus, but the bus driver agreed to let him ride for free.

When they arrived at the new town, no one was at the bus station to pick them up. They slept in the chairs at the station. The next morning Daddy and Mama came to get them. If Robert Lee had been afraid that he was never going to see them again, he never mentioned it. He was hungry when they got to the camp, and Daddy let him eat before they went to the cotton patch so that he could go to work.

Listening to Ruby Lee tell these things, I began to laugh and wanted her to tell me some more. Ronald Wayne and Larry Edward were playing in the yard, and we were sitting on her front porch. She thought and then said, "Oh yes, there are a couple of more things that happened a few years ago that make me laugh now."

Bo had a couple of twin brothers as I have mentioned before. They were the babies of the family. When they were about fifteen, they came home one day and found that their older brother, Billy, had a woman in the bed with him. She got up quickly and got dressed. The two boys tried to get her to go to bed with them. She refused. She thought they were just kids. Nig and Pete decided that they would hang her, so they got a rope, and tied it around her neck. She was pleading for her life. Billy thought the whole affair was funny.

The girl was taken to a big tree in the yard. The guys kept telling her that all she had to do was to go to bed with them. She finally consented. She figured it was better to be in bed, than to be dead. They were taking her down when their mother and daddy pulled up in the yard. Mrs. Paul, afraid that her sons might be in some trouble with the law, blamed the girl. She told the woman to go home and never to come to her house again, and that she was not to discuss this with anyone, especially the law. The girl agreed. They never saw her again. Ruby Lee suggested that the poor girl feared for her life, and probably left the state.

Bo was really fast with his hands and on his feet. On Saturday afternoon in Lindale the town officials decided that they would take a live chicken and throw it off a building downtown. The person who caught the bird could take it home and fry him, or he could sell it. Someone climbed on a building, threw the chicken up into the air. When it hit the ground, it started running as fast as it could. Bo outfoxed all the other guys. He took the chicken home for his mother to cook. It had been an honor back then to be the person to catch the first chicken to be turned loose in Lindale.

I wanted to tell something that I thought was funny too. I told Ruby Lee that sometimes I did really stupid things. "Like what," she asked. I told her about the time when I only had a dollar, and I had bought a billfold. I didn't have any money to put in it, or anything else for that matter, such as pictures or identification. "That's nothing," Ruby Lee said, "I once "borrowed" a dollar to buy a billfold. She had topped my story, and I laughed. My sister was country when country was country.

Ruby Lee told me two sad things too. She said that when Franklin Eugene was a young boy, long before I had been born, he had been a very good worker. Some man kidnapped him and took him to California to work. Mama was very unhappy about this. She left the kids with her brother, Uncle Jean, and hitchhiked to California to look for him. She, of course, could not find him.

If she had not had the other children at home, she probably would have ended her life in California. Somebody in California gave her enough money to buy a bus ticket back to East Texas. When she got back to Dekalb, Texas, Franklin Eugene was there. Somehow he had gotten away from the man and hitchhiked his way back to Uncle Jean's. Mama was so happy that she went to sleep and slept for several days. She must to have been extremely tired from her trip.

Ruby Lee continued with the other sad tale. She told me that once Mama had become really sick and had extremely high fever. Daddy would not let her go to the doctor. He took her to a tree on a hill, made a bed for her, and left her there in the shade. No one else was allowed to go near her. About once a day, Daddy would take her something to eat. She was sick for about four weeks before she got well enough to come back down the hill to see her children. The good thing about her being able to survive this ordeal was that she had never gotten sick again, not once, in all these years. She was a remarkable woman; that was a fact.

Although Ruby Lee had told me these two sad stories, I felt much better when I left her and the boys, but I knew that I was going to miss them terribly for the next few months. The next morning, when we pulled out of our yard to go to South Texas, Ruby Lee, Bo and the boys were there to wave good-bye to us. I was crying and they were too. All except Bo, he was a man, you know. Grown men didn't cry back then.

When we started our trip south, we had a new hobo to go with us. Daddy gave him the name Blackie because he had a lot of cold black hair. Blackie was very handsome. We had no idea where he came from or what he had been doing. We didn't even know his real name. Daddy said it was none of our business. Other families from Lindale helped make up the train leading to Sinton. Billy Ray and Ruth Evelyn were among them with Rickey. I thought at least I would have one baby to help see after.

We laughed as we read the Burma-Shave Signs: BOTH HANDS ON THE WHEEL...EYES ON THE ROAD-THAT'S THE SKILLFUL...DRIVER'S CODE."

"THE ONE WHO DRIVES WHEN...HE'S BEEN DRINKING-DEPENDS ON YOU...TO DO HIS THINKING."

We stayed in Sinton one night. I didn't even get to see Charles Roy. Most of the hands, as the workers were called, stayed in Sinton to work for Mr. Huey. Daddy took us on to the Valley to work for a couple of weeks. We stayed in Aunt Ellen's yard again. When we left, she gave us some clothes. I loved her.

We had stayed in McAllen for only one week. Daddy rented a house in Raymondville, the first town in the Valley from Kingsville. Across the street I met a Mexican guy who worked at a filling station. Dollie also met her a fellow. At night we would sneak out of the house, go over to the station, and sit in his car. The car was parked in the back of the filling station, so that Daddy could not see it. His kisses were almost as good as Charles Roy's. I enjoyed his kisses, but I knew we were going back to Sinton, and I would never see him again. One night during one of these petting sessions, Joe stuck his head in the window and said, "Annie Bell, Daddy is looking for you!" That statement scared me to death. I knew we were in for it.

I started to get out of the car to go meet my punishment. Joe then said, laughing, "I am just kidding you. Daddy is asleep." The scare had shaken me up, however, so the next night I went to bed and didn't get up. Dollie did though. Apparently she took turns kissing those fellows.

We went back to Sinton. I turned sixteen there. Charles Roy still had a car. A boy's girlfriend could put little trinkets on the sun visor of her boyfriend's car. The first week there I bought some and put them in his car. We were still kissing, but I felt something was not right. He seemed distant. In the field he seldom wanted to pick cotton on the row next to me. I tried to ignore the awful feelings I was having about him.

One weekend Billy Ray and Ruth Evelyn went to Corpus to the beach. They asked us to go with them. We did. It was a wonderful day. Billy Ray was a lot of fun to be around. He was always pulling some kind of prank. That day he covered me with sand. I thought I was going to die before they started digging it off me. We all went to the water and washed it off. Ruth Evelyn had packed a good lunch. *I thought that this was the way it was always going to be. After I graduate from high school, Charles Roy and I will marry.*

On the way back to Sinton, Charles Roy and I were curled up against each other in the back of the truck. We were kissing. I was in love and so happy. Ruth Evelyn was driving. All of a sudden, Billy Ray opened the truck door, reached into the back and pulled the covering off us. He thought it was real funny. Charles Roy did not. After that he seemed sullen.

When we got back to the camp, Charles Roy went into their trailer house. He did not come out that night to see me. I began to get a real sinking feeling. The next week at work he hardly spoke to me. *What was the matter? I could not live like this.*

The next weekend Nuse and Joe broke into an old building in town. The law paid us a visit. Daddy was so mad, but instead of just punishing the two boys, he punished all of us. He told us we could not go to the show or anywhere else until he decided it would be okay with him. This was not fair to Dollie and me.

I watched as Charles Roy got into his car and drove off. I hoped he was going to the show by himself. The next week Nuse told me that Charles had another girlfriend. He had taken her to the show more than once. Nuse also said that Charles had more than one girlfriend in the wintertime while we were in Lindale. I could not believe my ears. My dream that we would someday marry died right there in the same place that it had begun-Sinton, Texas.

I cried all night, never slept a wink. When it was time to go to the field, I was a wreck. I went to his car and retrieved the trinkets I had given him. I wanted to throw them as far away from me as I could. *Maybe when he sees the trinkets are gone, he will talk to me, ask for them back, and we will make up. He had to see that I was the only person for him. What about all the years we had been kissing? Didn't they mean anything to him?* I put the trinkets up for safekeeping.

I could not have bought an ounce of sleep, even if I had had any money. There was no one for me to talk to. Not even Ruth Evelyn. She might think that I was silly. Daddy and Mama were out of the question. They both thought of me as still being a kid. I didn't go anywhere that I thought he might be, except for the field. I did watch his trailer house though; saw him come and go. He never came around us with a girl, but we all knew he was going on a date with a local girl on Saturday night. On Sunday afternoon he was gone all day. He never said anything about my trinkets being missing.

One afternoon I saw him go off in the car with his parents. I went to his car and looked in. On the sun visor were some more trinkets; given to him I am sure, by his new love. I had thought that things could not get any worse for me, but they had. A decision was made to let him go. I would find a new boyfriend, even if I had to find one in Lindale. In fact, I thought that Nuse had probably told him about my kissing Treva's, cousin as well as the other guys. He was getting back at me. If Charles had talked to me, I would have told him that they meant nothing to me. It was hard for me to believe that he could ever like anyone but me.

The last time I had kissed him became my most treasured memory. I would never kiss him again. His parents didn't go very far north with us before they decided to go back to Sinton where they lived. Charles Roy and I didn't even tell each other good-bye. It was as if "us" had never existed. In a way I was glad that I would no longer have to hurt around him. I knew that I would hurt badly enough without him.

Days and nights ran together. I could not eat, and I lost weight that I didn't have to lose. *Would this misery ever end?* If

Mama and Daddy suspected anything was wrong with me, they never said anything about it. Ruth Evelyn didn't seem to notice either. I felt as if I was an open book, and that everyone in the whole world could read my thoughts. I tried to be happy, went to the shows on Saturdays and did all the things expected of me. I cooked, cleaned up the camp, read books, and I prayed. Prayed for a miracle that I somehow knew was not going to happen. The praying in the past that had come in handy was just a thing of the past. My past was catching up with me.

Our Sikes cousins were living in Deport, Texas. Deport was a very small town north of Lindale. They had a good cotton crop that year. Daddy decided that we would go there and work until school started. I decided I would not tell anyone about my heartache, not even my favorite Sikes cousin, Marie. She was pretty and had a lot of boyfriends.

Daddy rented an empty building that had once been a garage for us to live in. Across the road there was a filling station. A good-looking boy worked at it. We got to be fast friends. I never mentioned Charles Roy's name to him. Dollie also found her a boyfriend. She and I slept in the car. She slept in the front seat, and I slept in the back seat. Almost every night, after Daddy went to sleep, we would slip out of the car and walk up the road. The guys would be waiting for us. Marie would be there with her boyfriend too. Her daddy let her date, so she wasn't sneaking around.

We would ride around; sometimes we would go to a drive-in movie. One night we went all the way to Paris, Texas. We stopped at a filling station to use the bathroom. I grabbed the keys from the car and ran into the toilet. As I was turning on the lights in the room, the keys went flying from my hands and landed up in the commode. The commode looked awfully dirty. I had no choice; I had to put my hands in there and get the keys out. What a mess!

That night when we got back to the car, Daddy was there waiting for us. I don't believe I had ever seen him this mad. He told us to get into the house and that he would deal with us tomorrow. He also told us he was going to kill the boy working at the filling station.

Mama was sitting up waiting for us too. She looked as scared as we must have looked. We both lay down, but we could not sleep. Daddy started telling Mama that they had raised a couple of whores, just like his sisters were. I wanted to scream, "We are not whores; all we did was kiss those guys." I didn't say a word. Mama or Dollie didn't either.

Around three o'clock that morning it started raining. I was planning a way to get Nuse to warn the boy at the station. I finally dozed off. The sun was up by the time I woke up. Immediately I remembered last night. *Why had Daddy not yet killed me?* Dollie was lying beside me asleep. I got up. It was still raining a little drizzle although the sun was shinning.

I looked outside and saw Daddy talking to the boy at the filling station. My heart almost stopped. I had not warned him! Daddy was talking really loud. The owner of the station came out. He must to have told Daddy to get back across the street because a few minutes later I saw him coming in my direction. I met him at the door expecting the worse. His blue eyes were almost crying. For some reason, I asked him, "Did it rain much last night? He answered, "Yes, we won't get to start working until about ten or eleven o'clock."

Dollie got up. Daddy didn't say anything to her. *When was he going to whip us?* He never did. Daddy told Mama to make us a pallet inside to sleep on that night. I thought that he didn't have to worry; I was not going to sneak out anymore. The incident was never mentioned again. Not by him, us, or by Mama. I never got another chance to talk to the boy at the filling station.

The very next week Daddy announced that we were going home. School was set to start in Lindale. I will always believe that Daddy let us go home to get me away from the boy across the street. He had no way to know that I didn't really like him anyway: he was just a substitute for Charles Roy. Though, I will admit his kisses were pretty good.

When we left Deport to go home, Blackie stayed there. He had moved into a house with a woman and her mother. They were well to do, had a nice home, and several acres of land. I knew I would surely miss him. I remember Daddy's telling Happy that he didn't think the woman had ever had a man mess with her before, but Blackie would take care of that. *What was he talking about?*

I was elated about getting to start to school on the first day of classes of my junior year. I signed up to take English III, American History, Chemistry and Spanish. Since I had been around the

Spanish people in South Texas each year, I felt this would be a good course to take. That way I would be able to carry on a conversation with some of them in the summer when we went cotton picking.

At the first of school I was elected to be the reporter for our school paper and as a representative of the student council. As the reporter, I had to assist in writing the school paper, coming up with ideas and writing articles. I don't believe the student council did very much back then. If we accomplished anything, I surely don't recall what it was.

The first twelve weeks of Spanish were good. I studied hard and really tried to learn to speak, read and write this language. I thought it was funny that you didn't say the "red car" but you would say the "car red." It was different from English. After the first twelve weeks, things went down hill. Some of the guys began to be mean to the teacher.

One morning, she brought in a lovely vase full of fresh cut flowers. She asked one of the boys to take them to the bathroom to be watered. When he got to the bathroom, he urinated in them and brought them back to class. He sat the already wilting flowers in the window where the sun could hit them. The teacher had a hard time figuring out where the bad smell was coming from a day or so later.

At the end of the third six weeks, two of the boys took the report cards she had just completed and threw them all over the street in front of the school. For some reason, the principal called me in. He asked me if I had participated in the destruction of the cards or if I knew who had done it. I truthfully told him no. I just didn't tell him that I might have given someone the idea to begin with.

The gossip at school was that a girl had told the principal that I had actually done the deed myself. I was mad as I could be. I decided I was going to give her a good whipping, at least a tongue-lashing. I could not find her. She was absent. The girl never came back to school.

I bragged to the others that she was afraid to come back, as she knew I was out to get her, and that she was afraid of me. The truth was that she had run off and gotten married. You could not go to school in Lindale, Texas, in 1958 if you were married. In reality, she probably had not told the principal anything. She had other things on her mind other than a bunch of rowdy kids. I was secretly glad that she didn't come back; she was bigger than I was, and my whipping her might not have been as easy as I had made out like it was going to be.

Before school was out, the Spanish teacher quit. I don't think she ever taught school again. I know she didn't teach in Lindale. I didn't learn much in Spanish either. I have regretted that ever since. Looking back I can see many mistakes I made, and this one is right at the top of the list.

It was a warm morning in late September. We were outside after having eaten our lunch. A girl was standing around in the shade of one of the big trees. She found the money that I had buried there several years before. Do you think that I convinced her that the money belonged to me? No way! I tried though, even told her I would half it with her. Even if she had believed that I had hidden it there, she would not have given it back to me. She told me, "Losers weepers, and finders keepers." A couple of weeks later, her purse just happened to come up missing. Now I didn't take it, but I may have put the thought in someone else's head. I was told by my contact that there was no money in the purse, so the purse was put back where it had been found.

Sometimes at Sunday school, I would ask the class to pray for a friend of mine. A friend that wanted to do everything right, but at times would do just the opposite. I told them that the person I knew well always regretted committing these acts. Oftentimes, when I prayed in the class, I would ask the Lord to help her. Dollie would snicker at my praying about this. I hoped the kids in the Sunday school class would think that I was praying for her misdeeds and not those of my own.

The Lovings had their reunion. I, of course, was in their yard when the car with Pete came in. We had a wonderful few days. Every time I kissed him, I felt I was putting a nail in Charles Roy's coffin. *I will survive the winter, and next summer I will let him know that he is not the only boy in the world.*

Dollie, Joe and I walked home most days with Treva and Bobby. We all enjoyed this time together. Daddy developed a bad habit of coming to the school to pick his kids up. This embarrassed me; as I hated the old truck he drove. Now every kid in school knew who that truck belonged to, but I would act like I didn't see it, and Treva and I would take a different route home. Daddy could not see me. When I got home he usually got on to me, but I would just say, "I didn't realize you were out there."

A great thing happened in Lindale. At least I thought it was great. A portable skating rink came to town. Treva, Bobby, Dollie, Joe and I had learned to skate very well on the one pair of skates Treva owned. The first night Daddy gave us money to go. Most of the kids could not skate, and fell all over the place. Not us. Talk about showing off! It got to where all I wanted to do was to go skating. I saved my lunch money and baby sat as much as I could.

We all got better at skating. We learned to skate fast, backwards and dance on them. The owner of the rink would have times when he would call for couples only. Someone always asked me to skate. Other times he would do a ladies choice, and the girls could ask the guys to dance as a couple. The music at the rink was wonderful. I absolutely loved going skating. I was in my hey-day there. The owner was a very nice fellow, and sometimes if I did not have enough money to pay to skate, he would either let me skate free or at a reduced rate.

Things at school were going well too. One Friday our English teacher assigned each student one hundred lines of poetry to learn. We would have to recite them before the class. That weekend I learned all my lines. I worked hard. Everybody at the house got tired of listening to me. I practiced in front of the mirror in the bedroom. Getting in front of the class, saying the lines, and getting it over with were all I could think of.

I went into English class. The teacher asked if anyone were ready to say his/her poetry. She was not expecting any of us to be ready. I walked to the front of the class and said every line of the ones that she had assigned me. She was shocked. The teacher stated that she had not intended for us to learn all the lines at once. But she was proud of me, and told me so. She told us that we could say them all at once or twelve lines at a time.

After my performance, no one else wanted to say his or her lines that day. One of the guys told me I was just showing out. *I was not showing out.* I really had misunderstood and thought that we had to say them at one standing. The studying and bugging my family on the weekend had paid off. I didn't care what he thought. I had my poetry saying over with for this year.

This same English teacher asked each of us to write our own epitaph. Not a student in our class had ever heard of that word. When she explained to us what it meant, I knew it would be a difficult assignment; as I hadn't given much thought lately about my dying. I had thought about Daddy's death though. *Maybe I could write his.* Not so, it had to be our own.

I thought about it over the weekend and felt my lost love for Charles Roy. The next Monday I was the first to get up to read mine. It went like this: "Here lies the body of Annie Bell. She loved a boy she thought was swell. I don't love you anymore, he said. It broke her heart, so now she's dead."

That same old dumb boy who mouthed about my poetry reading asked, "What do you know about love?" "A lot more than you do, I bet," was my reply. *How could they understand about my broken heart?* After all, I had kept Charles Roy a secret from them. I went back to my desk. I was so mad that I felt like I could have crushed him like a bug.

I believe it was around November of that year that Daddy made a trip to South Texas. He was going to stop off in Corpus Christi to see Aunt Peggy and Aunt Leona. After that they were all going to travel on to the Valley to see Aunt Ellen and Uncle Harley. I was happy to see him go. He was still drinking and being mean to all of us. Even Robert Lee could do nothing to help when Daddy got on one of his drunks. I sometimes would wonder why Robert Lee had come back. In my heart I knew it was because of us kids that he had returned.

Daddy had been gone over a week. We didn't know exactly when to expect him back. He didn't have a job to go to so he could come and go as he pleased. Mama was making us a living at the rose nursery. I had spent the night with Treva. The next morning, we walked to school. Dollie had not come down to walk with us. I had been at school about fifteen minutes when she came in. She had on a new skirt. I knew then that Daddy was back. Aunt Ellen had sent us some more clothes. In one way I was happy about the clothes, but in another way, I was unhappy that he was back. I knew he would be drunk when I got home.

I was wrong. He was not drunk. Daddy seemed really happy to see all of us. We pretended that we were happy to see him too. Mama was very happy that he was home. I knew that she had missed him although I could not figure out why. Daddy had stopped in Alice, Texas, to see Billy Ray, Ruth Evelyn and Rickey. I was anxious to hear some news about them. The news that he gave me almost killed me. He was talking about them and as if an after thought he said, "Charles Roy got married."

I tried to conceal the shocked, hurt look on my face. I needed to get out of the room, but I stayed and listened to him. Mama and Daddy discussed who the girl might have been. Daddy had met her. He said that she sure was a pretty girl. I could not stand anymore of this. I slipped out of the house and sat on the porch.

The tears that I knew were coming came out like a river flowing. *Why had he done this? Why couldn't he have waited until I finished school?* I was almost sobbing when I heard the door open. I immediately began to dry my eyes with my hands. Mama sat down beside me. She took my hand and said, "You will get over this. There will be a lot of boys who will want to marry you. You must first finish school. Good things will come to you, you will see. I love you." My love for her had never been greater in my life.

Having said that, she got up. I turned to say something to her, but as I did, I saw Daddy standing on the porch. I hadn't noticed that he had come outside too. He was wiping his eyes with his handkerchief. That show of emotion from him was a surprise. I sat on the porch a little while longer before I went into the house, by-passing the living room where they were watching television. I went to bed. *I would cry no more tears for him.* For some strange reason there was peace in my heart, and I knew that I would like the girl he married. When morning came, I took the trinkets that I had saved to school. I threw them in a burn barrel. After that, thoughts of him were a thing of my past.

Twenty

It was getting close to Christmas. Daddy opened the firecracker stand in Mineola. I was looking forward to working in it during the holidays. Ruby Lee and Robert Lee had bought presents for all of us. Dollie and I again had opened them up, checked them out and rewrapped them.

During the holidays Nuse took a very big firecracker called a M-80 to a local filling station. He put it in the middle of the building, and then proceeded to light a match to it. Several people were sitting around a wood stove discussing God only knew what. The owner of the station told him in a very stern voice to put the firecracker out. Nuse had on work boots. He ran back over to the M-80 and stepped on it just as it was exploding. His right foot was broken. Daddy got really mad at him, as now he had a doctor bill to pay. The doctor told Daddy that if Nuse had not had on those work boots, he might never have been able to work again.

Nuse had to wear a cast on his broken foot. About a week later, the word was out; there was going to be a fight between two boys out in the woods. Teenagers jumped into their cars, wanting to see the fight of the year. As it turns out, the fight was between Nuse and one of his good friends. They didn't make it to the woods. The cars they were riding in were brought to a stop right outside of town. Nuse was kicking as hard as he could with his right foot and hit his friend in the head, knocking him into a ditch. The fight ended right there as Nuse figured he had broken his friends neck. Later the guy told Nuse, "I was doing pretty good until you hit me in the head with that "casket".

Robert Lee bought an old stripped down car to go with his good one. It did not have a top on it. We called it the "Sputnik." We drove that old car many miles. Gas was cheap, nineteen cents a gallon. We went from one end of the town to the other; then we would turn around and go back in the other direction. From north to south and back again, from east to west and back again, that is the way it was. All of the kids in town wanted to ride in that old car. Robert Lee let us take the car to school.

After the Christmas holidays, school began again. Someone brought about five hundred cracker-barrel firecrackers to school one morning and dropped them all over the halls. When it came time for the students to change classes, and their feet hit the halls, the firecrackers started popping. It sounded like a bomb had hit the school. The noise sure woke up the school officials. I never did understand why the principal interviewed me about any possible involvement in this. I also didn't know why he asked me if I had put string firecrackers in students' lockers fixing them so they would go off when the students opened their lockers. Sure couldn't figure that one out.

By the end of February, we were just about out of money. Daddy was not doing anything now to make anymore. He did plan to open up the fruit stand soon. One night someone came to our door soliciting money for the Heart Fund. Daddy had only fifty cents to his name. He gave the money to the lady. We all went to bed as broke as the Ten Commandments. The next day at school we didn't have any money for lunch.

That afternoon when we got home, Daddy and his friends were playing poker in our living room. I instantly got mad, until I saw the big pile of money Daddy had in front of him. After I sold the guys some coffee, I decided I was going to end the game, so that Daddy would not lose all the money he had won. I said, "Mama will be home soon, and she told me if she caught you men here again, she was going to town and get the law." Daddy turned red. Mustering all the nerve I had in my body, I looked at Daddy as if to say, "You had better keep your mouth shut." It worked. He didn't say a word.

The men started gathering up what little money they had left. Daddy had nearly all of it. They were cussing under their breaths, but they just didn't come right out and start a fistfight. They had wanted a chance to win their money back.

"Where did you get any money to gamble on?" I asked him. We had to do without lunch today. That was a lie. We all had asked someone to share their lunch with us. Daddy pretended to be mad, "Someone loaned me five dollars." "Did you pay him back?" I asked. "Hell no, you broke up the game before I had a chance to repay him," Daddy answered. By now he was laughing. He took me to the store with him, and we bought groceries. Daddy was a man of his word, and I am sure he did repay the man later on. The really good thing that came from my outburst was the fact that Daddy never played poker again at our house. I doubt any of his so called buddies wanted to come back over to our house just so they could get arrested.

By early April, Daddy had opened up a fruit stand down by Bo and Ruby Lee's house. They had fixed a shed for him to sit under while peddling his goods. A terrible thing happened to our family about this time. It seemed as if Mama had lost her mind. For a week, she would not go to work, and hardly got out of bed. Dollie and I were doing all the cooking and cleaning. I could tell Daddy was worried about his wife. We all actually felt sorry for him.

Mama would not talk to any of us. She went to the highway and tried to get herself run over. Joe had to run down to the highway to bring her back home. Daddy decided it was time to ask Dr. Kinzie to pay us a visit. He did. He went into Mama and Daddy's bedroom and shut the door. Daddy and the four kids and one grown one waited outside while Dr. Kinzie visited with Mama. After what seemed like an eternity, he came out.

He sat down with all of us on the front porch. Dr. Kinzie said to us all, "There are a few things that children don't understand about women when they get a certain age. Something happens to them, and they act strangely. Changes occur in their body. It is only a temporary condition. She will get over it. You will all need to be patient, especially you, Buford. I have given her some medicine. I believe she will be okay in a week or two. If she does not get better, I will have to send her to a mental hospital."

"No," I spoke up. "She is not going to a mental hospital." I remembered that her sister had been in one. "Damn it girl, shut your mouth," Daddy ordered. "Dr. Kinzie is talking." "It's okay," Dr. Kinzie said. "I told Dorothy about my decision. She understands that the law will require that I will have to carry it out." *It will be over my dead body.*

That night I was as worried as I had ever been in my life. *What would happen to all of us?* I remembered the time when I was much younger, and I had thought that she had left us. I just could not let it happen again. I went into her room and sat at the foot of her bed. Dr. Kinzie had told Daddy to stay away from her for a while. He had given her some sleeping pills.

I began to pray aloud, but softly, to the same God who had helped me so many times before. I told God that I had not understood what Dr. Kinzie had said to us, and that I was still a kid, and that we all needed her well again. I fell asleep at the foot of her bed. The next morning she got up, woke me up and said, "I am going to cook breakfast, find out what everyone wants to eat." After breakfast she announced she was going to work if Daddy would take her. I went to school, amazed at the wonder of it all.

I now realized the power of prayer. In my Sunday school class, I started asking God to help all the down trodden. My prayers asked for God's blessings for the people on the television soap opera who were having trouble in their lives. Once, one of the women on the show was about to have surgery. I asked God to help her through it. It worked too. She didn't die on the operating table.

I was given a part in our junior play. I was going to be a colored maid. A lady who lived up the street from us made my black dress complete with a white apron. I studied my lines. The play was a comedy and was a complete success with the audience.

Before school was out we had a Junior and Senior Prom. Because I didn't have a boyfriend, I had to go to the prom single. I didn't feel bad about it though as not many of the kids, boys or girls had dates. It was just hard to like boys who seemed like one of your brothers. Mama bought a new dress for me to wear. I had a terrific time at the prom.

Several of my girlfriends were practicing yells at Treva's house in the afternoons after school. They were going to try out for cheerleader for next year. I did not have any desire to try out, since I knew that I would never get enough money together to buy a cheerleading outfit. The whole junior class would vote to determine the winner.

The big day came. My friends were all excited. Our entire class went to the gym. The girls who were to try out had to do one yell each. When they had finished, the principal asked, "Does anyone else want to try out?" Someone sitting next to me said, "Why don't you try out, Annie Bell?" "I believe I will," I answered, jumping up and running down to the gym floor. All my friends were as shocked as I was when I got down there. I did my yell. I had practiced with them, just to help them out, so I knew all the yells.

All the contenders were sent to the girls' locker room to await the vote. My best friend, Ernestine, who was going to be the head cheerleader, came into the locker room. She was practically screaming, she was so excited, "Annie Bell you won!" In an instant all the other girls were hugging me. *What had I done? How was I going to pull this off?* We were planning to go south to pick cotton this summer. I will admit that I was very happy about it.

As soon as Mama got home, I ran to the car and told her that I had been elected cheerleader for next year. She smiled and said, "That's good." I realized that she had no idea what a cheerleader was.

The next day at school, the new cheerleaders met. We all decided that we would like to wear short skirts like the band majorettes got to wear. I was elected to go to the principal to discuss the prospect with him. I sat down in front of him and told him that the long cheerleading skirts would get in our way when did our yells, and that the girls wanted to dress like the leaders of the band.

For some reason, he got upset about this. He told me it would not be a good image for the school to change the dress code for the cheerleaders. He pointed out that no other cheerleaders in our district wore short skirts. I pointed out to him that things needed to change, and that we could start the change.

He told me to leave his office and not to come back in there with a request like that again. The cheerleaders could not wear short skirts. It would never happen as long as he was running the school. I did like he told me to; I got up and left. He had the authority to expel me. I told those girls that I was never going to him with one of their requests again. He had made a believer out of me.

On the last day of my junior year, our English teacher asked me if I would be the Editor for the school paper the next year. She told me that I had done a good job as a reporter. I told her yes. The Business teacher asked me if I would be the Subscription Manager for our annual the next year. I told her yes, too. The principal asked me if I would consider using one of my study halls the next year to be a Library Assistant as I had done this year. I told him that I would.

On my way home I thought about all the things that I was going to be when school started back in September. I had been elected to represent our class again on the Student Council. *What if Daddy decided not to let us come back and start to school on time? Would I have to give up all of this? Well, I might just have to put my praying abilities back into use.*

I didn't have long to ponder on all of this as blackberry season was beginning, and I had to go to work. We had to pay our grocery bill at Neeley's Grocery Store.

At the time there was no organized softball for girls in Lindale. We decided to organize ourselves. Our softball field was located on a corner lot in town. We didn't know who owned the land; we just started playing on it. We mowed the field with our push mower. We guessed at the number of feet between bases. I don't recall what our bases were made of, probably something like pasteboard boxes. Our coach had been a professional baseball player.

Dollie and I were players on the team. She played third base. I played first base, rover and sometimes pitcher. One could tell that I was the main player on the team. Here again, I was still thinking of how important I thought I was. When I pitched, I had good control of the ball. But, I didn't have any speed to go along with the control. I pitched it right over the home plate, and most of the time the opposing team members just hit the ball. That is when I could rely on my good fielders to get the batters out.

My sister and I didn't have a glove, so we had to borrow our brothers' gloves to play a game with. They also were playing on a team. If they happened to be playing a game at the same time, we had to borrow a glove from a member of the opposing team. Later, Dr. Kinzie gave me a glove to play with. I shared it with Dollie. We had a great time playing ball in neighboring towns.

We played a team from Yantis, Texas, a town in neighboring Wood County. You talk about big, stout girls! They hit our balls over every fence in Wood County. You have heard of some people being cornbread fed. Well, I know in what community that saying got started. One of their players hit one of my pitches so far over our center fielder's head that when she got to third base, she stopped, and with hands on the ground and feet in the air, she hand walked across home plate.

During the blackberry season, Daddy brought a new hobo out to the field one day. Unlike most hobos, he was clean cut and educated. Daddy let him move into the building behind our house. He fixed it up. We found out that he had worked for the railroad for over twenty years in Longview, Texas. He had a son who was fourteen years old. The hobo's name was Don.

Don told Daddy that he had come home early from work one afternoon because he had felt ill. When he went into his house, his wife was in bed with a man. Naturally, he was very upset about this. After divorcing her, he quit his job and "just took off."

Don always seemed sad, but he was very nice. One thing I was impressed with was the fact that he worked crossword puzzles with a pen. What little I had dealt with crossword puzzles, I used a pencil so that I could erase a lot. He quickly became a good buddy of mine. Don had never been around people like us who tramped around all over the state. He seemed pleased when Daddy asked him after the blackberry season if he wanted to go to South Texas with us to pull cotton. I thought, *boy you have no way of knowing what you are getting into*. I figured that he would not survive the cotton patch.

The trip to South Texas didn't take as long as it once had. All the families who went with us now had better cars and trucks, including us. Daddy had bought a newer model truck. He put the trap on top of it, and off we went.

I dreaded going south this year. My soul was as dark as clouds were on a stormy day. I didn't know if I would see Charles Roy and his new wife. *What would happen when I met them? Would I cry?* The best thing to do was not to even see them. I didn't. We did stop by and visited Billy Ray and Ruth Evelyn. Neither one of them mentioned him, and I didn't either. We stayed there two days, and I played with Rickey quite a bit. The next morning we went on down to the Valley; the cotton was ready to be picked.

Uncle Harley got us a job with a farmer who had a really good cotton crop. I was anxious for Don to get to the field. I wanted to see how he would handle the cotton sack. He asked me for help. I gave it to him. We all laughed at his first attempts to pick cotton. That first day he picked less than fifty pounds. I thought he would probably starve, or at least be a lot thinner by the time we returned to Lindale in September. The next day he picked a little more cotton. The other hobos were helping him out too.

Trying hard to keep my mind off my obvious unhappiness, I worked very hard in the field. *Maybe I should get my mind on the fun I was going to have when school started back in the fall.* On the third day, the clouds were covering the sun, matching my mood. If it rained, we would quit and go to the camp. I saw Daddy standing at the trailer that we emptied our cotton in. He was talking to my cousin, Larry Coomer, Uncle Harley's oldest son.

Larry was in college. He was a football star in the Valley and was very stout. He was a good-looking fellow, but, unlike Orville, he was older than me. Therefore, I had never paid much attention to him during the summers.

When the conversation ended, Daddy walked out to where I was working. He told me that Larry knew a guy who wanted to go out with me. "Go out with me where?" I asked. "I don't know." Daddy said. "I guess to a show." I could hardly believe my ears. Daddy had never said a word to me about going with a boy anywhere except for my brothers. I stood there in silence. I was embarrassed for my Daddy to be talking to me like this.

Daddy continued, "I told him that I didn't think you had ever been out with a boy." Apparently he had forgotten about last summer in Deport. I looked up at the trailer. Larry was standing there waiting for Daddy to return with my answer. "If you girls want to go out with the boys, I am going to let you," Daddy said as he turned to leave. "I will tell Larry to come out here and talk to you. Remember now you only have one more year in school. I don't want you to marry some boy and live in this Valley."

Daddy had never been concerned about my finishing school. *Did his statement mean that we were going to get back to Lindale in time for school to start?* All at once the sun broke through the clouds. Out of the blue I was free to go out with a guy. I looked down at my bare feet. *Why would one of these Valley boys want to go out with me?*

I sat down on my cotton sack, amazed at this turn of events. *If he had let me date last year, maybe Charles Roy would not have gotten married.* Daddy had said "you girls"; I guess that meant Dollie too. I wanted to be mad about that. She was a year younger than I; therefore, I figured she should have to wait another year. I decided not to make a federal case out of it. If we got into it about this, he might change his mind all together. *Would she believe me when I told her? What would Mama think?*

Larry came out to join me on the cotton sack. He told me that a friend of his had seen me the first day that we had arrived in the Valley. I agreed that I would go to the show with him and his friend on Saturday. A girl from one of the cotton picker's family offered to loan me a dress to wear.

Saturday finally came. I woke up full of happiness. I picked cotton until lunch, and then I went in to get ready for my first legal date. Dollie was as excited for me as I was for myself. All the hobos and the other cotton pickers knew about my going out that night. It was the talk among the work hands. I took a bath with a water hose that had been fixed up for this purpose. My clothes were ready. *What would this boy look like? Would he kiss me? Would I like it?*

Around two o'clock Larry came to our camp. He had bad news for me. He told me the guy could not go out with me as something had come up with him. "That's okay," I said. Larry seemed nervous and embarrassed. He left quickly before Daddy came up. I had no idea why the guy changed his mind, but I knew Daddy would be mad about it. He would have a few words for his nephew too. I didn't want to start a family feud. When Daddy came in, I told him that I wasn't going on the date because I didn't feel too well. There was no reaction from him. I cried myself to sleep that night.

Later I found out that my phantom date's real girlfriend came home early from a trip that weekend. He didn't want to get caught with a girl who was nothing but a cotton picker. He didn't know that back in Lindale that I was not just a cotton picker. I was going to be a cheerleader. I longed to be home among friends. I didn't see Larry any more that summer, but I was grateful to him. His talk with Daddy was the reason that I was now going to get to date. I was glad to leave the Valley and return north to work.

We didn't go straight back to Sinton. We stopped in Bishop, Texas, to pull boles. We moved into a house with two more families. We had the two front rooms. This house actually had a bathroom in it. The first weekend there Daddy let us go skating in Kingsville, Texas. Someone had loaned me his car to drive. Nuse,

Dollie, Joe, two other girls, and I were eager to show off our skating skills.

At the rink we met four boys who were stationed at the Naval Base in Kingsville. We paired up. When the skating rink closed, we made a date with the fellows. One of them had a car. We agreed to meet back at the skating rink the next Saturday night, and from there we would go to a drive-in picture show.

The boy who paired up with me was handsome. They all were. Another thing is this: they were from New York. I remembered what Robert Lee had told us about Yankees. He had told us that they were dumb. I was looking forward to finding out if he had been right about them.

On Saturday evening the four girls, Nuse, and Joe left Bishop to drive to Kingsville. We told Daddy we were going skating. He had said we could date, but I didn't think he meant we could date sailors. They were not boys; they were men. I felt they probably would not show up anyway. I was wrong. They were waiting on us when we drove up. It was obvious that they had not intended for Nuse and Joe to come too.

The guys let us know real quick that they were short on cash. Two of them didn't have any money at all. My date was one of them. We pooled our money. Two of the guys would have to be taken into the movie hidden in the trunk of a car. We drove up to the drive-in in two cars. One boy was in each trunk.

Nuse was sitting by me like he was my date. Joe was in the other car pretending to be a date for someone in the other car. This had been my brainy idea. It worked too. No one said a word when we purchased our tickets. The guys in the trunk were still and quiet.

We parked on the back row at the drive-in. Nuse and Joe hurried down to sit in some seats by the concession stand. My date was freed from the trunk. At the other car, a problem arose. The sailors could not get the trunk open. They could not figure out why it would not come open. A voice, full of hysteria, from inside the trunk said, "Walker, if I die in here, I'm going to kill you when I get out." *Yea, they were dumb all right. How could he kill anybody, if he died inside the trunk of the car?*

We were making a lot of noise, and other people were beginning to look in our direction. I began to worry that the owners were going to come out there to find out what the commotion was all about. *Would they arrest us?*

I sent Dollie to get Nuse and Joe. I knew they could figure out a way to get the guy out. Nuse came to the rescue. He got a tire tool from inside the car we had been in, and within a minute had the trunk pried open. *Robert Lee had been right about those Yankees.* The sailor had to be pulled from inside the trunk, as he appeared too weak to walk. He was scared to death. I guess he really had thought he was going to die.

The next weekend when we met them, I made sure we had enough money to pay everyone's way in. We shared a total of three weekends with these fellows. I could not tell you what any of the movies were about. Charles Roy Huey did not have a patent on this kissing business. Yankees were not dumb about everything.

One Sunday afternoon, while we were living in Bishop, we went to a movie. Nuse and Joe did not go with us. Some of the local boys were sitting behind us. We began to flirt with them, talking back and forth. One of the girls had long, pretty legs, and she had on a pair of shorts. She kept getting up, pretending to go to the bathroom or to get something from the concession stand. The boys took notice of her legs.

One of the guys asked her if she would wrap her long legs around him. They began to talk trashy to us. One of them asked me if we were cotton pickers. I told legs that we had to get out of there. These guys were not kids. We had no business messing with them. She, of course, didn't want to go. The rest of us got up and went home, leaving her there. I worried about her.

Around dark, two of the fellows brought her home. I was out in the yard when they drove up. Her mother and daddy were out looking for her. The boys got out. She was laughing, and I was relieved that she had not been hurt. I went into the house. One of the guys began to talk to Daddy in the front yard. I could see them from the window.

In a few minutes Daddy came in and told me that the boy wanted to have a date with me. I didn't want to go. The guy had scared me back at the movie. He acted as if he was sorry about the way he had talked. I told him to come back next weekend and that maybe I would go with him. I knew we were leaving in a few days, to go to another town to work. I often wondered how he felt when he came back to see me and discovered that we were gone. For some reason, I hoped that he felt as bad as I had felt back in the Valley, when my date didn't show up. *If one boy hurts a girl, she can punish another boy for it, now can't she?*

We went back to Wallis, Texas that summer to work. Don had gotten the hang of the cotton pulling business and he was saving his money. When we had been there two days, Slim Robinson came back into our lives. He had served a few months in prison and had been fully released. Our hobo family was complete now, except for Blackie.

We went everywhere with them, to the show, skating, and to the carnivals. They played endless hours of cards with us on rainy days. They shared their money with us, helped us in the fields, and shielded us from Daddy when he was drunk and belligerent. They were the best friends that we had. We teased them and called them "bundle stiffs", Daddy's nickname for them.

One of the bundle stiffs saved me from Old Man Henry Paul. He was Bo's daddy, and he was meaner than a snake. I was as afraid of him as a possum is an axe handle. He and his wife, Pearl, were picking cotton with us. One night all the men were drunk, and they got into a poker game. Mr. Paul won a lot of money and put all of it in his billfold. However, because he was so drunk, he got up but left his billfold lying on the ground. He went to bed. I found the billfold the next day. I didn't think about not returning it to him, but I did take out what I figured was the amount Daddy had lost and gave that much to him. When I gave Mr. Paul the billfold, instead of being grateful, he accused me of stealing some of the money and said he was going to whip my ass. When he reached to grab me, Slim knocked him out. I stayed away from Mr. Paul for a long time afterwards.

In August we went to Deport, Texas, to see Mama's brother and his family. We also went there to work. Daddy rented the same building that he had last year for us to live in. The hobos lived in the back part of it. Daddy went to see his friend, Blackie. Dollie and I went with him. We had all missed him last year. He was cleaned up and had on nice clothes. The two women acted like they were not happy about us showing up on their doorsteps, but Blackie was sure glad to see us.

Daddy asked him if he had married the woman, and he said no. After a brief visit, we left. As we were leaving I looked back at him standing in the manicured yard. I wondered why he had not married the woman. I would have married just about anybody who could have gotten me out of the fields.

The boy who had worked across the street at the station was gone. I was disappointed, since I wanted to tell him that I could go out with him now. My cousin, Marie, got me a few dates. Robert Lee, who was working at a full time job and living in Lindale, came to see us on the weekends. He bought a lot of good records for us to play on our record player, all rock and roll.

The state employment office had a man working in Depot helping the farmers find hands to pull their cotton. He just happened to be from Lindale, and Daddy had known him for years. He became a friend of ours too. Even though he was married and his wife lived in Lindale, he became one of the hobos. He was a retired Navy Chief and had money on him all the time. He also had a good car and didn't mind taking us to a neighboring town to skate. The work in the field was hard, but I truly enjoyed living in Deport.

My cousins living here was a good reason for me to be here also. I figured that when I graduated school, I might move back here to work and live. Lying on my pallet at night, it gave me something to think about.

One day in the field, a Mexican lady and her family were pulling cotton for Daddy. She got to talking about the black people and their wanting to go to school with us. I got mad at her, and told her that I didn't see any reason why they couldn't go if the Mexicans got to. Well, this made her mad. "It is legal for Mexicans to go to school in any state in the United States," she explained to me. "Why do you think you are better than I am?" She asked. "Why do you think you are better than black folks?" I answered her questions with one of my own.

Later in the day I felt bad about my statements to her. *None of us could help our nationality, her, black people, or me. We all needed to be treated the same.* They didn't return to the field to work for us the next day. Daddy wondered why. I told him that I didn't know for sure, but I thought that they had gone to Mexico. "I thought they were American citizens," Daddy said. "Why would they go to Mexico?" "To get their kids in school." I explained.

Twenty-One

The weekend before school was to begin, we moved back to Lindale. Blackie came with us. He told Daddy he was tired of that woman and her mother bossing him around. The girl was pressing him to get married and settle down. He did not want to do either one. Daddy told him that he had made a wise decision. Blackie also felt that the two women had kept him too clean. I thought he sure was stupid. He could have had a farm and all the land that went with it. *Didn't he know that the girl's mother would one day die?*

The other hobos came back to Lindale also, all but Slim. He told Daddy he was going to try to find a job in Deport. I didn't think much about it at the time. For several weekends after school started, we went back to Deport to see our cousins and pull cotton. We left real early on Saturday morning, and came back Sunday afternoon.

Our family was going to have another addition to it. Ruby Lee was going to have another baby. She wanted a girl, and had a named picked out. She was going to name her "La Quita." I was as happy about this as I could be. All I had were nephews, and a niece would be really nice. We would just have to wait to see what it was.

When school started, I enrolled in English IV, Bookkeeping, Civics and Speech. During the first week the students elected me Speech Class President. I also reported to work in one of my study halls as a Library Assistant. I was a happy, country girl. The business with the blind date in the Valley was completely gone from my mind.

During the first week of school, while I was walking to the drug store to eat lunch with some of my friends, I saw them. Driving by us in a car were three of the boys from the U. S Naval base that we had met during the summer. *What were they doing here?* I pretended not to notice them. They didn't see me. Daddy would not be happy about this, since we had not told him about those guys. *Maybe they would go away.*

I could not get them off my mind. When school was out, I did not see them. Dollie was nowhere to be seen either. As I turned the corner to our house, I saw their car. It was parked in our yard. Daddy was home. I went into the house and found the guys sitting at our kitchen table, drinking coffee. I acted surprised that they were here. Dollie explained that Joe had spotted them and sent them to our house to wait for us to get out of school. They had told Daddy about meeting us during the summer.

The guy who had been my friend expressed surprise that we had not told Daddy about them. I was nervous, but Daddy didn't seem mad. They were U. S. Servicemen, and he respected that. The guys stayed in Lindale for several days, sleeping in their car, before they returned to base. We never heard from them again.

Daddy had a telephone installed. Our local telephone company's operators would say, "number please" when you picked up the phone. She would then connect you. Our number was sixty-two. The year was 1959, and the Coomers had a telephone. *This was going to be a really good school year.* I would be wrong about that thought. Daddy would see to it.

I had to get ready to be a cheerleader really fast. The other cheerleaders had been practicing all summer without me. One of their mothers had purchased my sweater and shoes, and she had made a skirt for me. Everything fit exactly right.

I practiced the first four days of the week with the other girls after school. I knew I was in trouble with this cheerleading business. Doing yells was not as easy as it looked. At the first football game, they would go one way, and I would go another. I kept apologizing for my mistakes, but being Lindale girls, the cheerleaders laughed with me, and not about me. It was a fun football season even though I never did get any better.

Our cheerleader sponsor took the cheerleaders to Troup, Texas, for a cheerleaders' meeting at their local high school. The talk on the way to Troup made me realize that we would stop on the way home at a drive-in to get a Coca-Cola. I did not have any money, so, I decided to leave my purse at the school. That way I could pretend I had accidentally left it at the school, and the others would not find out that I did not have any money to buy a Coca-Cola with.

As it turned out, I would not have had to pay for the Coca-Cola as the teacher bought all of us one. *How as I going to get my purse back?* It contained my driver's license, a fact that I had over looked when I left it at Troup. Sometimes the things I did just didn't make any sense after I had time to think about them. As it turned out, the school counselor brought my billfold to me. She told me a student at the school had turned it in to the principal. I was relieved to get my driver's license back, and I never pulled that stunt again.

In late September, Dollie, Treva and I went to Tyler to the East Texas Fair. We rode with Dollie's boyfriend. Daddy had given us a little money to spend, but not much. As soon as we got inside the fairgrounds, Treva and I lost Dollie and her boyfriend. We were going to meet back at the gate around 10: 30 p.m. and then we would go home.

Treva and I were having a good time until I tried to talk to one of the men working for the carnival to give me a teddy bear. He agreed to do so, but then he told me I would have to go with him to the back of the tent. I asked him why. He told me he wanted to show me something back there. He also told me that he would give me a really big teddy bear. I really wanted the bear, but I just didn't trust that guy. He was dirty looking. We got away from him. I would go home without a teddy bear and wandering what it was behind the tent that he wanted to show me.

At 10:30 Treva and I were at the front gate waiting on Dollie and her guy. Dollie showed up, but the boyfriend did not. She told us that he had gotten mad at her about 10 o'clock and that he had gone home. Now was the time to panic. Lindale was fourteen miles from Tyler. I had no idea how we were going to get home. It was too far for us to walk. I was really mad at the old boyfriend, and I knew I would get even with him. *Maybe he would come back for us.* He didn't!

We stayed at the front gate, hoping that someone would come by from Lindale that we could hitch a ride home with. No one came out that we recognized. The fair gates closed at 12:00 midnight. The only thing that we could do was to start walking toward Lindale. We had walked about a block from the gates when I heard people talking behind us. I could not believe it; I recognized their voices. One of the voices belonged to a neighbor of ours.

We all piled into one car and headed toward Lindale. It felt good to get home. I knew not to tell Daddy about the boy leaving us. He would be so mad that he would probably kill him. It really didn't matter because I knew that I was going to kill the boy myself, as soon as I could find him. I didn't sleep much, plotting my revenge. The next week, before I had an opportunity to commit murder, Dollie's ex-boyfriend joined the U. S. Army and left town. I don't know if he was sad because of the break up with Dollie or if he had gotten the word that he was on my hit list. In reality, of course, it was neither one, but I knew that he would not stay in the Army forever, and that someday I would get a chance to tell him what I thought about him. I didn't see the guy until years later, when he retired from the Army.

The Friday of the last football game, the weather was freezing cold. The cheerleaders were required to go to the game anyway. We sat in the bleachers all wrapped up in blankets. There was no way we could do a yell. Very few fans were at the game, and they were mostly parents of the players or band members. At half time we decided that we would go to Van, a small town west of Lindale. They had a neat café there. They also had cute boys.

We went to the café and bought some coffee. Sure enough, just after a few sips, the guys began to come in for us to talk to. We sat at the café until it closed, warm as toast. I just knew that we were probably all going to get expelled for leaving the football game. The principal would surely talk with us about this stunt that we had pulled.

On Monday I went to school as usual. I was as nervous as I could be. It had been my idea for us to go to Van. All morning I waited for my name to be called over the loud speaker to report to the principal's office. It never happened. Apparently no one had even missed us. The principal probably had left too. I had worried for nothing.

I had the same bookkeeping teacher as I had had for typing two years earlier. I had quit chewing gum, so she would not have to get on to me all the time about spitting it out. The first week of school she had us tear our "practice sessions" out of our workbooks. She was going to use them as tests.

Thurman came home for a visit. He brought a surprise with him, a new wife. I had no idea that he and the first Mrs. Coomer had divorced. She had seemed to think that she was a little better than we were, and I had not liked her much. This new wife was friendly. She also was quite a bit younger than Thurman. She appeared to like us a lot. We rode her around in Robert Lee's "Sputnik." She enjoyed that. I don't think she had ever been in such a small town.

About this time I met a boy from Mineola and started dating him. He was taking bookkeeping also. They had the same workbooks as we did. However, their teacher was not going to use the practice sessions as tests. They were going to be just that, practice sessions, stuff the students could do at home. He gave all of them to me. I made almost a 100 on every bookkeeping test that year. I didn't have to cheat, but for some reason, it came natural for me to do it.

In Sunday school, our class elected me to be its first president. I had responsibility now. I kept up with attendance and ran errands for the teacher. Sunday school was still one of my favorite places to be. One boy, who was a year younger than I was, had been in my Sunday school class for several years. He was very funny, and kept us laughing all the time. His being in my class was one of the main reasons I liked to attend.

During basketball season, Daddy did something that tore our family apart. He left us! He moved in with a widow woman who lived in the same neighborhood as we did. He took all his clothes and the truck. We were left without transportation except for Robert's car. Mama had her job at Owentown. She was as unhappy as I had ever seen her.

I had always wanted Daddy to be gone, had even begged Mama at times to run him off. I had told her that we didn't need him, that we made the living. She always said, "I love him, I will stay married to him until one of us dies." Well, it seemed now that one of them had died. It was she!

We had to walk right by the house where he was now living to get to Treva's house. I hated to go by there in the mornings, seeing his truck, knowing he was in bed with that woman, and my poor Mama having to go to work. My hate for him had never been stronger. If Mama had been okay with it, I would have been happy about his being gone, but she was miserable. She just moped around the house, hardly eating. I could hear her crying in her bed, alone at night.

I didn't want anyone at school to find out that he had left us, so I pretended to be as happy as I could be while I was there. I never told a person, not even my best friend, Ernestine, about it. The boy from Mineola was not informed either. I baby-sat and saved my lunch money so that I could go to the skating rink. Everything appeared to be normal, but it was gloomy around our house.

Robert Lee and Ruby Lee visited Daddy trying to get him to come back home. It did no good. Bo went too. I felt if anyone could get him to come home, it would be Bo. Not so! Each one of them reported to Mama that Daddy was drunk when they tried to reason with him.

The woman had a daughter who had been in my grade at school before she had quit the year before. She was living at the house with them. One Saturday afternoon, as I was entering the show, I accidentally ran into her. When I realized who she was, my face turned red. Hers did too. We didn't speak, but I knew from the look on her face that she didn't like my Daddy being at their house anymore than I did.

After a few weeks, I realized it was time for our government checks to be put in our post office box. I knew that Daddy would get them out and spend them on the widow woman. I could not let that happen. The mail was always put in the boxes by 8:00 a.m. By 7:30 I was standing in front of our post office box, ready to open it. Each box had a secret combination that a person had to use to get in it. I, of course, knew ours. Looking around to make sure I was the only one in the lobby of the building, I opened our box. The checks were in there!

My heart was pounding; I didn't want anyone to see me stealing the checks. I put the checks inside one of my schoolbooks and went on to school. Saying that I was nervous all day is an understatement. I fully expected Daddy to come through the doors at school, or maybe even the law paying me a visit. Every thirty minutes I checked my book to make sure the checks were safe.

Daddy was at the house when I got home. Guilt showed all over my face, but I went right past him, not saying a word. I wanted to tell him that I hated his guts and for him to get back to the old woman's house, and that he was not welcome here anymore. It was best that I not open my mouth though. He asked each one of us if we had gotten the checks out of the post office.

When it came my time to answer, I said, "You know the mail is not put up until 8:00. We were all at school by then." "The postmaster told me that one of the clerks had put all the government checks in the boxes, and mine was included." Daddy said. "One of you kids got them, since you are the only ones in town to know the combination. Did your Mama put you up to getting my checks?"

"They are not your checks," I told him. "They belong to Mama." He was mad as heck now; no he was mad as hell! "Goddamn it girl, you black Dutch bitch, you had better give me my checks." I knew that he knew that I had gotten them.

He was taking his belt off. "You are not my Daddy anymore," I told him, "and you are not going to whip me ever again." I went into the kitchen and came back with a big butcher knife. "I will cut your no good guts out. Now you get out of this house." Dollie and Joe did not know exactly what had happened. They left the house. I went to the telephone and picked it up. "I am calling the law." Daddy left the house too. I don't recall which one of us was shaking the most. I was glad that I did not have to follow through with my call. *Would I have had the nerve?*

He was still in the yard when Mama got out of the car. He told her that I had gotten his checks, and that she had better get them from me and bring them to him. *Over my dead body!* Mama told him to go on back to his other woman. She would talk to me about it. Seeing Daddy in the yard had shaken Mama up, and she was shaking when I helped her into the house.

"I will burn them before I give them to him," I told her as soon as I had her calmed down. "Let Joe take the one that has his name on it to him," she instructed me. "No, I will not do it. If he comes back here, I am going to cut his head off," I informed her. Mama became upset again.

The next day I went to town and cashed the checks at the bank. No one said a word to me. They knew I was their daughter and assumed I had permission to cash them. I paid our gas, electric, water and telephone bills. Dollie, Joe and I went to the grocery store and bought a lot of groceries. Mr. Neeley offered to take us home, but I told him no. I wanted to walk right past the house where

Daddy was living so that he could see what "his" check had bought-groceries for his family.

Daddy did not immediately come back to confront me, but since it was obvious it would be hard for him to survive without the checks, in about two weeks, he came home. When we got home from school, his truck was parked in our yard. He was in the kitchen cooking supper. "What are you doing?" I asked him. "I am cooking you kids and your Mama something to eat," he answered. "Put the dishes on the table."

Dollie and I were crying as we got the plates out of the cabinet, but we did not let him see our tears. When Mama came home, she ate without saying much. After supper, we left them alone in the kitchen. About thirty minutes later, they called us back in the house. "I am coming home," he said. "Your Mama has asked me to move back." "I don't believe you," I told him, and "neither does Dollie or Joe. You had better be gone by the time Robert Lee gets back here."

Mama said, "Now kids I have forgiven your Daddy and you should too, for my sake." "I can't do it, Mama, not even for you." I told her. "He will just do it again." Dollie and Joe shook their heads in agreement. "No he won't," Mama said, looking sternly at him. "Look at your Daddy, kids, he is an old man. He won't do it again." Daddy was shaking his head as if to say, "No, I will never leave my family anymore."

Dollie and I started cleaning up the table. Mama and Daddy went outside. Finally we went outside. I could see the old woman standing in her back yard looking toward our house. I wanted to go up there and really tell her off, but for one moment, I felt sorry for her. *Would I trust Daddy?* I had to, my Mama loved her man, and I loved my Mama. I wanted her to be happy. *Had he come home because of the checks?* What a mixed blessing I thought. One good thing came out of this; Daddy never struck Mama or another one of his kids again.

The very next week, I got a letter from Slim Robinson, the hobo who had stayed in Deport when we moved back to Lindale. It was a happy thought, getting a letter from him. I hurriedly opened it. The words on the pages shocked me. He told me that he loved me and wanted to marry me.

Slim stated that the reason he had stolen the pick-up last year was because he felt he just could no longer be around me without my finding out how he felt about me. He had known that he would be sent back to prison. Being in prison was easier than being around me all the time. In prison he had realized that he had to come back to us so that he could let me know how he felt. The reason that he had not told me before was because of the difference in our ages.

Sometimes when we were all having a good time, he had suspected that I might love him too. Slim wanted me to write him if I felt the same way about him, and he would come to Lindale to talk to Mama and Daddy about our getting married. By the time I finished reading the letter, I was crying. I read it again. Never had I imagined he was in love with me. He was right, I did think of him as an old man, almost as old as Daddy. I had never thought about him in a loving kind of way. He was my good friend. I held the letter close to my heart. "Slim, Slim, how could you feel this way?" I said aloud. I knew our friendship was over.

I was afraid that if I showed the letter to Daddy he might go to Deport and kill Slim. He might also run all the other hobos off. *Mama probably should see it*, I thought, but I didn't show it to her. *What if the rest of them felt the same way about me?* I would never again look at them the way as I had before, but I would still treat them as nice as I could.

The letter was too much for me to handle by myself. I showed it to my best friend. She told me to tear it up and forget it. I did. About three weeks later, Mama and Daddy got a letter from Slim. *What was in the letter?* I watched Mama's face as she was reading it to herself for some clue as to its contents.

When she finished, she announced, "Slim is moving to Arkansas. He has married some woman in Deport. He is thanking us for our love and support of him. If he comes back this way, he will stop by and see us, and he will write to us later." I secretly thanked God. "P.S.," Mama began again, "tell all the kids good-bye for me, and tell Annie Bell to have a good life after she finishes high school." *I will, my friend, I will.* I still have one special thing he made for me, a small table scarf with my name on it.

One afternoon a man drove into the yard in a used pick-up truck. Another car pulled in behind him. Both men got out. I recognized the man in the back car; he was the local Constable, as you may know, the law. Daddy came outside to talk to them. Nobody shook anyone's hand. After speaking with the men briefly, Daddy called Robert Lee outside to join them. I watched with interest as they talked. What would the law want to talk to my brother Robert Lee about? He was the best brother I had. What could he have done?

I found out later that what the conversation was all about. The first man's unmarried daughter was going to have a baby. The Constable showed Daddy a list of names with at least ten boys on it. Robert Lee's name was at the top of the list. The man told Daddy that anyone of the boys might be the daddy of the baby. He wanted each one of them to pay $25 so he could pay the doctor bills for the baby.

Daddy asked Robert Lee if he had been with the girl and Robert Lee said that he had. Daddy told the girl's daddy that his gal had kept her drawers on, then the boys would have kept their play pretties in their pants. He, was mad, but being the honorable man that he was, paid the $25 for Robert Lee's part in possibly getting the girl pregnant. It was $25 that we could have used for groceries. I didn't realize at the time that it took ten boys to get one girl pregnant. But this is East Texas, and things can be different here.

The two men left. Walking back into the house, Daddy did a strange thing; he put his arm around Robert Lee's shoulder. Robert Lee, even though he was an ex-Navy man, was scared to death, knowing he might be about to be killed by Daddy. But, Daddy, just said to him, "Buddy, the next stuff I pay for, I am going to get myself."

The next week, the girl's daddy was driving a new used pick-up truck. It was rumored that the people who were adopting the child had actually paid the girl's doctor bills, but the daddy had to be paid for the shame and humiliation his daughter must have brought to him.

The Tucker family had a very pretty 1955 Ford car. It was pink. Barbara and I went to Mineola quite often to flirt with the boys. Another girl, Karen Hester, and I also drove over there. She was petite and very pretty. Her step-father had a 1955 Chevrolet. He let her drive it during the day. For some reason, we thought we had to sneak off in it at night. The car was parked in a detached garage.

After he went to bed, we would get in the car and back it out real quiet like, and then we were Mineola bound.

Later when we returned home, we would turn the ignition off and let the car roll down into the garage. We would pee outside, so that we would not have to do that when we got inside the house. Then we would climb through a window that we had left open and go to bed.

One Saturday night as we were returning from Mineola, we had to pass a slow moving car. We had just gotten past it when we realized a pick-up, that didn't have its lights on, was coming in our direction. We were able to get back into our lane about one second before we hit the pick-up head on. This incident shook both of us up, and we never sneaked the car out of the garage again.

Dollie and I had a bad habit of "borrowing" Robert' Lee's car while he was sleeping. This usually happened early on Sunday morning after Robert Lee had had a major date the night before. We would get the car back before he woke up. Robert Lee had gotten suspicious of what we were doing, so he began to hide his keys from us. We were looking for them one morning when I realized they were in his pillow, and his head was safely on it. Dollie got the scissors, and very carefully cut the end out of the pillow, and the keys fell right into my hand. We went to town and rode around a long time. When we got home, Robert Lee was still napping. We had brought his car safely home, empty of gas.

One Sunday afternoon Robert Lee had left his car parked at a local service station. He had gone to a car race with some other fellow. The car was headed north. We looked, and the keys were inside. Dollie and I went to Mineola and rode around and talked to several guys. We finally decided it was time to go back to Lindale. All at once I realized that the brakes had gone out. I was approaching a traffic light, and it was red. I pushed the brake pedal in as far as it would go. The car would not stop!

I had to run the light, but I did turn toward Lindale. Two guys were following us home, and we were going to go the show with them later. They were behind us all the way to Lindale, but they did not know that our brakes were out. We went very slow, and finally got the car back to the place where we had gotten it. I said a silent prayer. The car came to a stop. We got out of it and got into the car with the boys. When we pulled out, I remembered thinking that the car was now headed south. Robert Lee was going to know that we had been joy riding in it.

I didn't think about his getting into the car and having a wreck because he had no brakes. All I could think of was that he was going to kill us. There was no enjoying the rest of the afternoon. When Robert Lee returned to town, he didn't even notice the car had been turned around. He jumped into and headed home. He had a date that night. Robert Lee had to cancel the date, since he noticed the brakes were out by the time he had gotten to the house. We were not accused of a crime, but I had learned my lesson. We never did take the car again without his permission.

I began to get serious about a boy who lived in Mineola. He was the one who had given me all the practice sheets from his bookkeeping workbook. When we went on a date, I enjoyed the way it felt when he kissed me. He began to want the relationship to go a little farther. In a way I did too, but I really didn't want to "go all the way". I was a good girl. He began to pressure me about this. I agonized over it.

One Saturday night we had a date set for seven o'clock. He did not come, nor did he call. I went to Treva's house. We got her folk's car and went to Mineola to see if I could find him. When we first got to Mineola, we went to the Dairy Bar to buy a Coca-Cola. While we were there we met two boys who were in a convertible. They asked us to ride around, and we said yes.

My boyfriend worked at a part-time job at a grocery store in Mineola. As we drove past the store where he worked, I saw him putting groceries in someone's car. He saw me too, sitting on the backseat of that convertible. I felt badly. *Why hadn't he called me to let me know that he had had to go to work?* We finally got back to our car, and we went home.

The next day my boyfriend called me, and he was mad. He was also sad. We made a date for the next weekend. I had decided that maybe I should go all the way with him. This was a sure way to get him over his mad spell. He picked me up. He hardly said a word to me. We were going to Mineola to go to the drive-in movie.

After we parked at the show, he let into me. He told me that he had told one of his friends to call me to let me know that he was going to have to work. I explained to him that his friend had not called me until after I had left to go to Treva's. He told me how bad he had felt when he saw me in the car with the other guys, and he could hardly believe his eyes. He had figured that I was safe at home watching television with my parents.

He also told me that because he had been so mad at me, he had gone "skinny dipping" in a lake with some other guys, and that one of them had drown. I had already heard about the boy's death. My boyfriend told me that he felt that if he had not agreed to go swimming, his friend would not have died. His conscience was bothering him. I felt bad about all of this. *What could I do to make it better?*

We got into the back seat of the car. He was still mad at me. *This was the night that I was finally going to "do it."* The temperature in the car was rising, and so was ours. *I just could not do it!* Something like this would change a girl's life forever, and I was not sure if this was the boy I wanted it to change with. I asked him to take me home. He was really mad now.

When we got to the house, he told me good-bye and that he was not going to call me again. "Why?" I asked, acting innocent. "Because," he said, "I like to do things, and you do not. Do you want me to walk you to the door?" "No," I said, "I think I can find my way into the house." I jumped out of the car, slammed the door, and started running toward the house. A tree that had always been there got in my way, and I ran into it. My head was down, and I was crying. I fell to the ground.

He had been watching me from the car and jumped out to help me up. I told him to get away from me, go back to Mineola, and crawl under the rock that he had crawled out of. He kept his word and did not call me again. I saw him several times after that riding around in Mineola. Other guys from Mineola did call me, and I went out with them, but it took me a long time to forget the boy that I had almost become a woman with.

I woke up out of a sound sleep, realizing someone was pounding on our front door. I knew it was very late at night as I had been asleep for quite sometime. About the time I got to the door, Daddy was already up; dressed only in his drawers, opening the door to a very mad, mad man. "I am going to kill your no good son," he shouted at Daddy. Daddy pulled the guy into the house. "What in the hell are you talking about man, are you drunk?" "That boy of yours left my daughter in the woods and she made it to the highway where she flagged down a car and was brought home."

"I'll get him up; I don't blame you for being mad." Daddy told the man. I had already gone to Nuse's bed and told him he was in some really bad trouble. He knew it too. As it turned out, Nuse had gotten mad at the girl and had just driven off and left her at their parking spot. Daddy had to really do some apologizing and so did Nuse. This father actually wanted to kill him. Later, after things had calmed down, I thought about how scared she must to have been. I remember thinking, "I am glad I am a Coomer so I would never have to marry one of them."

Robert Lee got a good offer for his old car "Sputnik", and he sold it. I was mad at him. I loved that car as much as anything that we had ever had. I went into the house and fell across the bed crying. Mama put her arms around me, and she told me not to worry, that someday they would get a car for us. Robert Lee would regret selling "Sputnik." I think he missed it as much as I did.

In November, Ruby Lee had her baby. It was another boy. His name was Mark DeWayne. His being a boy was okay with me, as I would love him just as much as I did other two boys. Ruby Lee and Bo lived in their new brick house. No one who was remotely kin to me lived in a brick house. They also had two rent houses. All their hard work sure was paying off for them. They always had a pretty new car. I was proud of them. I baby sat for them as much as they wanted me to, since I liked spending the night in their nice new home. During these times I would read books, such as Tom Sawyer and Huckleberry Finn to the two older boys as the baby slept in his bed. I pretended these were my kids, and this was my house. It was only a dream though, since I felt I would never ever be able to have any of this. I was just not the worker that Bo and Ruby Lee were.

One week Bo went out of town to work. He was to be gone all week. About midweek, Ronald got sick, and I went to their house to help Ruby Lee with the boys. She wanted to sleep with Ronald, so I got in her and Bo's bed and went to sleep. During the night I woke up, terrified; someone was in the bed with me. He pulled me up close to him and said, "Ruby, honey, I'm home."

I realized it was Bo, but I could not say a word. It was as if I were frozen. Finally, I found my voice, and I said, "This ain't Ruby honey." He let go of me like a hot biscuit. Bo jumped out of the bed and said real loud, "My God, I didn't know that was you, girl. Where is Ruby Lee?" "In bed with Ronald Wayne," I answered. He was embarrassed. We both were. He left the room. I got up and put on my clothes.

Bo woke Ruby Lee up, but did not tell her that he had gotten into the bed with me. I didn't tell her either. I thought she might get mad at me. We exchanged beds. The next day, Ronald Wayne was feeling better. As we were eating breakfast, Bo explained to his boys and me that the weather had turned bad in West Texas. The workers had returned home early. His crawling into bed with me was not mentioned.

In December our Speech teacher decided that our class was going to put on a play. She selected a boy and me to pantomime the song, "I'm Getting Nothing for Christmas." She had to order the record for us. Everyone in the class had a part. It was a Christmas play. The guy and I practiced, and learned the song. We were to dress up like little kids. He didn't like that very much, but he did agree to do it. Three days before the play was to be held, my partner discovered that the record was warped. He had left it in the back of his car, and the sun had shone down on it. The Speech teacher was not pleased.

Not only was she going to be out some more money for the record, she would have to go to Tyler to get it. She also didn't know if it would come in soon enough for the play. She told us that if the record didn't get to Lindale in time, we were going to have to sing the song ourselves without any music. *Sing the song! I could not sing. What was she thinking about?* I didn't want to get laughed at. Luckily the record got to Tyler on the morning of the play. Her husband drove there and got it for us. We had fun putting on that Christmas program.

I had a few dates with a guy from Mineola who painted my name "ANNIE' on the side of his car. I didn't like him much though, and the romance didn't last very long. He began to date another girl in Lindale whose name was Fannie. He promptly painted an F in front of my name to make her name. She was a friend of mine, and we both enjoyed a laugh about that.

It was a few days before we were to be dismissed from school for the Christmas holidays. Daddy and Mama were running the firecracker stand in Mineola, giving us the night off. Fannie had her boyfriend's car. He worked at night during the week. Fannie picked up Dollie, Treva, Patsy, one other girl and me. We decided that we would stay out all night. I knew where my parents were; they had plans to spend the night in Mineola in the firecracker stand.

First we went to a movie and then we went to Kilgore, a town east of Lindale. Kilgore had a lot of oil derricks and they were decorated with lights during the Christmas holidays. We decided to drive over there and ride around. After spending some time in Kilgore and getting cokes at a local dairy bar, we started back to Lindale. Patsy was asleep in the backseat. I had discovered that Fannie's boyfriend had left her Christmas present in the glove compartment, and I was about to open it up.

The red lights came up behind us. It was past midnight. We pulled to a stop. The highway patrolman came to our car and shined his light in our faces. Patsy appeared to be passed out in the back. "Where are you girls going this time of night?" He asked us. Fannie told him we were going home and that we had driven over to see the lights. We were nervous. *Would he haul us in?*

Shinning his lights on Patsy, who was beginning to wake up in the back seat, he asked, "Have you girls been drinking?" "Just cokes," Fannie told him. I was shocked that he would ask us that. In the first place, he could tell that we were too young to buy liquor, and besides, we didn't have enough money for that. I almost spoke up, telling him what I thought about his questions, but decided against it. He told us to go on home. We assured him we would.

We drove through Lindale going to Mineola. After driving around there for a while, we all got tired. We had driven by our firecracker stand several times. Mama and Daddy were in bed. I began to wish that I were in my bed at home asleep. We came back to Lindale and parked the car. Lying across each other, we all went to sleep. It was now after three o'clock.

When it got morning, we all went to Treva's house and told her mother what we had done. She fixed us all a good breakfast. We went upstairs and everyone but me went to sleep. Going to school that day was an option for the other girls, but I had to go. When school had started back in September, I had made myself a promise that I was not going to miss any days.

At school I told several of my friends about our staying out all night. I also had one of them go to Treva's house after lunch to

269/Baldwin/Meager Beginnings

tell the girls that the principal was looking for them. It was a lie, of course, but it scared those girls. It scared Mrs. Loving too. I had not meant for that to happen. I loved her. They all had to go to the principal's office to get an excuse to go back to class the next day. That was not a problem, as each girl told him they had been sick the day before. He did not suspect a thing from that bunch of good girls.

The worst thing that happened because of this was that Fannie lost her boyfriend. It turned out that his car needed some oil in it, which we knew nothing about, and the car sort of tore up. He wasn't too happy about that. He also wasn't happy about our opening her Christmas present. Before long he had a new girl friend and a different car, without anyone's name painted on it.

On a Saturday during the holidays, Treva went to Tyler with her parents to shop for clothes. When they returned in the afternoon, I was sitting on their side porch. She got out, carrying several packages. We took the clothes out of them. I was happy for her, but I was sad for myself. I had never been on a shopping trip with my parents by myself. As she took the clothes out, I noticed a beautiful tight skirt and an orange sweater to match it. The skirt had pleats on each side. It was the prettiest outfit that I had ever seen. Tears began to come into my eyes. *Don't let them see you crying.* We hung all the clothes in her closet upstairs.

I went home because I was going to go to Mineola to work in the firecracker stand. All I could think about was that skirt and sweater. That night, lying on the pallet in the floor of the firecracker stand, I dreamed I had a date with a nice looking guy. I was wearing Treva's outfit.

Twenty-Two

After the Christmas holidays, I got a job at the Lindale Candy Company after school and on Saturdays. I was a waitress, and I made fifty cents an hour. I knew that I would not get to keep the money, but it did get me out of having to cook supper every night. Daddy took over that chore. I ate at work, usually a hamburger or a barbecue sandwich. When the job ended around ten o'clock, I walked home, down the highway. I was not afraid. If I saw a car coming, I didn't pay any attention to it. Because I could study at school, I did not have any homework to do. I took a bath and went to bed, tired.

The Lindale Candy Company was better known as Jim and Ruby's. They made homemade candies and sold fast foods. Working there had its fringe benefits. Boys! They came in to eat and to play pool. I loved this part of the job, seeing them. It kind of made up for the fact that I would not get to keep my money.

I had worked seventy hours over a two-week period. When Jim, the owner, gave me a check for $35 on a Saturday morning, Daddy was waiting on me to give it to him. He took it to the grocery store and bought groceries. He apologized for having to take the money, but then he said, "Everyone has to eat, so everyone has got to help buy the groceries."

For some reason I knew that he was really sorry for having to take my money. Thirty-five dollars would have bought several dresses for me back then. I didn't dwell on my loss. I could hardly wait for Monday afternoon to come around so I could get back to work to see the boys.

As a member of the annual staff, Billy Ramsey, a cute little thing, and I, had to go to Mineola to sell ads for the annual. I had on a short dress, and when he started the car, he pulled a vent open and my dress blew up around my legs. He looked at me and said, "That is my trick." I tried to act like I was embarrassed, but secretly, I enjoyed it.

When we got to Mineola our first stop was at the home of Doris Chritzeberg who owned a wholesale candy company and operated the business from home. We knocked on the door. A nice looking lady came to the door. We assumed that she was Doris Chritzeberg. I begin to give her the spill about how she should renew her ad in our annual. Mrs. Chritzeberg said, "Oh, my husband is Doris, and you would need to talk to him." Image our shock learning that Doris was a man. We found him and renewed his ad. On the way back to Lindale, I reflected on his name and thought, "A Man Named Doris." That could have been a song. He might have been the daddy of a "Boy Named Sue." Where was Johnny Cash when I needed him?

Something else happened concerning that annual. I was the Subscription Manager and talked a lot of students into buying one. I wanted to buy one for myself, but, of course, did not have the money to do so. But, you know what? When those annuals came in right before school was out, there was one for me. Well, miracles do happen. Or it just could have been that I used another student's money to buy one for me. I really just don't remember which way it was, a miracle or the other way. Anyway, I still have the annual.

Nuse had started to date Treva. I could not understand why she would go out with him. He was like a brother to her. I was jealous because I could not spend as much time at her house as I would have liked. It seemed now that every Saturday night she had a date with him. That was okay if I happened to have a date too. I wanted to do something about the relationship, but she seemed so happy to be his girlfriend.

It was in February when Daddy took me aside and said to me, "I know that you hate me, and you have reason to. Your Mama and you kids have put up with a lot of bad things that I have saddled you with. The past cannot be changed, but I am telling you now that I will never drink again. I will not ever do one bad thing to any of you again." He was crying. *Was he asking me to forgive him? I will tell him, "No!"*

He continued, "You are the one who has stood up to me. I feel you have suffered the most because of me. *No, Nuse is the one that you have been the meanest to,* I thought. The worst thing I ever done was to leave all of you. I want to ask you to forgive me. Mama has. I will love her forever, and I will love you, even if you say no."

I sat down on our front porch. This was what I had hoped for all my life, to have a really good Daddy, no drinking and no fighting with Mama or his kids. But, I could not say to him that I would forgive him for all the years of physical and mental abuse, for all the years of our not getting to go to school a complete year, and all the hard work in the fields.

I stared into his blue eyes with hatred showing from my brown ones. No words came from my soul or out of my mouth. I got up from the porch and left him crying there. I hoped that he was hurting as bad as he had hurt us. *This was something I would have to think about. He would have to prove to me that he was truly going to change.*

I talked to our preacher about it. I knew it was the Christian thing to do, but it was going to be a hard thing for me to do. The preacher reminded me that Jesus had asked forgiveness for those who had crucified Him on the cross. Forgiving Daddy was something that God would have me do. He said that he felt that I wanted to. *I knew he was right, but could I do it? Would Daddy change?*

He did. He began to go to church with Mama on Sunday and Wednesday nights. I was, however, always afraid that he was going to come back drunk every time he went somewhere without one of us. It was something that had been with me for seventeen years, and the fear would not go away over night. Uncle Earnest came to visit one morning, and Daddy left with him. I knew that when they returned, Daddy would be drunk. I was wrong. He somehow knew that I was proud of him. Daddy never come home drunk again.

Mama talked Daddy into letting us have a party at our house. We invited everyone in the entire high school. Daddy and Mama went to Ruby Lee and Bo's to spend the night. Robert was to be our chaperon. The only rule was that there could not be any drinking alcohol.

The party was a huge success. Robert Lee had bought all kinds of snack foods and cold drinks. Everyone had a wonderful time. We played all sorts of games. Robert Lee had to take four different girls home from the party. He had more fun than any of the younger people. It was after midnight before the last person went home. I went to bed tired, but extremely happy.

One of the guests, a guy named Maynard Neeley was in attendance. Maynard was a really funny person and always enjoyed a good time. His folks owned the grocery store where we bought groceries on the credit. He had brought a lot of empty whiskey bottles and set them in every room of the house. Mama and Daddy came home early the next morning. Picking up the whiskey bottles, Mama said, "Well, I see that Maynard was here."

Daddy bought the family an old car, just like Mama had promised that they would do. It was a 1949 Chevrolet. Dollie and I were going to get to drive it to school. She could have it for one week, and I could have it the next one. Dollie and I shared good times in that old car. We went to drive-in movies, to the skating rink and to Tyler State Park. Daddy no longer objected to our going there, since we were grown up girls now. The car had a standard shift, and the gears would get stuck. We would have to stop it, get out, raise the hood and get them unstuck.

It was Dollie's week to drive the car to school. Joe took it for a joy ride. He backed the Chevrolet into the brick fence when he was returning it to school. The back bumper was dented. Did he tell her what he had done? Of course not! When we were getting into the car after school, I said, "I don't remember your backing the car in this way this morning." We did not notice the dent until after we had arrived home. It was later in life when Joe confessed what he had done. The dent, of course, was never repaired.

Dollie went to work at Jim's too. We now had the car to drive to and from work. It seemed to me that we got some more friends after Daddy purchased the car for us. He began to let us keep half the money that we made. This was a real happy time for us. Our happiness would, of course, not last.

The senior teachers picked the players to be in our senior play. Another student and I were picked for the lead girl role. One of us would play the part in the morning for the grade school kids and in the afternoon for the high school. The other person would do it for the evening performance when the town folks could come. I started learning my lines, and there were a lot of them. I began to have my doubts that I would be able to learn all of them, mainly because of my working after school.

None of us had any idea that a tragedy was about to happen that would end a life, but would make us closer. It was a normal Saturday night. Robert Lee and I were at the skating rink. Dollie had a date with Maynard. When the skating ended, I asked Robert Lee if he would take a guy home that lived in a neighboring town. His friends have left him in Lindale on purpose, because they knew that he was sweet on me. I sure had a crush on him.

We took the fellow home. On the return trip to the girl's house, Robert Lee let me drive. He rode in the back with her. I was going to spend the night with her. He let us out at her house. We stayed up for over an hour talking and enjoying ourselves before we went to sleep. Maynard took Dollie home and she went to bed.

I was still asleep at 8:00 the next morning when Mama came to the house to get me. I was startled to see her. *What was wrong?* Dollie was with her and she was hysterical. Mama explained that Robert Lee was in the hospital with a broken neck and was not going to live. We had to get to Tyler right away. I became weak in the knees. This could not be happening. He was with us just a few hours ago. *How could he have gotten his neck broken?*

Dollie was inconsolable. I had not heard the worse of it. Maynard had gone back to Jim and Ruby's after he had taken her home. There he had met up with Robert Lee and three more boys. They had gone to Tyler, driving two cars, to get something to eat. This was a common thing for them to do on the weekends. Robert Lee had left his car in front of the Jim and Ruby's.

On the way back to Lindale, one car was attempting to go around the other one. Somehow the two cars' bumpers had gotten tangled together, and both cars had rolled over. Maynard drove a beautiful 1959 Ford convertible. He had been killed instantly! Another one of the boys had a broken back, and one had a broken arm. Mama was not sure about the other boy. Robert Lee was the one on her mind.

When we got to the hospital, Daddy and the others were there. So were what seemed like half the people who lived in Lindale. The doctor explained to us that Robert Lee had broken his neck where a man's neck would break if he were hung from a rope. He could not live. He told us to get all our family members home, including Thurman, who was now stationed in Germany. It was a very upsetting time for us, as well as other people in our community.

The first time I went into his room, I began to cry loudly. Someone was trying to comfort all of us. Robert Lee looked as if he was already dead. His neck was in some kind of contraption, and he had holes drilled in the sides of his head to keep the thing in place. His eyes were closed, and he did not respond to us.

Maynard's parents, although grieving, came to see all the guys. They felt like it was his fault that this tragedy had happened. He always drove fast. My parents did not agree with them. Both cars apparently were traveling too fast. It was hard on me, seeing my parents so torn up this way. I knew Daddy was regretting the way he had treated him when he was a kid. Robert Lee had turned out to be a good son, in spite of Daddy.

Robert Lee did not immediately die as the doctor had predicted. He kept breathing. The days passed. The other guys went home from the hospital to heal. We stood vigil by Robert Lee's bed. The doctor could not understand how he could still be alive. He was, and that was all that mattered to us. I wanted him to wake up, so that I could tell him that my classmates had selected me as "Most Typical Teen." He could not die without knowing that! I had always thought that I was anything but typical.

One day a miracle happened! Robert Lee opened his eyes, but he did not speak. A couple of days later, one nurse had come into the room and had put a washrag on the sink in the bathroom. She was going to come back later to bathe him. She left the room. For some reason, another nurse came in and bathed him, using the washrag.

Later, the first nurse came back in. Seeing the washrag was gone she asked, "Where is my washrag?" She was talking to me. Before I could answer her, Robert Lee said, "Annie Bell has it stuffed down her brassiere." The second miracle had happened! He was wide awake. The news spread quickly in Lindale. By the afternoon it seemed at least one hundred people had come to see the miracle talking.

From that day on, his recovery came pretty quickly. We had to turn his body over in that contraption every two hours, and he would be upside down for two hours until it was time to turn him right side up. I came up with the idea for Robert Lee to help me study my lines in the play, while I was there nursing him back to health. When he was turned upside down he could read. He would read the lines before the ones I was to say, and then I would say my lines. It seemed to me that learning the lines became an easy thing to do.

The doctor told Daddy and Mama that Robert probably survived the wreck because he had been in such good physical shape. All the hard work in the fields and his physical conditioning in the Navy had paid off.

When it came time for Robert Lee to go home, he was in a cast from his waist to the top of his head. He had insurance from where he worked to pay the hospital bills, but a hospital spokesperson told Mama and Daddy that they would have to have to pay for the private duty nurses that had been hired to stay with Robert Lee. Mama and Daddy did not have the money to pay for them.

Mama went to the welfare office to ask for help. I went with her. Since Robert Lee was grown, the lady at the welfare told Mama they could not help her. My Mama said to her, "If I leave here and paint my face black, I bet you would help me then." I was embarrassed, and the lady was getting mad. We left the building.

What were we going to do? How were we going to get Robert Lee out of there? It just so happened that the answer was at our house when we got home. His name was Bo Paul. Mama explained the situation to him. He said, "Mrs. Coomer, don't worry about it. I will pay the bill." Daddy thought about how wrong he had been about Bo when he and Ruby Lee had gotten married. Bo went to Tyler with us. When we returned home, Robert Lee was with us.

All the family members did our part to help Robert Lee get well. Daddy stayed with him during the day. He had to be spoon-fed. At night, Dollie or I would sleep in the same bed with him to make sure he didn't have any problems during the night and make sure he took his medicine. Since he was in the half body cast, the only thing he could do was eat. There were holes cut where his ears, nose and mouth were.

At first, the cast was too tight around his Adam's apple, and it was hard for him to swallow. The doctor cut a hole there too. Since he could not be shaved, the whiskers could not be cut off. As they grew, they became plastered to the inside of the cast. We stuck long sticks down his cast to scratch where he itched. He could walk some, but not for a long period of time. We took turns walking him.

One night a big storm came up. Daddy made all of us get out of bed and get to the safety of the car. We had a hard time getting Robert Lee stuffed in it, with that cast on. I told Daddy that if another storm came up, Robert Lee was going to stay in the house. He had survived a broken neck. He could survive a little old storm. After a few weeks, part of his cast was removed. After that he had freedom to do a few more things, like ride in a car.

It was a hard time for us, but it was also a time for us to bond. Robert Lee let Dollie and me drive his car to school. Mama drove him to the doctor's office. I wanted to do this, but I was not going to miss school. We were determined that Robert Lee was going to get well. We had to be ever so careful with him. One of my favorite memories about his recovery was taking him riding in the car. He looked like a ghost, riding in the car with his cast on. People would almost have wrecks turning their necks to look at him. I began to act like his car belonged to me. I kept the keys with me all the time.

We talked a lot about Maynard. Mama remembered the time when he had been riding around town at Christmas time in a pick-up, and they were shooting firecrackers from the back of it. Robert Lee parked his car, and when Maynard and his crew pulled up, Robert Lee got in. They had made about half a block when the city marshal pulled them over. He told them they were going to have to pay a fine.

Maynard said that he was not going to pay a fine, and he was taken to jail and had to spend the night. Every time Mama saw him after that she would ask him, "What kind of birds don't have wings? Jail birds! Jail birds!"

Robert Lee went before the Justice-of-the-Peace to plead his case. He told the judge that he had just gotten into the back of the pick-up, and he had not shot any firecrackers. The judge fined him

278/Baldwin/Meager Beginnings

five dollars. Robert Lee wadded the money up and threw it in the floor at the judge's feet. That had cost him five more dollars for contempt of court. The judge told him if he threw that money at him, he would go to jail. Robert Lee paid the ten dollars and left, madder than he was when he had come in.

We remembered another time when Maynard took three of us girls to Mineola to ride around. We sat on the back of his convertible seat. After pulling up to the Dairy Bar, Maynard put on one of the girl's headscarves, went up to the window and put in our order, talking and acting as if he were a girl.

Once, when he had been riding around with some guys in his new car, they put a blindfold on his eyes, while he was driving. They then proceeded to tell him how to drive. "A little to the right, go to the left, turn here, stop." Another night he had backed his car everywhere he went. Everybody had loved Maynard.

After his death, his grieving father would sometimes call Jim at the Candy Kitchen late at night. He would ask Jim if he would tell Maynard to come on home for it was time for him to go to bed. Mr. Neeley knew that the Candy Kitchen had been one of his son's favorite hangouts, and that he had loved the game of pool.

Robert Lee was unable to return to work for a year. At the doctor's office, when his cast was removed, Robert Lee looked bad with his long beard and its being plastered to his face. He also smelled bad. Half of the patients waiting in the doctor's waiting room got up and ran out of there when he came out of the office. After Robert Lee went back to work, he paid Bo back all the money that he had given Mama to pay the nurses with. It took him a long time.

The senior play was a big success. The name of the play was "My Cousin from Texas." The part I played was of a girl who was getting married to one boy, but was in love with another one. In one scene of the play, a doctor was going to tell my parents that I had measles so that the wedding would have to be put off. The doctor was to look down my mouth and say, "Ah ha!" and pretend to see red bumps in my mouth.

I had eaten onions right before practice one night. During practice when I opened my mouth, the smell of the onions floated to the doctor's nose. He said, "Good Lord!" I understand that this boy was about ready to ask me for a date. After that, it never happened. I was always opening my mouth when I should have kept it shut.

In another scene, a boy, who played my little brother, was supposed to come running into the room with a lariat rope trying to lasso a lamp. He missed it. Then he would say, "Oh, shucks, I missed." It worked every time during practice. On the afternoon of the play, he accidentally hit the lamp. He went right ahead and said his line, "Oh, shucks, I missed." The lamp lay broken on the floor. The audience got a good laugh out of that misspoken line.

The next day after the play, I went to see Mr. and Mrs. Brown to tell them about the success of the play. I had been close to them all these past years and had visited them often. Mrs. Brown had cooked a lot of meals for me. The Coomer kids had been sort of a replacement for their dead sons. On this particular day, Mrs. Brown was not there. A friend had come and taken her to her house for a visit. I bounced into the house unannounced. Mr. Brown was reading a book. They did not have a television.

I began to talk, telling him about the play. All of a sudden he reached out and grabbed me, trying to kiss me. "I want you," he said to me. "I don't want my wife." Mr. Brown was very strong for an older person. He dragged me to his bedroom. I was struggling, trying to get away from him. I was pleading for him not to hurt me. *What is wrong with all these old men?*

Apparently he thought someone was coming up, because just as quickly as he had grabbed me, he let me go. I fell to the floor. I got up and ran from the house. When I got home, no one paid any attention to me. I never told anyone about this encounter. Later, I saw Mr. Brown and his wife at the grocery store. She asked me why I had not been to visit them. I did not look at him when I lied to her, telling her that I had been busy. Whenever I went to visit them after that, I always tried to go at a time when I thought Mr. Brown would not be home. They later moved to Athens to be close to some of their nieces and nephews.

I heard that at Troup High School there was going to be a talent contest, and students from the surrounding school districts could take part. Now, I knew I sure didn't have any talent, but I figured that we might be able to fool the judges. I talked three more girls into joining me in this. We decided to pantomime a song and also dance while we were singing.

The song that we picked out was "Mr. Sandman." We practiced at Treva's house, and before the big night, we all knew the song frontwards and backwards. When we got to Troup, all of us were excited. I had brought my record player with us. We decided to wear pajamas to wear in our act. Of course, I had to borrow a pair. Another girl went with us so that she could start the record. Our chance to go out on the stage finally came. If anyone of us were nervous, it didn't show. We sang the song beautifully. If the judges thought we were pantomiming the song, they apparently didn't care. We won first place and got a trophy.

On the way home, we got into an argument as to what to do with the trophy. I stated that since it had been my brainy idea, I should get to keep it. Treva thought it should stay at her house, as that is where we had practiced. Before we got back to Lindale, we were all mad. I didn't care. We had won. The trophy came home with me. The next day I took it to school and put it in a place where all the students could see it. The trophy later disappeared. To this day, I do not know where it is.

In April, we had our Junior and Senior Prom. Thurman's new wife had sent me several nice prom dresses. I picked out a really pretty one to wear. Again I did not have a date. I rode to the prom with three more girls. They were all going steady with boys who were already out of school. Two of them were engaged and were to be married after graduation. We did enjoy the dance. After it, we rode around, going to Mineola, looking for a boyfriend for me. On the way out of Tyler, we ran a red light. There was not a red light in Lindale, and we were just not used to them. No one saw us. We acted like we had really gotten away with something.

It was getting close to the end of school. Daddy had planted some tomatoes. The weather had been dry, so water had to be carried to each plant. One morning Daddy told us that we would have to stay out of school for the morning, as the plants needed watering today. They were dying he said. The next day was Saturday. I told him that we would water tomatoes tomorrow. He was getting mad and told us that they would be dead by tomorrow. It was important for us to water them today. I reminded him that I had not missed a class all year. "Well, you are going to miss this morning. I have a lot of money in those plants, and the tomatoes will bring us a lot of money when they get ripe and we sell them at the stand."

I went with him, and Dollie and Joe went too. We worked all morning. I cried the entire time. I went to school in the afternoon. Dollie and Joe stayed home. The plants lived, but I had missed a half-day of school and would not have a perfect attendance for the year. Daddy tried to console me by telling me that he had not had a choice; we were the only hope that he had of saving the tomatoes. I believe he truly was sorry, but I grieved about it anyway.

We had another play in our Speech class. I was a member of the "Crooked Mouth Family." In the play, each family member had a crooked mouth and could not talk plainly. During the play, another crooked mouth person came into our store where I was working. He said, "Is your daddy here?" "No," I answered. "He has gone down to Lem Jones to get them eggs." "Will you marry me," he asked. "Yes, I will," was my answer. "By the way, what is your name?" I asked him. We get married. When I attempt to blow out the candles on the wedding cake, I can't do it, because of my crooked mouth. Each person takes a try at blowing at the candles. We finally try all at once to do it, and it works. The candles are out. I also had a part where I was a window washer. We had a lot of fun putting on that "Speech Spectacular."

It came time for us to go on our senior trip. I had saved my money. We were going to Shreveport, Louisiana. The plans were for us to eat lunch at a park, go skating, visit an Air Force base, eat supper at a nice restaurant, and then go to the Louisiana Hayride.

We would have to come back to Lindale after the Hayride since seniors were no longer allowed to spend the night. A few years before, some boys from one of the senior classes misbehaved badly on their trip. They took beds from the hotel and put them outside. I don't really know what else they had done, but the senior trips now lasted for only one day.

We ate our lunch at the park and then visited the Air Force Base in Bossier City, a town immediately past Shreveport. They showed us how they trained K-9 dogs. I was sitting by a window looking at the servicemen. They all looked happy, healthy and well fed. *I might join the service myself when I finish school.*

I was glad to leave the base. We were on our way to the skating rink. I wanted to show off my skills. When we got to the rink, it was closed. Just my luck! We had to return to the park to kill some time. At the park I found a billfold. When I looked inside, I realized that it belonged to Whan Boaz. He had not missed it. It must have fallen out of his back pocket when we had stopped there for lunch. If we had not returned to the park, his billfold and his money would have been lost to him forever, not to mention his driver's license.

When we went to the fancy restaurant to eat, we had to ride an escalator to the second floor of the building. I had never heard of one. I had never heard of a café being upstairs before either. I was scared to step onto the escalator. All the other kids were doing it, but they were just as afraid of the thing as I was. Finally I had to do it. I was the last one though. I was not near as tough as I wanted my classmates to think I was. We all survived the ride upstairs. I did not enjoy my meal, since I was dreading the ride back down. I survived that too!

It was time to get our tickets for the hayride. As soon as we got settled inside, I started looking around at all the people there. Up in the back were several good-looking guys. Four of us girls left our group, and went up there to talk to them. We sat there the entire show. When it ended, we said good-bye to the boys. It was a long bus drive home, not only because it was a hundred mile drive in a school bus, but also because I knew we were going to be in trouble when the principal found out that we had left our group.

Sure enough early Monday morning, I heard my name being called over the loud speaker to report to the principal's office. *Would I tell him the names of the other girls?* I didn't want to get expelled all by myself. *After all* these years *of struggling to get to go to school, why had I done such a stupid thing?* It had been for boys, of course. I thought about how Daddy and Mama would be so disappointed in me. I had failed them, and I had failed myself as well.

Even though his office was a short distance from my room, I felt that it was taking me a long time to get there. My legs felt like they were made out of jelly. I went in and stood and waited for him to come out of his office. I could feel my heart thumping inside my clothes.

He appeared to be ten feet tall as he asked me to come in. He told me to have a seat. As soon as I sat down he said, "Annie Bell I want to apologize to you for what I had to do. I had no other choice." *It was coming now, his decision to expel me.* Instead he told me that when he averaged my grades for my class ranking, he had had to give me a zero in three classes when I had not gone to school the first six weeks of my sophomore year. He had averaged in the grade that my Algebra teacher had given me. Having to add in the zeros, of course, put me down a couple of numbers in the rankings. He told me it would not have been fair to the other students if he had not averaged in the zeros.

I was so relieved. *Who cared about class rankings?* The only person who was eligible for a scholarship anyway was the class valedictorian. That person was Whan Boaz, and my grades would not have out ranked his if I had gone to school all year round. I told him that I understood, and thanked him for telling me. I always felt though that he could have ignored my zeros if he had wanted to. Later, when he died, I didn't shed any tears.

The other girls were anxiously awaiting my return to class. They were as nervous as I had been, for they knew they each had a date with him. I was smiling as I went back into the room. They knew they were off the hook. As far as I know, he never found out about our leaving the group. If the teachers, who had gone with us, had noticed we had left, they did not tell him.

I sent out graduation cards, and the gifts began to come in. I did not send out as many as I would have liked to. We just didn't have the money to buy them. I got several gifts from people that I had not sent a card to. They just wanted to give me something. The gift that Mrs. Clinton, our good neighbor from across town, gave me was a beautiful "short pink gown." It had lace on it. I had always wanted something with lace on it, but never had received anything with lace. It was several weeks before I could bring myself to sleep in it. It was just too pretty.

My aunts from South Texas all sent me nice gifts also. Aunt Peggy's card was titled "Be the Best of Whatever You Are." It had several versus in it, but the last verse was my favorite. It read, "If you can't be a highway, then just be a trail; if you can't be the sun, be a star; it isn't by size that you win or you fail; be the best of whatever you are!"

The gift that I will always remember is the one I got from Don, the educated hobo. He gave me a brand new one hundred dollar bill. He also gave me a card. On it he had written, "Never give up on your dreams." I told him that he should never give up on his dreams either. A week later Don came into the house to tell us good-bye. He had decided to go back to Longview to see his son, and try to get his job back with the railroad.

Daddy told him that he would take him there. "No, thank you, Mr. Coomer," he said. "I came here walking, and I want to leave here the same way." He came over to me, as tears were beginning to fall from my eyes. He put his hand on my right cheek. "I hope you have a good life," he told me. I was embarrassed by this show of affection. I looked to see what Daddy thought about this, but he had walked outside. I suspected he was crying too. We never saw or heard from Don again.

By the time our senior year ended, Ernestine was secretly married. I had introduced her to a boy that I had met in Mineola, and she had fallen in love with him. She had not told a person, not even me that she was married. She knew that she would have had to quit school.

Treva was married too. They were living at the Loving house. She and Nuse were expecting a baby. The school officials let her finish school at home. She only had to complete her two required courses, as she had taken an extra course each year and had the necessary number of credits to graduate. The teachers let me take her homework to her each day, and I would take it back the next. They even let me bring the tests home to give to her. She had always made good grades and didn't have any trouble passing them.

Treva had gone to beauty school in Tyler two nights a week while going to high school during the day. She had her cosmetology license and could go to work after the baby was born.

Concerning her having a baby, I wasn't going to stand by the window waiting for the stork to make its delivery. I was happy that the Coomers were getting another grandbaby, but I sure was going to miss all the fun Treva and I had had in the past years. I thought of all the years to come and the fun we would have as sisters-in-law.

When the baby was born, it was the girl that all of us wanted. They named her "La Quita", the name that Ruby Lee had picked out for Mark Dewayne if he had been a girl. Ruby Lee said it was okay with her for them to name the baby that. She did not plan to have any more children; she was too old. I thought so too; after all, she was twenty-seven years old.

Twenty-Three

On Sunday, May 15, 1960, a baccalaureate service was held at the Methodist Church in Lindale. My mama went with me. She had been almost thirty-eight years old when I was born, and by the time I had started school, she was in her forty-fourth year. The other mothers in our class had been in their twenties and early thirties. I had always thought of Mama as being old. She certainly was the oldest mother of anyone in our class. As a child, I had thought that she would never live to see me become grown.

She looked more like a grandmother than a mother. She may have been old, but looking at her at this service, I knew that none of the other mothers could love their children any more than she loved us. They surely had not had to survive all the things she had been through. She was proud of me too, her first child to complete high school.

I smiled as I thought about the boy at the church who had never heard of a cotton picker that could read and write. I wished that he could see me now, sitting at this service. *He would know his first cotton picker to finish high school.* I grinned as I thought *he might still be at the church, afraid to come out.* I had sad thoughts of all those other cotton-picking kids who didn't get to go to school very much. All of them had quit, and most of them were married, some with babies to raise.

I sat through the rest of the activity happy with myself. I realized that I loved my mama more than ever. Her stability had made this day possible. She had stayed with us, with Daddy, had taken us to church, and shielded us against a lot of stormy days.

Because of her, I would never have to work in the fields again, unless I wanted to.

When the service was over, I made a point to tell her that I loved her. She asked me, "Aren't you glad now that I stayed with your daddy?" "Yes, Mama, I am." I lied. Her love for Daddy was as strong now as it had ever been. I gave her another hug.

The next day at school, during my time as Library Aide, a boy came to the front of the class and gave me a note. I looked up and noticed that everyone was looking toward the front of the room. I opened the note and it read, "If you wet your pants last night, smile." I began to laugh aloud. Realizing that all the students but me knew what was in the note, I knew the joke was on me. What a great bunch of kids!

Later that afternoon I related the incident to Treva at her house. We began to reminisce about some of the things that had happened at school in the years we had spent there. One boy had brought a pig to school, and turned him loose in the halls. Another time, just as soon as the teacher left the room, the boys began an eraser fight. Some boy threw one, just about the time the teacher walked back into the room. The eraser hit her in the face and knocked her glasses off.

Another upper classman had brought a #3 washtub full of bullfrogs and dumped them out at school. We laughed as we remembered how he must have looked jumping around, acting like he was one of them. One day a guy rode a motorcycle through the school. Some of the kids had the job to hold the doors open so that the motorcycle could start at one end and go right out the door at the other end. Another boy rode his horse into the post office and asked for his mail.

Sometimes the smoke was so bad in the boys' bathroom; the teachers were afraid to go in there in fear of getting lung cancer. A girl, walking down the hall, lost her panties. They just fell off her. Some boy behind her picked them up, put them in his pocket, and would not give them back to her.

Treva and I had fond memories of the night that her mother let us have a slumber party at her house. The boys had to leave at ten o'clock. Two of them left the party, and went to work knocking down several mail boxes on their route. They had been so smart; they even knocked down the ones that belonged to their own families. This way, they would be above suspicion. Well, I think someone told the laws before the sun rose the next morning who the guilty parties were. You know, boys back then had to brag about things like that. One of these boys left his shoes at the house, so that Mrs. Loving would think that he had spent the night.

When I was about thirteen, one of these guys asked me if I would sit in his lap at the movie. He had been standing behind me in the line as I was buying my ticket. He told me that we would talk about the first thing that popped up. As the other guys were laughing, I remember thinking that boys were so stupid. *What on earth could pop up?* I declined his offer.

A lot of the roads in the country were unpaved. When it rained, the dirt roads became very muddy, and the buses got stuck many times. Oftentimes, the bus drivers would ask the older boys to get out and push the bus out of the mud. But instead, they just pulled the bus into the ditch.

Our history teacher would leave the room each time he gave a test. Some of the students used this time to get a little help on the test. Another upper classman had told me about the time, when the teacher was out during a test, that a girl, who was the official lookout, got on her hands and knees and crawled to the door so she could stick her head out to see if the teacher was coming. As she got to the door, there was the teacher on his hands and knees, and she came eyeball to eyeball with him.

When we were in the fourth or fifth grade, a boy was standing in the yard waiting for the school bus to pick him up. A skunk came into his yard, and this young lad decided that he would try to catch him. Just as the bus turned the corner, the skunk sprayed him. He got on the bus, not saying a word to anyone. The boy got into his seat. All the kids were trying to determine where the smell was coming from. He sat with his eyes rolled up toward the top of the school bus. The principal sent him home as soon as he got to his first class.

This guy would later run a scam on some of the guys in our class. He wore a coat with a "trick pocket" in it. The boys played a game called "Drop Knife." After both of them had shown his knife, the boys would hold the knife clenched in his left hand. The right palm would be open and facing up. On the count of three, both boys would drop their knife into the other boy's pocket. The way our skunk guy tricked the other person was that he would show them a good knife, but then he would quickly put it into his trick pocket, bringing out a bad knife; the one that he would exchange with the other boy.

That same year, it was determined that some of the kids in school had not had their smallpox vaccinations. The school officials decided to have those students vaccinated. There were two brothers in one family who needed the shots. When the day came to get them, only one of the boys came to school. The other one was sick. The student got his shot. His brother, back at home, had an open sore on one of his arms.

As they were sleeping together in the same bed that night, the two arms came together. The boy, who had not taken the shot, got his open sore in touch with his brother's smallpox vaccination. In a day or so, it was evident that both boys were vaccinated. The teachers could hardly believe what had happened. I just thought it was purely brotherly love, taking a shot and giving it to your brother in a way that he felt no pain.

Treva and I remembered how some of the guys had nerves of steel. Seven of the guys had gotten on one Indian motorcycle all at one time and had ridden it to State Park. One had operated the steering while another one operated the gas pedal. They were practically riding on each other's backs. If they had had a wreck, it would have probably killed all of them.

In band hall one day, an upperclassman, who was guilty for some infraction of the rules, was about to get a whipping from the teacher. He ran from the room, up the tree he went, right to the top of the band hall. He felt pretty safe, as he knew the band director would not climb after him. Wrong! Much to the boy's surprise, the band director climbed right up there with him, thus making him have to jump from the top of the building to get away.

Treva and I remembered the day in our American History class when we were studying about the American Revolution. The Battle of Bunker Hill was taking place. The teacher told us that the American soldiers ran back down the hill acting like Egyptian spirits saying, "I want my mummy, I want my mummy."

In World History we were studying about the army who was building a wooden horse, so they could get inside the enemy's walls. He said that one of the soldiers was bragging to a member of the opposition about how they were going to get inside the walls. "Yes, and this is what is going to happen to you when you get inside," the enemy said. With that remark, he killed the soldier. Our history teacher had always entertained us.

One day I had gone home with a girl in my class to spend the night. She rode the bus home, and this was a treat for me to get to ride the school bus. Her daddy raised turkeys. He bought day-old bread to feed them. The bread was brought home in the trunk of his car. That afternoon we were standing in the yard when he drove up with the bread.

I opened the trunk of his car to help him unload the loaves. I climbed in it. All at once I looked up; there were at least fifty turkeys trying to get into the trunk with me, and the bread. I was terrified. The turkeys must have thought I was going to eat all their food. *What was I going to do*? They were about to assault me. I opened a loaf of the bread and began to throw it out, over their heads. Finally they turned around and got away from the car. I shook right up until suppertime.

We discussed the fact that our superintendent's last name was Fight, the bank president's last name was Crook and the druggist's last name was Wolfe. We had always said that we had a fight at school, a crook in the bank and a wolf in the drug store.

I went home from Treva's laughing from the thoughts of all these memories, realizing that after a week, I would no longer return to the school that I loved so much. I knew that I wanted to continue to learn, but I would have to go to work full time now. College was not a dream for me. Therefore, I didn't dwell on it. I was about to accomplish something that had been a dream. I was going to walk down the aisle and get my diploma!

It was the last day of school. I had mixed emotions about going into the building. I knew that when I left later in the morning, I would never again return to it as a student. I had loved being here all these years. I could not imagine anyone loving school anymore than I did. As I entered the building, I was crying.

We were only going to be in each class for five minutes, just long enough to get our report cards. Then, as was the custom on the last day of school, the kids were going to Tyler State Park for a fun filled day, dancing, skiing, riding in paddleboats, and swimming. One of the senior girls had nothing on but her bathing suit. After all, we were only going to be at school for about thirty minutes. The principal and superintendent were mad at the girl for her state of undress. Before school started back the next year, a dress code was in place at Lindale High School.

As I was leaving the school building, everyone was hugging each other. Tears were running down my face. I could not stop them, and I didn't try to. I was not ashamed to cry. I was both extremely happy and extremely sad. There was a feeling in my soul that I would never feel again. The next day we would all graduate.

The morning of graduation day finally dawned. It was Friday, May 20, 1960. I woke up with an incredibly, wonderful feeling in my body. It was as if no one but I had ever reached this day in her life. No one was going to dampen my spirits this day. Daddy told me he wanted to talk to me alone. He had been really good lately, but I had not forgiven him for his past. I was working on it though.

We went to a local café. He ordered a cup of coffee, and I got a Coca-Cola. *What was he going to talk to me about?* He started in by telling me how proud he was of me for staying in school and making such good grades. He apologized for not letting me start to school on time, and for taking us out each year to pick strawberries. He stated that if he had let his older kids go to school; they too, probably would have graduated.

Daddy told me his drinking was the main thing that he wished he could erase, and the times he had whipped us so hard. He said something that I will never forget, "We shouldn't look back; we are not going in that direction." Daddy knew that I had not forgiven him yet, but he hoped that I would do so before he died. I told him I was trying, and I was. It just had not happened yet.

He told me that he was not going to come to my graduation that night; that he didn't have a suit to wear. I had not expected that he would. He had never been a part of my school life. He had never gone to any of my plays or to see my cheerleading mistakes. Daddy had never met any of my teachers. I couldn't remember him ever being in the schoolhouse. I really didn't think that he had a right to watch me get my diploma.

My daddy said something to me that I would never had expected him to say, "If I had the money, I would let you go to college." "It is okay," I said trying to convince myself as well as him. "I know that I cannot go." I was not the only one of my classmates who did not have plans for college. In fact, very few of them did. We went back to the house.

Ruby Lee, Ruth Evelyn, and Dollie, as well as Mama, were going to my graduation. We made pictures with my cap and gown on. We even let Daddy get in on the picture taking. We ate lunch together and had a wonderful afternoon.

When it came time to go to the school for the big event, Daddy hugged my neck, and I hugged his back; his beautiful blue eyes were full of tears. We got into the car. As we drove off, I looked back at him. He was crying really hard now. *Let him cry, this was not his dream; it was mine.* Strange, but for some reason, I wanted to turn around and go back to get him.

The superintendent called my name. As I walked across the stage, I looked at my Mama and my three sisters sitting in the audience. The Coomer women were watching another one fulfill her lifetime ambition; they were all smiling, and crying some. I felt as if I were the only one on the stage at that moment. I thought of the little baby who had been born in a tent with a dirt floor. There had been no diapers for her to wear. I had come a long way. There had been a lot of rough roads to brighter days ahead.

The President of the School Board handed me my diploma and shook my hand. It was the most wonderful thing that I had ever had in my hands. No one could take it away from me!

After the ceremonies, I went home with my family. Daddy was still up, and I showed him my diploma. We hugged again. That night lying in my bed, thinking about this day, I decided that I would forgive him. At times, there had been good times in my life while growing up. He had given me life, and I would give him a second chance. I got up, went into their bedroom and told him so.

They let me sleep late the next morning. Dollie had placed the diploma next to my face. When I got up, they had all left the house. Mama had left my favorite breakfast, eggs and fried potatoes, on the stove. Eating those potatoes, I got a warm, fuzzy feeling in my bones. I thought about something I had once read, "The decisions you make when you are young are the ones that you will live with when you are old." *I have finished high school, and I am still a virgin. I can do anything. I will go to college, one way or the other! I have the whole summer to figure it out.* After I made that decision, I got up and cleaned up the kitchen. I was as happy as I had ever been in my life.

My past was behind me. My future was ahead of me. I, Annie Bell Coomer, Miss ABC, was on my way! The baby who had been born into such meager beginnings, now had wings, and she could fly.

Epilogue

Annie Bell (Coomer) Baldwin-She picked cotton the summer she graduated high school in 1960. When September came, her mother went to the home of the president of the Lindale State Bank and borrowed $50 from him. Annie Bell started to college that next week. She retired from the Texas Employment Commission after thirty years as a Program Specialist. She has been married for over forty-five years to her husband, Arthur Earl Baldwin. They still reside in Lindale, Texas.

Dorothy Coomer-She lived to be 101 dying in 2006 in Lindale, Texas. Dorothy out lived her husband twenty-six years. Her children absolutely adored her for all the love she had given to them.

Buford Coomer-He quit drinking at age sixty and stated that he was not going to do another mean thing to his family. Buford lived to be 80 dying in 1980 in Lindale, Texas. He spent his last years making up to his wife and children for the bad things he had done to them. They all forgave him and loved him dearly when he died.

Thurman Harris (Bud) Coomer-He retired from the U. S. Army. He now resides on Emerald Bay in Smith County.

Ruby Lee (Coomer) & H. L. (Bo) Paul-They became multi-millionaires. Both became home builders and developers. Ruby Lee died in 1998 from lung cancer. They had been together for fifty years. Bo did not remarry. He died in 2003.

Robert Lee Coomer-He returned to work at Tyler Pipe & Foundry and retired as a Supervisor. He still lives in Lindale, Texas.

Ruth Evelyn (Coomer) Huey-She and her husband Billy Ray lived in Victoria, Texas, where he died in 1998. Ruth retired from the Texas Public School System and the Arkansas School System and now resides in South Carolina.

William Henry (Nuse) Coomer-He is a retired brick layer and still lives in Lindale, Texas.

Dollie E. (Coomer) Weems-She is a widow and lives in Troup, Texas in Smith County.

Harvey Joe Coomer-He served a term in Vietnam and then became a bricklayer. He is retired and still lives in Lindale, Texas.

About the Author – Annie Baldwin

Annie Bell retired from the Texas employment commission as a Program Specialist. She has served on several boards for the city of Lindale, the Smith County Appraisal District, Smith County Fire District, and presently serves as a volunteer clerk for the Smith County Emergency Services District #1. She is on the board of directors of the Lindale Economic Development Council and serves on cemetery and street committees for the city of Lindale. Mrs. Baldwin is a representative for the city of Lindale for tax increment financing.

In 1995 the International Association of Personnel in Employment Security honored her as *Retiree of the Year* for the state of Texas and she was named first runner-up at that organization's international convention in Montreal.

In 2002 she received the first *Hershel Duncan Volunteer Award* from the city of Lindale. In February 2006 the Lindale Volunteer Fire Department named their new substation in her honor. Annie Bell has written several articles for her local newspaper. On April 14, 2008, she received the *Citizen of the Year Award* from the Lindale Chamber of Commerce.

While employed with the Texas Employment Commission, Annie Bell co-authored several training packets and manuals on the state unemployment insurance, work incentive, and food stamp programs.

Mrs. Baldwin has been married for 45 years and has one son and two grandchildren. She was born in Lindale and has lived here her entire life. She graduated from Lindale High School, Tyler Junior College with an Associates Degree in Business and attended the University of Texas at Tyler.

Made in the USA
Monee, IL
10 July 2023

38622256R00164